Explore the

NELLES

GW00373819

SOUTH AFRICA

Author:
Marianne Fries

An up-to-date travel guide
with 168 color photographs
and 17 maps

**First Edition
1996**

Dear Reader,

Being up-to-date is the main goal of the Nelles series. To achieve it, we have a network of far-flung correspondents who keep us abreast of the latest developments in the travel scene, and our cartographers always make sure that maps and texts are adjusted to each other.

Each travel chapter ends with its own list of useful tips, accommodations, restaurants, tourist offices, sights. At the end of the book you will find practical information from A to Z. But the travel world is fast moving, and we cannot guarantee that all the contents are always valid. Should you come across a discrepancy, please write us at: Nelles Verlag GmbH, Schleissheimer Str. 371 b, D-80935 München, Germany.

LEGEND

▣	Public or Significant Building	Tzaneen	Place Mentioned in Text	▬	National Border
■	Hotel	✈	International Airport	▬	Provincial Border
▣	Shopping Center	✈	National Airport	▬	Expressway
○	Market	🐘	Wildlife Reserve	═	Principal Highway
✝	Church	🌳	National Park, Nature Reserve	═	Main Road (Paved/Unpaved)
✡	Synagogue	\25/	Distance in Kilometers	═	Other Road (Paved/Unpaved)
☾	Mosque			—	Railway
✳	Place of Interest	Mt. Anderson 2284	Mountain Summit (Height in Meters)	N 1	National Road
🏖	Beach			R 23	Provincial Road

SOUTH AFRICA
© Nelles Verlag GmbH, 80935 München
  All rights reserved

First Edition 1996
ISBN 3-88618-411-0
Printed in Slovenia

Publisher:	Günter Nelles	**Translations:**	Sue Bollans
Editor-in-Chief:	Berthold Schwarz		Lesley Booth
Project Editor:	Marianne Fries	**Photo Editor:**	K. Bärmann-Thümmel
English Editor:	Anne Midgette	**Cartography:**	Nelles Verlag GmbH

                                                                        - X01 -

TABLE OF CONTENTS

FEATURES

GUIDELINES

MAP LIST

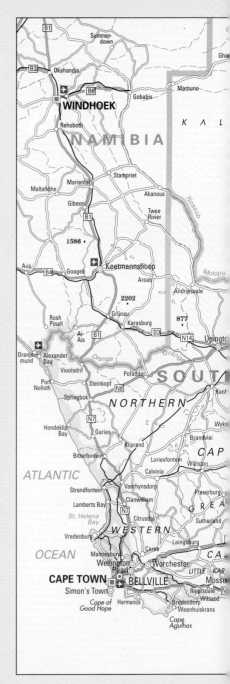

South Africa is redefining itself, politically and culturally. One part of this process is the reorganization of the country's administration, which entails renaming entire regions (such as the former homelands), provinces, buildings, and the like.

When this book went to press, this process was far from completed, note that additional changes may have been made in the meantime.

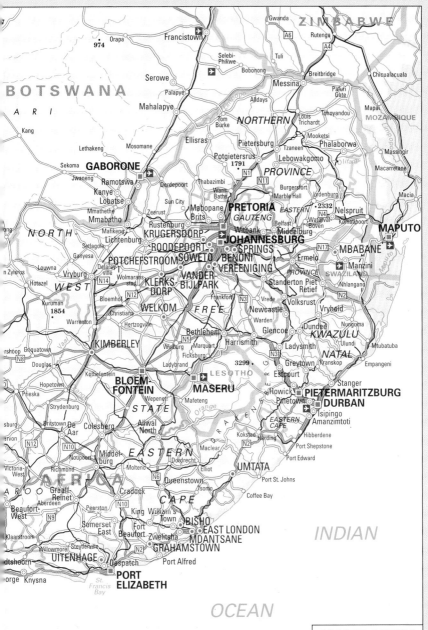

SOUTH AFRICA

0   50   100   150 200 km

GEOGRAPHY AND HISTORY

THE COUNTRY AND ITS PEOPLE "A WHOLE WORLD IN ONE COUNTRY"

South Africa is a traveler's dream. There are vast, undulating plains and precipitous mountains; wide sandy beaches and wild rocky coasts; fertile agricultural land and regions as dry as deserts; big cities like Cape Town, with a long history, and Johannesburg, which is relatively new. The country's unique animal and plant world is protected in numerous ' national parks, game and nature reserves. With all of this in addition to the many friendly people of a wide variety of different origins and cultures, South Africa is veritably "a whole world in one country."

Geographical features

With an area of 480,000 square miles (1.22 million square km), the country is about five times larger than Great Britain, but has only about three-quarters the population. The distance from Johannesburg to Cape Town is around the same as that from New York to Florida. Durban is approximately as far south of the Equator as Cairo is north of it. South Africa surrounds the territory belonging to the independent kingdom of Lesotho and borders Namibia in the northwest, Botswana and Zimbabwe in the north, and Mozambique and Swaziland in the northeast. The coast, which has a total length of approximately 1,860 miles (3,000 km), faces the Atlantic on the western side,

Preceding pages: On photo safari. A magnificent panorama – the "amphitheater" in the Drakensberg. Left: Women in Transkei.

and the Indian Ocean on the south and east. Coming from the Equator region, the warm Agulhas current flows south along the east coast, while the cold Benguela current from the Antarctic flows north along the west coast.

Most of the country is taken up by the vast interior plateau, flat in some parts, slightly hilly in others. The heart of this plateau is the highveld, 3,925 to 5,885 feet (1,200-1,800 m) above sea level and extending over the provinces of Free State, Northwest and Gauteng and parts of the Northern Cape, Eastern Transvaal, and Northern Provinces. The monotony of the scenery is only occasionally broken up by valleys and small isolated ridges or table mountains. To the west it changes to the rather flat, stony semi-desert of the Upper Karoo. North of Upington, the highveld gradually drops to the Kalahari, a relatively flat, dry area, 2,125-3,925 feet (650-1,200 m) above sea level. Most of the Kalahari is covered with red sand, which the prevailing winds have piled up into massive dunes, especially in the southwest.

The interior plateau is bordered to the west, south and east by the Great Escarpment, the most striking feature of the South African landscape. It varies in steepness according to the type of rock and separates the plateau dramatically from the land around it. Its most impressive part is the Drakensberg, a range of mountains extending some 620 miles (1,000 km) to form the eastern edge of the plateau. In the northern section, this range is predominantly formed of quartzite and dolomite, with Mount Anderson (near Lydenburg) the highest point (7,469 feet/2,284 m). In KwaZulu/Natal, along the Lesotho border, these mountains mark the edge of what was once a vast basalt plateau, and the highest summit, Champagne Castle, is 11,040 feet (3,376 m) above sea level. Around Beaufort West, at a height of 2,785 feet (851 m), it practically disappears for 50 miles

(80 km): through this opening runs the main arterial route of the country linking Johannesburg and Cape Town. West of this it rises again to a height of 6,210 feet (1,900 m), and parallel to the west coast it varies in height from 620 to 5,560 feet (1,000-1,700 m) above sea level.

Bordering the Great Escarpment are the fertile lowveld of Eastern Transvaal in the northeast, 500-1,950 feet (150-600 m) above sea level, and the hills of the Natal Midlands, Zululand and the region of Transkei in the southeast. Along its southern and southwest edge, it is bordered by the Cape mountains, almost parallel ranges of very rugged mountains divided by wide longitudinal valleys, such as the Little Karoo. In the west, north of the Olifants River, is Namaqualand, a very dry region which is flat in the south and hilly in the north.

Above: By the Great Escarpment in the lowveld of Eastern Transvaal. Right: Iron oxides give the sandstone rock of the Cedar Mountains its glowing color.

Along the coast, there are only a few bays able to provide good natural harbors, such as those of Cape Town, Durban and Port Elizabeth. The only extensive coastal plain with beach lakes and high dunes is in the east of the country, north of Richards Bay.

Geology

South Africa is geologically part of a very old, stable block of the earth's crust. Magmatic and metamorphic rock, in particular gneiss and granite, dating back approximately 3,800 million years and hence among the oldest in the world, is to be found in the northeast (e.g. near Barberton); similar rock, but "only" 1,000 to 1,800 million years old, is found in Namaqualand and in the eastern part of KwaZulu/Natal. Sedimentary rock, in particular sandstone, quartzite, slate and dolomite, is deposited in various basins above the bedrock. Herein lies the country's mineral wealth, such as the richest gold deposit in the world and sub-

stantial quantities of uranium at Witwatersrand, or, west of this, rich iron and manganese ore deposits.

Almost 2,000 million years ago in the bushveld, which extends north of Pretoria for around 27,300 square miles (70,000 square km), vast quantities of hot molten rock (magma) penetrated the old rock beneath the earth's surface. This solidified to form one of the largest ore deposits in the world which is particularly rich in platinum and chromium, as well as in tin, wolfram, molybdenum, copper, and the like. The volcanic chimney of Phalaborwa in the lowveld of Northern Transvaal, which dates back to roughly the same period, also has abundant mineral resources, primarily copper, phosphates, iron ore (magnetite) and mica (vermiculite).

In the most recent period of the Paleozoic era, around 300 million years ago, strata containing the country's main coal deposits (north of KwaZulu/Natal; Free State; Eastern Transvaal) were deposited in the Karoo Basin, which takes up 75%

of central southern Africa. These sediments are interspersed with volcanic veins, which have given rise to the dolerite caps on ridges, koppies and table mountains that give the landscape its characteristic appearance. In this period, Africa was still joined to South America, India, Australia and the Antarctic as part of the continent of Gondwanaland; when this broke apart, it gave rise to the continent of Africa in its present form. Massive quantities of lava were forced up from the earth's interior in the process; remnants of these have been preserved as a layer of basalt layer in the Drakensberg and Lesotho.

The most recent mountain formation in southern Africa took place in the Mesozoic era (around 200 million years ago), when the strata already deposited in the Paleozoic era were folded upwards to form the Cape ranges. Much later (140-80 million years ago), the volcanic rock forced kimberlite into the earth's crust, the source of South Africa's rich diamond deposits. In the most recent period

15

of the earth's history, from 65 million years ago to the present day, apart from the creation of a few coastal elevations and terrace formations, the geology of South Africa has been characterized by progressive erosion, in the course of which the Great Escarpment was formed and as a result of which it has been being constantly shifted inland ever since.

Climate

Since South Africa is located in the southern hemisphere, the sun reaches its highest point here in December (and is in the north at midday!), and the seasons are therefore the opposite of those in Europe and North America: summer begins shortly before Christmas. The country's climate is determined by its position south of the Tropic of Capricorn, its coasts and the height of the interior plateau. It is primarily moderate; only the areas east of the Great Escarpment have a subtropical climate, and the southwest has a Mediterranean climate.

Although the country extends over 13 degrees of latitude, temperatures are relatively uniform; they are lower in the interior than they would normally be, given the proximity of the Equator, because of the height of the land. Thus the average annual temperature of Pretoria, which is 4,477 feet (1,369 m) above sea level, is 63.5° F (17.5° C), not appreciably higher than that of Cape Town (62.6° F / 17° C), although it is much further north. Because of the warm sea current, the east and south coasts are considerably warmer than the west coast, which is cooled by the Benguela current. In summer, temperatures may rise to between 86 and 104° F (30 and 40° C) and sometimes go even higher. In the interior, however, they drop noticeably at night. None-

Right: The Sterkfontein Dam, the largest in the country, is part of the important "Tugela Vaal Project."

theless, there can hardly be said to be a real winter, in our sense of the word: during the cold season the days are sunny in most of the country and temperatures may rise to 68° F (20° C), although it is very cool at night. In the interior, there is also frost on clear winter nights (in July), but the coastal areas are more or less frost-free. In Cape Town, the sun shines an average of 8.7 hours a day, in Pretoria for 8.9 hours and in Durban for 6.3 hours (Madrid, by comparison, has 7.9 hours of sunshine, Rome 6.5, Paris 4.8 and Frankfurt 4.2).

South Africa is a very dry country. The average annual rainfall is only 18 inches (464 mm). 65% of the total area receives less than 19.5 inches (500 mm), the quantity necessary for agriculture without irrigation. It rains most on the coast of KwaZulu/Natal and the eastern Great Escarpment, and least in the Great Karoo and the Kalahari, where years can go by without any rain at all. Like almost all the countries within this proximity to the Equator, South Africa is occasionally struck by drought (the last one was in 1992/3). In most of the country, the rain falls in the summer, when there are brief, violent thunderstorms, generally in the late afternoon. In the southern coastal area, west of Port Elizabeth, the rainfall is distributed throughout the whole year, and in the southwestern part of the Western Cape province it rains in winter. Snow falls on the summits of the Drakensberg and occasionally also on some of the mountains in the Cape ranges.

The relative humidity is very low in the interior, but in the coastal regions can reach 85-90%; on the warm east coast, in particular, it is very sultry in the summer. On the cool west coast, on the other hand, there is frequent fog in the summer, which can spread 19 to 22 miles (30 to 35 km) inland at night, but disperses in the day when the temperature rises. It is also often foggy on the eastern section of the Great Escarpment.

Bodies of water

Because of the high rate of evaporation, only 9% of the total precipitation reaches the sea (by comparison with the worldwide average of 31%). The total discharge of all South Africa's rivers is no greater than that of the Rhine at Rotterdam. Together with its tributaries, the Orange River (Oranje), Africa's fifth-largest river at 2,250 km (1,395 miles) long, drains half the country. As a result of the abundant rainfall at its source it has water in it year-round, but is not navigable because of its great variations in depth and its many rapids and waterfalls. A number of dams along it, however, have harnessed it to provide irrigation and hydroelectric power. Like the Nile, its source is in a different country from the main part of its course; it traverses the Kalahari without any tributaries. In its lower reaches, west of Upington, it has cut deeply into the outcroppings of granite and gneiss. From here until it flows into the Atlantic at Oranjemund, it forms the boundary with Namibia.

The Vaal, its largest tributary at 776 miles (1,251 km) long, is also used for irrigation and as a source of energy. The most important rivers flowing into the Indian Ocean are the Tugela, which runs through KwaZulu/Natal, and the Limpopo, which forms the northern boundary with Zimbabwe and flows into the sea in Mozambique. There is always water in the many short rivers flowing from the eastern part of the Great Escarpment, and there are numerous waterfalls. The rivers from the Cape ranges in the south and southwest are also used intensively for irrigation, especially the Oliphants, which is 186 miles (300 km) long. North of this, as well as in the western part of the interior (in some half of the area) there are only dry rivers, here called *riviere* (*wadis* in North Africa); a heavy rainfall can transform them into raging torrents.

There are hardly any natural lakes in South Africa, only salt pans which sometimes fill with water. But there are, in addition to many large reservoirs, a number of smaller ones, known as *dams*,

17

created mainly for irrigation purposes. The lakes near the coast, such as Wilderness Lake Area or St. Lucia, are in fact lagoons.

PEOPLES AND LANGUAGES

Peoples

When the Europeans first arrived in southwest Africa, it was inhabited by Hottentots and Bushmen (Khoikoi and San); the blanket anthropological term for these two related groups is Khoisan, and their language are the Khoisan languages. The Hottentots, cattle and sheep herders, have, except for a small group of Nama in Northern Cape Province, died out or been absorbed in the colored population. A few small groups of nomadic Bushmen living as hunter-gatherers have survived in the Kalahari.

Above: Hottentot woman (South Africa), copper engraving, 18th century. Right: The Huguenot Museum in Franschhoek.

The country's 40.3 million inhabitants are anthropologically, ethnically and culturally very different from one another. Even within the large groups created by the apartheid laws – blacks (around 76% of the population), whites (around 13%), coloreds (around 9%) and Asians (around 2.5%) – there are big differences, which were maintained by the politics of apartheid.

The blacks are Negroids, and their languages belong to the Bantu group, which is also to be found outside southern Africa. The nine most important black peoples are the Zulu, Xhosa, Tswana, Sotho, Tsonga/Shangaan, Swazi, Pedi, Venda and Ndebele. Each group has its own independent culture and traditions, and is divided up into numerous tribes. Many Tswana, Southern Sotho and Swazi live outside South Africa; they are the national peoples of the neighboring countries of Botswana, Lesotho and Swaziland.

Livestock – mainly cattle, but also sheep and goats – were the traditional economic basis of the Bantu peoples. Crops were cultivated primarily for the growers' own use. Work in the fields was women's work, and stockpiling was unknown. Herd animals were kept more as a status symbol than for their practical use. Cattle were, however, also necessary to pay the *lobola,* payment to a bride's family as compensation for her loss to the family. This custom is still followed, although payment is now often in money rather than cattle.

Contact with white settlers and their taxation system necessitated the changeover to a money economy, which, in the face of a rapidly growing population, increasing devastation of the land, and the use of traditional rather than technological farming methods, it was almost impossible to support by agriculture alone. Men, in particular, began moving from the countryside into mining and industrial centers; and this left a permanent

mark on the traditional social structures of the extended family, village community, and tribe. Such traditions as ancestor worship or belief in witchcraft and magic, which Christianity attempted to abolish, have survived in various forms in the approximately 400 independent black churches (African Indigenous Churches). With over 7 million members, these form the largest religious group in the country, and their supporters are constantly growing in number. Many of the religious communities, also collectively termed "Zionist churches," were created under the influence of the Pentecostal mission from Zion City, U.S.A. Largest of these is the Zion Christian Church (founded in 1910) with 1.5 million members, which has its headquarters in Zion City Moria, Northern Transvaal. The Zulu Isaiah Shemba, who founded the equally influential Nazareth Baptist Church in Ekuphakameni, Kwa-Zulu/Natal, is today revered as a prophet. 30% of the black population belongs to other Christian confessions.

Until 1994, the white population dominated the country's political, economic and cultural life. More than half of this group speak Afrikaans; they originate from Dutch, as well as German and French, settlers who came to South Africa after 1652. They were primarily farmers and hence came to be known as "Boers" (the Dutch word for farmer). The English-speaking whites are descendants of the British settlers who came to South Africa in 1795 and managed, after prolonged conflict, to gain the upper hand, especially in the profitable branches of the economy (gold and diamond mining). Although all the prime ministers from 1910 on were Boers, the Boer National Party didn't become the major political power in the country until 1948. French (Huguenots) and German immigrants also contributed substantially to the country's development, and left their mark everywhere, including in family and place names.

The coloreds, sometimes incorrectly called "half-castes," are also a very

mixed group. They include white and Hottentots of mixed blood, Bushmen, slaves from West Africa and the East Indies, members of the Bantu peoples and the Griqua, a surviving group of Hottentots, and the approximately 200,000 Cape Malays in the Cape Town area. The latter are descendants of Malays brought to South Africa as slaves by the Dutch East India Company. As strict Muslims, they are held together as an independent community by their religion, but also by the cultivation of their traditions. The destruction of the area where they lived, District Six, earmarked as a "white" residential area and razed to the ground in 1966, aroused worldwide indignation and has never been forgotten; the area (Zonnebloom) remains undeveloped. Most coloreds live in the Cape provinces, and their culture and way of life strongly

Above: The Cape Malays are strict Muslims.
Right: The Taal Monument in Paarl commemorates the establishment of Afrikaans as an independent language.

resemble those of the whites, with around 85% speaking Afrikaans and belonging to the Christian faith. It was with their votes that the "white" National Party was able to retain its majority in the Cape region in the 1994 election.

The Asians in South Africa are primarily of Indian origin. They were brought to Natal starting in around 1860 to work on the sugar-cane plantations. After their contracts expired they had the option of returning to India, but most of them stayed on, and others, especially merchants, followed them over. Among the Indians, particularly in the province of KwaZulu/Natal, there are also considerable linguistic and cultural differences. The younger generation increasingly tends to speak English, and traditional Indian dress, which once dominated the streets of Durban, is being worn less and less. 70% of the Asians are Hindus, 20% Muslims and 10% Christians.

57% of the total population lives in cities (96% of the Asians, 91% of the whites, 83% of the coloreds and 42% of

the blacks). As a result of the continuing flight from the land, the existing slum areas have spread and new ones are developing.

Languages

According to the 1994 constitution, English, Afrikaans and the most important black languages – Zulu, Xhosa, Swazi (Siswati), Ndebele, Pedi (Sepedi) Tswana (Setswana), Sotho (Sesotho), Venda and Tsonga (Shangaan) – all share equal status as the country's official languages. English, however, remains the main language of communication.

Afrikaans, the newest language in the world, is spoken by 14.5% of the population (85% of the coloreds, 58% of the whites, 1.4% of the Asians and 0.4% of the blacks). As the language of the original Dutch settlers continued its independent development, words were retained which have ceased to exist in Dutch; others acquired a different meaning; and still others were incorpor-

ated from Malay and African languages, seaman's language and English. A teacher from Paarl compiled a grammar and a dictionary and, in 1876, published the first newspaper in Afrikaans; the language officially replaced Dutch in 1925.

English, the mother tongue of 8.4% of the population (95% of the Indians, 39% of the whites, 15% of the coloreds and 0.2% of the blacks) is understood practically everywhere.

The languages of the blacks belong to four main related groups of Bantu languages: Nguni (Zulu, Xhosa, Swazi and Ndebele), Sotho (Pedi, Tswana and Sotho), Tsonga and Venda. 22.4% of the population speaks Zulu (primarily in KwaZulu/Natal, Eastern Transvaal and Gauteng) and 18.3% Xhosa (mainly in the provinces of Eastern Cape, Northwest, Free State and Western Cape), which has taken over the clicks from the Hottentot and Bushman languages. Zulu, which has almost become the lingua franca, is now also spoken to an increasing extent by other Bantu peoples. Fana-

kalo, created as a vernacular for black workers (including those from neighboring countries), is based on a mixture of Zulu, English and Afrikaans. It has to be mastered for communication and safety underground by everyone who works in South Africa's mines.

HISTORY

Prehistory and early history

Numerous fossils and skulls, found mainly in Transvaal, demonstrate that around 3 million years ago there were hominid early forms of man living in Southern Africa. In Taung, north of Kimberley, a child's skull was found in 1924 which proved to be the "missing link" predicted by Charles Darwin between primates and hominids; this world-fa-

Above: Rock paintings ten thousand years old attest to the hunter-gatherer lifestyle of the Bushmen. Right: Jan van Riebeeck founded Cape Town in the 17th century.

mous find was the first piece of evidence in support of the now generally acknowledged thesis that mankind originated in Africa and not, as had previously been assumed, in Asia. Further significant evidence of this genus, *Australopithecus*, was found in 1936 in Sterkfontein and in 1947 in Makapansgat. The oldest remains of *homo erectus* in South Africa date from the Pleistocene era and are around 1 million years old.

Southern Africa was inhabited approximately 10,000 years ago by Bushmen, nomadic Stone Age hunter-gatherers; examples of their culture have remained in the form of numerous well-preserved rock paintings, in particular in the Drakensberg and Free State. Around the time of the birth of Christ, they came into contact with the Hottentots, nomadic herdsmen who were gradually moving south from the north of present-day Botswana. The two peoples, now termed San and Khoi (or Khoikhoi) by anthropologists, are genetically related; their similarly related languages, which feature clicks, are known as the Khoisan languages.

Evidence of settlements of farming peoples with an Iron-Age culture, who gradually moved south from Central Africa in around the 5th century AD and who were the ancestors of the present Bantu peoples of South Africa, has been found in Transvaal and Natal. Recent archaeological and historical research has shown that Mapungubwe in Northern Transvaal was the precursor (1050-1200) of the Iron Age culture of Greater Zimbabwe, which controlled trade with the Islamic settlements on the East African coast. In the late Iron Age (14th/15th century), black peoples spread to the open grassland. They farmed the land, herded animals, and smelted iron and copper.

The age of European discoveries

In the 15th century, the Portuguese started to look for a sea route to India along the coast of Africa. In 1488, Bartolomeu Dias reached the "Cape of Storms," later renamed the "Cape of Good Hope;" in 1497, Vasco da Gama was the first to sail to India using this route. The sailors stocked up on fresh water in Table Bay and bought cattle from the Hottentots. Towards the end of the 16th century, the Dutch, English and French began challenging Portuguese marine and trading ambitions, founding trading companies and bases in South and Southeast Asia. On April 6, 1652, the Dutchman Jan van Riebeeck arrived with three ships in Table Bay at the southern end of Africa's Atlantic coast, and, in the name of the Dutch East India Company, established a supply and maintenance station for ships en route to South and Southeast Asia and a hospital for sick sailors. Out of this rapidly-developing, fortified base with its good natural harbors grew the modern city of Cape Town.

In 1657, some of the company's employees were allowed to settle as farmers.

These "free burghers" were still nominally under the control of the Dutch East India Company, but it did not have to pay them. Dutch, German and French immigrants were gradually added to their numbers and slaves were brought from West and East Africa, Madagascar and the Netherlands' Southeast Asian colonies, who mixed with the whites, Hottentots and each other. The settlement developed apace under the governorship of Simon van der Stel and his son (1679-1707). While around the Cape the immigrants had concentrated on agriculture, the settlers ("trekboers") who were pushing into the dry interior and gradually claiming more territory began to keep livestock. The number of whites, which was around 2,000 at the beginning of the 18th century, had risen to 20,000 by 1800. The Hottentots, decimated by the diseases brought in by the Europeans, forfeited more and more pastureland to the advancing settlers and had, by the end of the 19th century, to a large extent lost their identity as an independent people.

23

The Bantu peoples

As their settled territories expanded steadily eastwards, it was inevitable that the white settlers would encounter the Bantu peoples, who had gradually penetrated south as far as Natal; the first clash took place in the second half of the 18th century. The first armed conflict between the whites and a Bantu people, the Xhosa, took place in the area between the Great Fish River and Bushman territory, between 1779 and 1781; this was followed by eight more violent conflicts, the last of which was in 1878.

The political and social structures of the Bantu peoples in Southeast Africa underwent profound change after around 1815, when there began what were to be a number of violent tribal wars. The dominant figure in these events was Shaka, chief of the Zulus, originally a small and unimportant tribe that was part

Above: British troops fighting against the Zulus to capture their capital Ulundi.

of the Nguni language group. Shaka, the "Napoleon of Africa," was an important military organizer. He subjugated the other Nguni tribes in the area with great brutality and welded them into a strong military nation which was given the name of his tribe. As he pushed forward into Transvaal, Botswana and the northeastern part of the Cape, he sparked a major population migration (called *mfeqane* by the Nguni and *difaqane* by the Sotho), which lasted until the middle of the century, temporarily devastating the highveld and emptying it of people. Plundering soldiers, conquerors and refugees wandered in all directions, even beyond the borders of present-day South Africa. Old social structures were destroyed, and new, powerful and well-organized communities of Bantu peoples were formed, such as those of the Ndebele, the South Sotho (today the national people of Lesotho), the Swazi, and others. Shaka, who was murdered in 1828 by his half-brothers, became the Zulus' national hero.

The Boers and the British

In order to protect the sea route to India that was all-important to their country, the British established themselves in the Cape, which they conquered in 1795. In 1814, after the end of the Napoleonic Wars, the domination of the Dutch East India Company came to an end and the area was formally ceded to Great Britain. It was now the British who were in charge of the region's administration, justice and trade. In 1820, they were reinforced by around 5,000 British immigrants, who settled in the eastern border area, along the Great Fish River. British missionaries now also began to turn their attention to the blacks and half-castes. In 1828, the British improved the situation of the colored labor force, and even, in 1833, abolished slavery. This went quite against the sentiments of the Boers, who felt themselves increasingly suppressed; as English was introduced as the official language in schoolrooms and courtrooms, their own language was being systematically ousted from public life.

In protest against this situation, thousands of Boers left house and home starting in around 1835, and embarked on the "Great Trek" northwards with their livestock and all their possessions. They first crossed the Orange, and one group also crossed the Drakensberg; other groups traveled further north across the Vaal. Although the British at first annexed the newly founded Boer states (Natal) or temporarily occupied them, in 1852 they recognized the independence of the Boer state of Transvaal, which from 1853 on called itself the South African Republic; and in 1854, they also recognized the independence of the Orange Free State.

In 1857, members of the German Legion, which had fought on the British side in the Crimean War against Russia, settled in the Ciskei area. In addition, many Indians came to work on the sugarcane plantations in Natal; most of them settled in the country after their work contracts expired, and they were joined by numerous Indian merchants.

For immigrants from Europe, who left their own countries in large numbers during this period, poor, economically backward South Africa had few attractions. This changed overnight with the discovery of the first diamonds. Fortuneseekers from all over the world poured into the country, paving the way for major economic and political changes. The mining rights were claimed not only by the Boers and the British but also the Tswana, a Bantu people, and the Griqua, a group of Hottentots who had been pushed out of the Cape by the white settlers in the 17th century. The financial wrangle ended – perhaps predictably – with the British occupying the diamond fields in 1871 and turning the area into the crown colony of Griqualand West, which was incorporated into the Cape colony in 1884.

The Boer War and the unification of South Africa

As Great Britain became more and more involved in South Africa – with Cecil Rhodes in charge of the Cape Colony after 1890 – it started to work toward the goal of uniting the British colonies in southern Africa with the Boer republics and placing them all under British rule. The Zulu area became a British colony in 1887 and was incorporated in Natal in 1897. The greatest obstacle to unity, Transvaal, was no longer just Boer farmland: in 1886, mining of the largest gold deposit in the world had commenced at Witwatersrand. Johannesburg, which began as a gold-diggers' camp, rapidly grew into a big city, which after 1890 was connected by railway lines with harbors in Natal and the Cape colony.

The Boers' fear and hatred of the British grew. On October 11, 1899, the Boer states, led by their president Paul Kruger,

non-white inhabitants. The Boer general J.C. Smuts, who became a member of the British war cabinet in World War I, represented South Africa at the Versailles peace conference and played a major part in the founding of the League of Nations, helped draw up the constitution. From 1919-24 and again from 1939-48, he was prime minister of the Union of South Africa.

Between the two World Wars, in which South Africa fought on the side of Great Britain, the country slowly developed an industry, a process which continued at an impressive rate and with great success after World War II. After 1946, new mineral resources were discovered and mining was increased. In 1931, the Union of South Africa was granted full sovereignty as a Commonwealth state.

Apartheid and its abolition

The National Party, which ruled from 1948 on and was primarily a Boer party, stepped up the policy of racial separation begun in colonial times. This system, which became known as apartheid, isolated South Africa from the rest of the world. In Afrikaans, the language of the Boers, the meaning of apartheid is "separation." After a referendum held among the whites, South Africa became a republic in 1961 and at the same time left the Commonwealth.

The constitution of 1910 had already denied blacks the right to vote. A law passed in 1913 (Natives Land Act) set aside 7% (since 1936: 13%) of the country's land as so-called "homelands" for the blacks, who formed some 75% of the country's population. All non-whites were assigned to specific areas. Since the early 19th century, non-white men had been required to carry identity documents at all times; after 1952, this applied to the women, as well. Further laws and regulations forbade mixed marriages, excluded black people from certain occupations,

finally declared war on Great Britain, represented by the prime minister of the Cape colony, Cecil Rhodes. Initially successful, the Boers fiercely resisted the superior British forces, but were finally forced to abandon the struggle in 1902. The "Boer War" was hard and cruel: the Boers lost around 40,000 people, including women and children incarcerated in concentration camps; and the scorched-earth tactics of the British left the land ravaged and livestock destroyed.

The Peace of Vereeniging (signed on May 31, 1902, in Pretoria) set the seal on British domination in southern Africa. Transvaal and the Free State were granted internal autonomy in 1906/07; in 1910, they united with the Cape colony and Natal to form the Union of South Africa, a dominion of the British Empire with 1.2 million white and 4.6 million

Above: Paul Kruger, leader of the Boer states in the Boer War. Right: Nelson Mandela pledges to reconcile the black and white populations (1994).

stipulated separate education, and finally also divided the races in everyday life to the extent of separate park benches, beaches and public transportation.

The African National Congress, founded in 1912, attempted to unite the blacks in peaceful resistance to the apartheid system, initially with little response. Its president from 1952-67, Albert Luthuli, received the Nobel Peace prize in 1961. In 1959, a radical militant wing (Pan African Congress) split off from the main organization. After violent unrest in Sharpeville in 1960, both organizations were banned. In 1961, ANC vice president Nelson Mandela founded the militant underground organization "Spear of the Nation"; he was arrested in 1963 and sentenced to life imprisonment. When, in 1976, young people protested in Soweto against the specification that Afrikaans was to be used in black schools, the security forces shot more than 600 people; as a result, there was an increase in the resistance of numerous black groups as well as in international pressure in the form of sanctions and boycotts. The business world wanted the government to abandon the policy of apartheid, foreign firms withdrew, and white South Africa gradually realized it was being branded the pariah of the world; the sport-obsessed South Africans were also upset by the country's exclusion from international sports events.

One of the first steps on the way to a new South Africa was taken by President Botha, who repealed the pass laws and the law prohibiting mixed marriages. The breakthrough was achieved by F.W. de Klerk, who became state president in 1989. In 1990, he lifted the ban on all opposition parties and ordered Nelson Mandela's release from prison.

After tough negotiations, all the parties, including the largest organization after the ANC, the Inkatha Freedom Party of the Zulu chief Buthelezi, agreed to participate in preparations for the first

free general elections and the drawing up of a provisional constitution (Convention for a Democratic South Africa, CODESA). For a time, violent conflict between supporters of the ANC and Inkatha made civil war seem imminent; in 1993, Mandela and de Klerk were jointly awarded the Nobel Peace Prize, rather as if the world were offering them payment in advance.

At the elections on April 27, 1994, it was as if the country dramatically liberated itself from its unhappy past. For all South Africans, the event became a splendid festival of reconciliation. After Mandela was inaugurated as the first black state president, a government of national unity was formed including the three largest parties (ANC 62.7%, National Party 20.4%, Inkatha 10.5%). Together, they represent more than 92% of the electorate. The homelands were abolished, and nine new autonomous provinces were created to prevent too great a concentration of power in the central government.

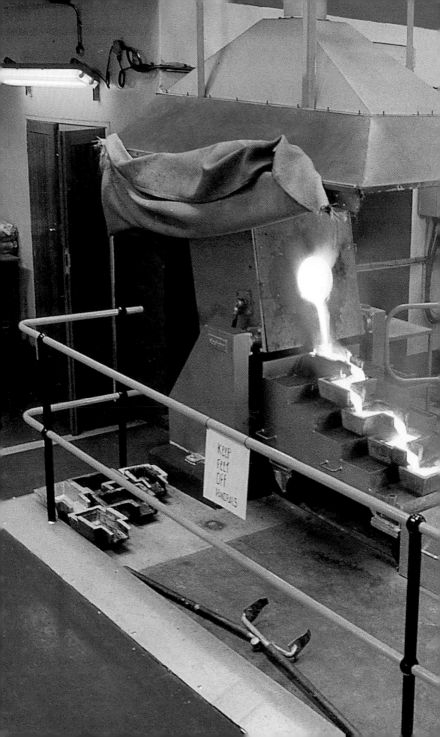

KEEP
FEET
OFF
HANDRAILS

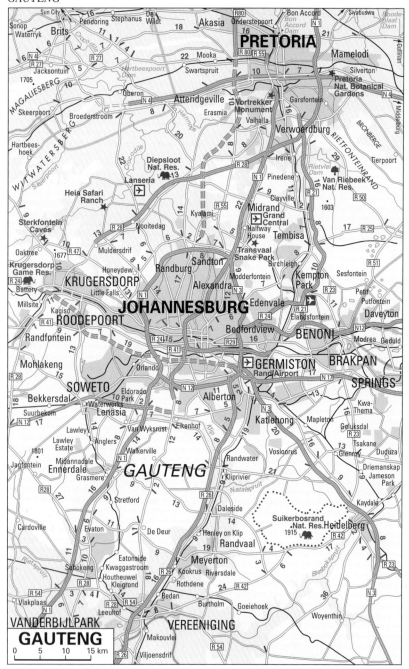

GAUTENG

0   5   10   15 km

GAUTENG

JOHANNESBURG
PRETORIA
EXCURSION TO THE NDEBELE
EXCURSION TO SUN CITY

GAUTENG

The province of Gauteng (which in Sotho means "Place of gold," and which, until 1995, was the region of Pretoria-Witwatersrand-Vereeniging, PWV), with its surface area of 7,316 square miles (18,760 square kilometers), occupies only 1.5% of the country and is thus its smallest province. Its 6.8 million inhabitants, however, give it the second-largest population (16.8% of the total) and the highest population density (365 per square kilometer) of all the provinces. 28% of the inhabitants speak Sotho, 20% Afrikaans, 18% Zulu and 15% English (which, however, is understood in most places).

After the start of gold mining in 1886, this area became the main economic center of South Africa. Over one-third of the country's gross national product comes from Gauteng, where 27% of South Africa's jobs are concentrated, and the population has the highest per capita income in the country.

The province consists primarily of the population center along the Witwatersrand range, as well as the concentration

Preceding pages: Ndebele women express themselves in the colorful painting of their houses. Gold smelting in Randfontein.

of heavy industry around Vereeniging and Vanderbijlpark in the south. Its main center is the capital Johannesburg with its surrounding townships, of which Soweto is by far the largest and the best-known, along with Alexandra.

JOHANNESBURG

What is today the largest and most important city in South Africa grew out of the settlement in Witwatersrand, known as Rand for short, where in 1886 – 20 years after the first diamond finds in Kimberley – an Australian prospector discovered an exposed vein (or reef) of gold. Within a very short time, thousands of fortune-seekers were pouring into the area. Johannes Rissik and Christian Johannes Joubert, authorized representatives of the government, founded a town in a farm area that they called Johannesburg after the Christian name they shared. Three years later, it was already the largest town in southern Africa, and by 1892 it was linked by rail with the Cape Colony. In 1960, its population passed the million mark.

The city known to the blacks as *Egoli*, City of Gold, and called "Joburg" for short by the whole country, is situated 5,732 feet (1,753 m) above sea level. It is not unjustifiably dubbed the Chicago or

33

Manhattan of South Africa: most of the leading companies in the country have their headquarters here, while the stock exchange, founded only a year after the first gold was discovered, is the central financial and capital market for the whole of southern Africa. As a consequence, Johannesburg has also become the country's most important transportation hub, not least because of its airport (**Johannesburg International**), 15 miles (24 km) east of the city center, or downtown.

Johannesburg, the center of which is laid out like a chessboard, has never been a city which attracted sightseers, and the discrepancy between the first and the third world is more evident here than anywhere else. Would-be visitors may initially be put off by the numerous residents of the black townships, who are now thronging into the downtown area –

Above: Night skyline of Johannesburg. Right: Demonstors take to the streets to demand a living wage.

minibus taxi drivers and street vendors dominate the scene – but the real deterrent to the tourist trade is the high crime rate for which the city is known the world over.

To get an overview of the city, the best place to start is the **Carlton Panorama**, a 660-foot (202 m) platform on the 50th floor of the Carlton Center, which is reached by lift.

In the north part of the city are attractive, spacious garden suburbs such as Parktown, Saxonworld and Rosebank; in recent years, good hotels, high-class shopping centers and other establishments have relocated here from the city center. The densely populated, cosmopolitan district of **Hillbrow,** north of downtown, is dominated by the **J.G. Strijdom Tower** (880 feet/269 m high). To the south is the mining area, its resources now largely exhausted; here, there are no high-rise buildings. Along the once-rich gold vein, or reef, are small ponds, formed from water that was pumped out of the mines, and the dumps

that were once such a characteristic feature of the city. These dumps consist mainly of floury, golden-yellow dust: the color comes from the chemicals that are used for gold extraction, in particular cyanides. Since 1977, workers have been reprocessing this material, since new, improved technological methods enable them to extract the last vestiges of the gold which still remains in it. The process also yields uranium, which no one was interested in when gold-mining first began, as well as iron pyrite, which is used to make sulfuric acid. After the conclusion of this extraction work, the dumps are to be planted and developed into parkland.

On the lower floors of the high-rise office block of the **Carlton Centre**, there's a shopping center (which has lost some of its original high-class air). Near the reception desk in the once-renowned **Carlton Hotel** is an American Express office which is also open on Saturdays and Sundays. Not far from this, on the corner of Market and Kruis Streets, is the local **tourist information office** (Johannesburg Publicity Association).

Hardly any of the city's original buildings have remained. One of the few exceptions is the fine old **Rissik Street Post Office**, a brick building dating from 1897, to which an extra story and a tower were added in 1902. Today it is a national landmark, but still functions as a post office, even though in 1935 a new building was put up in Jeppe Street to serve as the **Main Post Office**. In a small park behind the old post office is an attractive fountain that features 18 bronze impalas leaping through a jet of water. **City Hall**, built from 1910-15 and home base of the National Symphonic Orchestra, is also still in use, but most of its functions have been transferred to the large modern **Civic Centre**, near the **Civic Theatre**, one of the main stages in Johannesburg. East of the Civic Center, on Korte Street, is the **Adler Museum of the History of Medicine**, which, in addition to historic medical equipment, also displays the herb and plant stores of a medicine man.

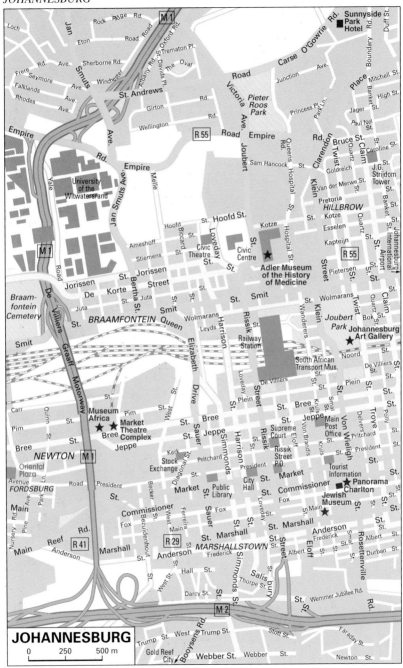

JOHANNESBURG

0   250   500 m

There is sometimes a surprising contrast between older buildings, such as the **Public Library** (1936), the older part of the main train station (1935) and the Supreme Court in Pritchard Street, and such super-modern edifices as the Holiday Inn Garden Court Hotel, faced entirely in reflecting blue glass. This hotel is located in Smal Street, which has been transformed into a modern shopping gallery, the **Smal Street Mall**. The contrast is even more evident in **Diagonal Street**, the only street downtown which doesn't conform to the grid of the streets' chessboard pattern. The houses in the neighborhood are mostly one- or two-story buildings with numerous little shops, many of them owned by Indians (notably No. 14, where there's a shop selling African herbs of the kind the *sangoma,* or medicine man, uses to treat illnesses). Juxtaposed with these is the ultra-modern high-rise office building at 11 Diagonal Street, also known as "Diamond Building" because of its many-faceted facade which reflects the cityscape around it. Caught in its mirrors is another high-rise nearby, the **Stock Exchange**, erected in 1978, which is open to visitors.

The **Johannesburg Railway Station** at the junction of Rissik/De Villiers Street, built in 1966, is the largest in Africa; it has a left luggage office. On the lower floor of the older part of the station on Villiers Street, you'll find the **South African Transport Museum**. Buses to the airport depart from the adjacent rotunda.

About a mile (1.5 km) west of downtown, in the district of Forsdburg, there's a large, modern shopping center with a number of shops and restaurants. This facility, built in 1974, is the main Indian market in Johannesburg: because of its eastern atmosphere, it's been dubbed **Oriental Plaza**.

Above: "Diamond Building," an example of modern architecture in Johannesburg.

Not far from here as you head downtown is the **Market Theatre**, which has been cleverly and imaginatively set up in an old market building. The complex includes three stages, an art gallery and a famous jazz cellar (**Kippies**). Even before the end of apartheid, this was a venue for black theater groups and experimental theater, and the world-famous musical *Sarafina* had its premiere under this roof. Also successful here, as well as on other local stages, were performances by Pieter-Dirk Uys, the cabaret artist, actor, and author of satirical comedies about Johannesburg, who has also become well-known outside his own country.

Adjacent to the Market Theatre Complex is the **Museum Africa**, opened in 1994, which documents the geology, archaeology, anthropology and history of southern Africa from the Stone Age to the Nuclear Age. The adjoining **Bensusan Museum of Photography** is a source of information not only about the history of photography but also about

state-of-the-art equipment and technology. Many of South Africa's rock paintings are kept protected in the **Museum of South African Rock Art**. **Gramadoelas**, a good restaurant in the old market building, offers South African specialities such as venison and sometimes even crocodile. Opposite this is the pub Yard of Ale, which tends to attract a younger clientele.

Among the works of art in the **Johannesburg Art Gallery** in Joubert Park, not far from the train station, are masterpieces of European painting, including pictures by French impressionists, Picasso's chalk drawing "Tête d'Arlequin," and paintings by Rodin and Maillol.

If you leave downtown on the N 1/M 1, you'll come, shortly after crossing the railway lines, to the buildings of the **University of the Witwatersrand**, the largest English-speaking university in the country with around 18,000 students. A

Above: In Kippies jazz club. Right: In the slums of Soweto.

little to the northeast in the suburb of Parktown is **Sunnyside Park Hotel**, a very attractive, quiet place to stay with historic connections: it's the former residence of the British governor Lord Milner.

Anyone interested in things having to do with gold and its extraction can visit **Gold Reef City**, southwest of the city on the M1. Here, on the site of a disused mine, is an attempt (in a vaguely Disney-landesque style) to recreate the atmosphere of Johannesburg as it was 100 years ago. The staff wear period costume, and visitors are transported by coach or steam train. The complex also includes entertainment and shopping facilities, bars, restaurants, businesses and banks, and there are performances of tribal dances in a roofed theater. The **Gold Reef City Hotel** is an authentic period-style building offering modern comfort and luxury. For another perspective, you can go down shaft 14 of the disused Crown Mines, once some of the richest gold mines in the world, and learn about

gold-mining and the extraction of gold. A visit to Gold Reef City is included in most standard city tours.

Much more interesting, but not so easy to arrange, are the tours of working gold mines which are organized at intervals by the South African Chamber of Mines. To participate, you have to apply at least two months in advance (minimum age 16).

Soweto

Just before Gold Reef City, the M 70, the Soweto Highway, branches off to the west from the M 1 and leads to the oldest, largest and internationally best-known of the residential townships built for the blacks in South Africa. Soweto, an abbreviation of the English name **So**uth **We**stern **To**wnships, is approximately 9 miles (15 km) southwest of Johannesburg, and occupies an area of 37 square miles (95 square km). Its current population is officially estimated at 3 million, but as people continue to move from the rural areas into the towns, the actual figures

are much higher. Soweto, until 1994 a ghetto which was administered semi-autonomously, is now part of Johannesburg. Since black tradition does not permit anyone to live at a higher level than anyone else, the houses are almost all single-story. It was only recently that rented apartment blocks several stories high were built at the edge of Soweto; these have gradually been occupied by members of the younger generation, who are more accustomed to city life and not so bound by tradition.

In addition to the unrelieved monotony of the many small houses – the oldest of these, in the Orlando East district, were put up as long ago as 1930 – there are equally grim, barrack-like buildings for single men, and depressing slum areas. But there are also, surprisingly, villa districts inhabited by famous, very wealthy black people such as Winnie Mandela or Archbishop Tutu, as well and up-and-coming members of society: the owners of taxi firms, brewers, and the like. The number of schools and kindergartens, or-

phanages, sports facilities and supermarkets is woefully inadequate for the size of the population. In the hospital called **Baragwanath** after a British immigrant, founded in 1948 and with 3,000 beds the largest in Africa, black and white doctors work together side by side. Several hundred thousand people commute every day from Soweto to Johannesburg or other Witwatersrand cities. Numerous taxis, most of them minibuses owned by small-scale black entrepreneurs, solve some of the transportation problem, but also add to the traffic chaos in Johannesburg.

Around Johannesburg

Just north of Soweto is the garden city of **Roodeport**, which you can reach by taking the M 18 from downtown. The

Above. Mzumba dancers at the Heia Safari Ranch are accompanied by singing and rousing drum rhythms. Right: Blossoming jacaranda in Pretoria.

Witwatersrand National Botanic Gardens, 562.5 acres (225 hectares) in area, specializes in the typical vegetation of the highveld as well as its wealth of bird life.

The **Heia Safari Ranch**, a hotel in the hilly highveld with thatched, luxuriously furnished rondavels, is thronged on Sundays with people from the city. Around 22 miles (35 km) northwest of Johannesburg, it is accessible on the M 18 and the M 5 to Honeydew. On the grounds are ostriches, springbok, impalas, blesbocks and zebras, which sometimes come up to the swimmingpool. Here you can experience the main pastime of many South Africans, the "braai" (barbecue), and after lunch watch performances by a very good group of about 30 black men and women dancers (Mzumba). The lively dances of many peoples of southern Africa are accompanied by singing and the intricate rhythms of a variety of drums. You can also arrange to be collected from your hotel for a visit to the Ranch. By the Aloe Ridge Hotel, only a few miles away, is **Phumangena**, a traditional Zulu village built by Zulu craftsmen; here, Zulu families live according to centuries-old traditions, and demonstrate their handicraft skills.

From Krugersdorp, 19 miles (30 km) northwest of Johannesburg, the R 563/R 47 leads to the **Sterkfontein Caves**, large stalactite caves with six chambers linked by passages where, in 1896, significant finds were made of the skulls and bones of prehistoric people. Some of these finds are exhibited in the adjacent museum.

Sandton, north of Johannesburg, an independent district formed by the fusion of three suburbs, is a sprawling green residential area with luxurious shopping centers, banks, department stores, and restaurants: one of the most attractive districts of Johannesburg. It also includes **Kyalami**, the car and motorbike race track built on a large tract of land once occupied by a farm, where the Formula-One race "Grand Prix of South Africa" is held every year. Not far away, the South African National Equestrian Centre holds dressage shows every Sunday with **Lippizaner** horses, first brought here from Hungary after World War II and trained in the same way as the horses of the Spanish Riding School in Vienna.

On the N 1 to Pretoria, 30 km (19 miles) from Johannesburg, is the former mail coach station **Halfway House**. Here, in the **Transvaal Snake Park**, visitors can watch poisonous snakes being "milked" for the production of snake serum.

Johannesburg International, the largest and busiest **airport** in the country in **Kempton Park**, 15 miles (24 km) from downtown, is connected by a regular bus service with Pretoria and Johannesburg. From here, you can make excursions into neighboring countries, notably Botswana (Okavango Delta) and Zimbabwe (Victoria Falls). Time and money permitting, a detour of this nature is well worthwhile, and a good selection of tours is offered by South African travel agencies.

PRETORIA

Johannesburg was created practically overnight with the help of British capital and people converging from all over the world 100 years ago. Pretoria, by contrast, reflects a slower, more organic development from the rural metropolis of the Boer state of Transvaal into today's administrative capital and research and education center of the modern industrial state of South Africa; the city harmonically blends new and old. In area, it's the largest city in the country (246 square miles/632 square km); and its population is approximately 550,000 (Greater Pretoria, including such neighboring communities as Verwoerdburg, Mamelodi, and others, totals around 1.5 million). Surrounded by long chains of mountains, Pretoria is located 980 feet (300 m) lower than Johannesburg, at an altitude of 4,457 feet (1,363 m) above sea level; it therefore has milder winters, but also hotter summers. This climate, together with the ample summer rain, creates the ideal con-

ditions for the lush subtropical vegetation of this garden city. The city presents an especially charming picture in spring (October/November), particularly when viewed from the surrounding heights; the 70,000 flowering jacaranda trees which line its streets and adorn many of its gardens seem to envelop it in a sea of delicate mauve blossom. Jacarandas, which come from Argentina, were first brought to Pretoria in 1888.

Tourists who want to avoid Johannesburg, with its hectic pace and bad reputation as a center of crime, generally prefer to use this quieter city as a base for tours of the area.

At the heart of downtown, which is, like Johannesburg, laid out in a chessboard grid, is **Church Square**, with a statue of President Paul Kruger at its center. Pretoria's two main streets intersect here: Paul Kruger Street, which runs north from the main train station in the

Above: Church Square, Pretoria, with the Paul Kruger statue and the Old Raadsaal.

south, and Church Street, more than 11 miles (18 km) long, bisecting the city from east to west. The south side of the square with the **Old Raadsaal** (the seat of the South African Republic government, dating from 1860), is said to have been modeled on Trafalgar Square in London, while the north side with the **Palace of Justice** was based on the Place de la Concorde in Paris.

Paul Kruger Street leads north to the **Zoological Gardens**, the oldest and, with its aquarium and reptile park, most important zoo in South Africa. A cable car provides unusual views of the animals in their outdoor enclosures. South of Church Square, set amidst attractive gardens, is **City Hall**: its tower contains a carillon with 32 bells. The highlight of the natural history collections in the **Transvaal Museum** opposite is the unique exhibition in the Austin Roberts Bird Hall. It contains all 887 species of bird occurring in southern Africa, classified and described by A. Roberts in his book *Birds of Southern Africa*, which

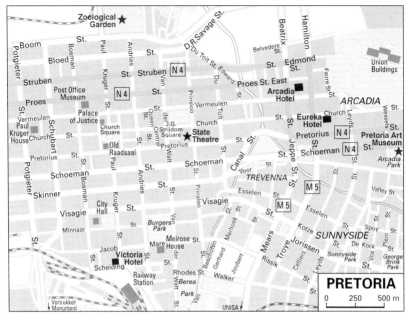

was first published in 1940 and is highly regarded by all ornithologists and amateur bird-watchers. Anyone interested in geology and mineralogy will find the collection in the adjacent **Museum of Geological Survey** very informative.

A little further south, opposite Burgers Park, the oldest park in Pretoria, is **Melrose House**, built in 1886 and a good example of Victorian architecture. Here, in 1902, the end of the Boer war was sealed with the signing of the Treaty of Vereeniging. In Church Street, west of Church Square, is the inconspicuous **Paul Kruger House**, where Paul Kruger lived during his presidency from 1883-1900. Today, the building is a national monument and a museum.

The **Pretoria State Theatre**, opened in 1981, is the largest and most modern theater complex in South Africa, with stages for both opera and drama. The neighboring high-rise building of the **South Africa Reserve Bank**, which was completed in 1987, is the tallest building in the city, 490 feet (150 m) high; the facade of black polished granite and glass is one of the city's signature landmarks. **Strijdom Square** is surrounded by an interesting juxtaposition of buildings with historical, neoclassical and Art Nouveau facades. Its most striking feature is the monument to the former prime minister Hans Strijdom (1954-58), protected by a tent-like roof.

To the northeast, Pretoria is dominated the **Union Buildings,** designed between 1910-13 by the English architect Sir Herbert Baker as the seat of government, which tower above the city on their hilltop site. Made of light, orange-red sandstone with a red tiled roof, the complex is 900 feet (275 m) long and consists of a semicircular section decorated with columns flanked on both sides by towers with domed roofs and two identical wings. It commands a magnificent view of the city with terraced gardens full of flowers and spacious lawns sweeping down to Church Street.

South of this, in Arcadia Park, is the **Pretoria Art Museum**; the works on dis-

play here are, for the most part, by South African artists.

4.3 miles (7 km) east of the city center, Church Street crosses the N 1, which runs through the city from north to south. As the N 4 it continues to Eastern Transvaal; at the beginning of this highway, on the left-hand side, it passes the **Pretoria National Botanical Gardens**. The plants here are grouped according to the climatic zone in which they originate. Next to the gardens are the impressive grounds of the Council for Scientific and Industrial Research, a research organization founded in 1945 and run according to market principles since 1988.

Approaching Pretoria from the south on the R 21, you can't miss the large buildings of the University of South Africa, the **UNISA**, which were put up in 1972. The largest open university in the world, it has never observed any kind of

racial segregation since it opened in 1951; it also has a high academic reputation. At present, more than 125,000 students are enrolled here.

From the N 1 south of Pretoria, you can take the R 7 westward to the **Voortrekker Monument**, a prominent landmark and the "shrine" of the Boers. The massive granite building 130 feet (40 m) high on a pedestal 130 feet square (40 by 40 m) was commenced in 1937 and inaugurated in 1949. In a large domed "Hall of Heroes," 27 marble friezes illustrate the Great Trek of 1835; through a round opening in the floor a granite cenotaph is visible in the hall below. The monument is enclosed by a wall made of 64 stone oxcarts representing the "barricade of wagons" with which the trekkers surrounded themselves when they were expecting an attack. From the roof, reached by a flight of 260 steps inside the building, there is a panoramic view of Pretoria and its surroundings. Adjoining the monument is a small museum devoted to the "Voortrekkers."

Above: The stone "barricade of wagons" around the Voortrekker Monument. Right: Hot-air ballooning.

Around Pretoria

As you go north, the R 513 branches off east from the N 1 after approximately 4 miles/7 km, and reaches **Cullinan** after a further 14 miles (23 km). It was here that the 3,106-carat "Cullinan," the largest diamond ever found, was discovered in 1905. The diamond was split in Amsterdam and one section of it, the 530-carat "Star of Africa," is among the British Crown Jewels. The **Premier Diamond Mine** can be visited on application (minimum age 10 years).

The **Heia Safari Ranch**, recommended above as an excursion from Johannesburg, is also easy to reach from Pretoria on the R 28, which branches off southeast from the N 1 (Honeydew exit).

Hartebeespoort Dam, a large reservoir west of Pretoria (N 4), is a popular day-trip destination, especially for anglers and water sports fans. East of the dam, a cable car (1,308 feet/400 m up) runs to the highest point of the 74-mile (120-km) **Magalisberg Range** (6,056 feet/1,852 m), with a magnificent view of the surrounding countryside. The attractions of the area include hang-gliding, paragliding, and hot-air balloon safaris.

EXCURSION TO THE NDEBELE

The Ndebele, like the Zulus and Xhosa, are members of the Nguni language group. Unlike the Ndebele in the Matabele area of Zimbabwe, a former Zulu tribe that migrated there in the course of the *mfeqane*, the Ndebele in Transvaal have been in this region for centuries. Since the 16th century, they've been divided into two groups. The northern Ndebele, in the former Homeland of Lebowa in the east of Eastern Transvaal province, have to some extent merged with the Tswana and Sotho around them, while the southern Ndebele have been more successful in preserving their own culture and language. They are probably the most artistically creative of all the peoples in southern Africa. Their homes, originally round, beehive-shaped huts

thatched with grass, were arranged round the cattle kraal in an open courtyard surrounded by a wall. Since the beginning of this century they have used clay to create entrances and walls in a great variety of designs and occasionally also decorative sculpture. It is only quite recently that they have also started to build rectangular houses. The women alone are responsible for painting the house and courtyard walls with abstract forms and motifs; they are now increasingly tending to use acrylic paints because of their greater brightness and durability. The Ndebele women's appreciation of color and form is also evident in their jewelry. A woman wearing chignon made of woven grass and embroidered with beads is showing that she's married; if her husband has

built her a house, she will also wear one or more metal bands round her neck, depending on how wealthy they are. Headgear, aprons and other clothing are also colorful and ornately decorated. The Open Air Museum in **Botschabelo**, near Middleburg, Eastern Transvaal, documents not only the development of the architecture, but also other aspects of the culture of this highly talented people.

From Pretoria, you can reach their former homeland of KwaNdebele in the province of Eastern Transvaal, northeast of Pretoria, which is not scenically particularly attractive, by taking the R 573 to Marble Hall. Visitors who have read about the culture of the Ndebele and are interested in seeing examples of their art will initially be disappointed: there are few houses with the characteristic painting. Their search will however be rewarded at Siyabuswa, the former capital (just off the R 573) and at **Weltevreden**, a little to the north of this, with the seat of the chief ("Court of the King") and other impressively decorated buildings.

Above: The headgear and neck bands of a Ndebele woman indicate her social status. Above right: Ndebele woman cooking for a festival. Right: Resting after a sprint – a cheetah in Pilanesberg National Park.

EXCURSION TO SUN CITY

The legendary entertainment center **Sun City**, the "Las Vegas of South Africa," 82 miles (132 km) west of Pretoria and 111 miles (179 km) from Johannesburg, is located in Northwest Province, in the formerly "independent" region of Bophuthatswana. Built in the midst of unspoilt countryside by a hotel concern, there is scarcely any form of entertainment and recreation facility it does not provide. Recently the luxury palace **Lost City** was added, taking as its theme the legend of the "Lost City" which gives it its name.

The complex with its luxury hotels, restaurants, snack bars and bars is surrounded by well-tended, subtropical greenery. There are artificial lakes for sailing, windsurfing, water skiing and boating; there are also swimming pools and facilities for playing tennis, golf, squash, bowling and other sports. You can ride, have a sauna, spoil yourself with a massage or beauty treatment or spend your money in the boutiques and jewelry shops. For day visitors, there are lockers and changing rooms with showers. There are all the enticements of games of chance in the casino, and there are amusement arcades filled with one-armed bandits. Further entertainment is provided by discos, an 8,000-seat theater with performances by international stars, pop concerts and sporting events.

For those more interested in nature, a visit to nearby **Pilanesberg National Park** (137,500 acres / 55,000 hectares, opened in 1980) is recommended. In the hills, an interesting geological formation arranged in an almost complete ring made of basic volcanic rock (the park is named after the highest peak, 5,500 ft / 1,682 m above sea level), more than 12,000 wild animals, including lions, rhinos and elephants, were resettled alongside the indigenous leopards, cheetahs, baboons, warthogs and other animals and around 300 species of bird. The park is open all year round (accommodation in the luxurious **Tschukudu Camp**).

GAUTENG
Transportation

Pretoria, the country's administrative center, and the economic capital of Johannesburg are the country's main traffic hubs, with excellent transportation links.

Bus: Intercity/long-distance buses (Greyhound, Translux) run regularly from Pretoria (main railway station) and Johannesburg (rotunda at the main station; Mainliners also run from here); these connect both cities with numerous other cities and towns along a wide variety of routes. Greyhound also runs to Harare / Zimbabwe and Gaborone / Botswana, Translux to Harare / Zimbabwe, Mainliner to Windhoek / Namibia. For day excursions in both cities, as well as trips to Gold Reef City and Sun City, or for a trip to and through Soweto, there are a number of companies: one that can be recommended is "Jimmy's Face to Face Tours," 130 Main Street, Johannesburg, 2nd floor, Budget House, tel: 331-6109, fax: 331-5388.

Train: Johannesburg and Pretoria are departure points for the Blue Train and for most other long-distance train lines. Rovos Rail departs from the Victoria Hotel in Pretoria.

Air: Johannesburg International Airport (tel. 333-6504) is still the country's most important airport for international flights from overseas and Africa. There's regular bus service to Johannesburg (rotunda, every half-hour from 5 am - 10 pm; 15 mi/24 km), Sandton and Pretoria (30 mi/48 km). Domestic flights are available from SAA (Bloemfontein, Cape Town, Durban, East London, George, Port Elizabeth), South African Express (SAX; Kimberley and Upington), and the airlines Airlink (Bloemfontein, East London, Nelspruit, Phalaborwa, Pietermaritzburg, Pietersburg, Tzaneen, Port Elizabeth, Hluhluwe, Durban and Richards Bay), Comair (Gaborone, Richards Bay, Skukuza, Cape Town and Durban), Transkei Airways (Umtata), Sun Air (Mmabatho, Sun City, Cape Town), Inter Air (Nelspruit, Phalaborwa and Messina). From Johannesburg-Lanseria (tel. 659-2750) to the northwest (25 mi/41 km), Theron Airways flies to Pietersburg and Thohoyandou; National Airlines to Sishen. Charter flights also depart from Johannesburg-Rand Air Port (tel. 827-8884) in Germiston (9 mi/15 km), Grand Central (tel. 805-3166) in Midrand (about 1 mi/2 km NE of Halfway House).

Tourist Information

Five of the region's most important tourist offices have combined to form the **Egoli Tourism Authority**: **GJTA, Greater Johannesburg Publicity Association**, corner Kruis/Market Street, PO Box 4580, tel: 337-6650, fax: 333-7272; **ERTA, East Rand Tourism Association**, PO Box 14133, Farrameer 1518, tel: 011/422-3651, fax: 421-6462; **MI-**

TRATOUR, Mid Transvaal Tourism, PO Box 50 521, Wierdapark 0149, tel: 012/313-7694; **WESTOUR, West Rand Tourism Authority**, P/Bag X033, Randfontein 1760, tel: 011/412-2701, fax: 692-3531; **THABISO, Vaal Triangle Tourism Authority**, PO Box 2720, Vereeniging 1930, tel: 2716/55-1377, fax: 55-1399.

JOHANNESBURG and environs

Telephone and fax area code: 011; post code: 2000
Taxi: tel: 725-3333, 725-1111, 648-1212.

Accommodations

JOHANNESBURG: *LUXURY:* **Carlton Court** (Silver), Main Street, PO Box 7709, tel: 331-8911, fax: 331-3555. **Sandton Sun & Towers** (Silver), corner 5th/Alice St., PO Box 784 902, tel: 780-5000, fax: 780-5002. **Sunnyside Park Hotel** (Sun Chain), 2 York rund, Parktown, tel: 643-7226. fax: 642-0019. *MODERATE:* **Rosebank Hotel**, corner Tyrwhitt/ Sturdee Ave., PO Box 52025, Saxonworld 2132, tel: 447-2700, fax: 447-33276. **Gold Reef City**, PO Box 61, Johannesburg 2159, tel. and fax: 496-1626. **Protea Gardens Hotel**, 35 O'Reilly Road, Berea, PO Box 688 Houghton 2041, tel: 643-6610, fax: 484-2622. **Holiday Inn Garden Court Johannesburg Airport**, 6 Hulley rund, Private Bag 5, Jan Smuts 1627, tel: 392-1062, fax: 974-8097. **City Lodge Airport**, Sandvale rund, Edenvale, PO Box 448 Isando 1600, tel: 392-1750, fax: 392-2644. *BUDGET:* **Mariston**, corner Claim/Koch St., PO Box 23013, Joubert Park 2044, tel: 725-4130, fax: 725-2921. **Springbok Hotel**, 73 Joubert St, tel: 337-8336, fax: 337-8396. **Diepkloof Protea Hotel**, 8651 Zone 6, Diepkloof 1868 (Soweto), tel: 938-1637, fax: 933-2041. **Someplace Else Guesthouse**, PO Box 9249, Edleen, Kempton Park 1625 (near the airport), tel. and fax: 393-2291. *YOUTH HOSTELS:* **Berea Youth Hostel**, 4 Fife Ave. Berea, tel: 643-1213, fax: 643-1412. **Fairview Youth Hostel**, Fairview, tel: 618-2048. **International Travellers Hostel**, 55 1st Street, Bez Valley, tel: 614-4640, fax: 642-2793. **ENVIRONS**: *MODERATE:* **Heia Safari Ranch**, Swartkop, Muldersdrift, PO Box 1387, Honeydew 2040, tel: 659-0605, fax: 659-0709.

Restaurants

El Em Prawns (fish, shellfish), 109 Kerk St., tel: 337-8083. **Gramadoelas at the Market** (South African, with game specialties), Bree St., in the Market Theatre Complex, tel: 838-6960 (closed Sun). **Ma Cuisine**, 40 7th Avenue, Parktown North, tel: 880-1946 (closed Sun & Mon). **Linger Longer**, 58 Wierda rund West, Wierda Valley, Sandton, tel: 884-0465 (closed Sun). **Jasper's 108**, Shop 108 Rosebank Mall, Craddock Av., Rosebank, tel: 442-4130 (closed Sun & Mon).

Museums and Sights

Carlton Panorama, open daily 9 am-11 pm **Adler Museum of the History of Medicine**, Mon-Fri 9 am-4 pm. **Johannesburg Stock Exchange**, guided tours Mon-Fri 11 am and 2 pm; advance reservation advised, tel: 833-6580.

Museum Africa with the **Bensusan Museum of Photography** and **Museum of South African Rock Art**, Tue-Sun 9 am-5 pm. **South African Transport Museum**, Mon-Fri 7:30 am-3:45 pm. **Johannesburg Art Gallery**, Tue-Sun 10 am-5 pm. **Geological Museum** and **Africana Museum**, Mon-Sat 9 am-5:30 pm, Sun 2-5:30 pm. **Gold Reef City**, Tue-Sun 9:30 am-5 pm; African dances performed twice daily (weekends 3 times daily).

Witwatersrand National Botanic Gardens, Roodepoort, daily 8 am-6 pm. **Sterkfontein Caves**, Tue-Sun 9 am-4 pm; guided tours every half-hour. **Lipizzaner** dressage, Sun 11 am (reserve through Computicket). **Transvaal Snake Park**, Mon-Sat 9 am-4:30 pm, Sun 9 am-5 pm, performances Mon-Fri 11 am and 3 pm, Sat also at 2 and 4 pm, Sun hourly from 11 am-5 pm. **Rondebult Bird Sanctuary**, daily 8 am-5 pm.

Tourist Information

SATOUR, corner Kruis/Market St., PO Box 1094, tel: 333-8082, fax: 333-0896. **Automobile Association**, AA House, 66 De Korte St., Braamfontein 2001, tel: 407-1000. **The Greater Johannesburg Tourism Authority** has branches in the International Arrivals Hall of the international airport as well as in the rotunda at the train station; for information, call "What's on", 400-2222. **Chamber of Mines**, 5 Hollard St., tel: 838-8211, fax: 838-4251. **American Express**, in the Carlton Hotel, tel: 331-7291.

Weather forecast: tel: 975-5671.

PRETORIA and surroundings

Telephone and fax area code: 012, post code: 007. Pretoria has a smoothly-functioning public transportation system; information (tel: 313-0839) and bus departure at the southeast corner of Church Square. Taxi: 325-8072, 08011-11-611, 324-4718.

Accommodations

PRETORIA: *MODERATE:* **Victoria Hotel**, 200 Scheiding St., PO Box 2837, tel: 323-6052, fax: 323-0843. **Holiday Inn Garden Court Pretoria**, corner Van der Walt and Minnaar St., PO Box 2301, tel: 322-7500, fax: 322-9429. **Boulevard Protea Hotel**, 186 Strouben St, PO Box 425, tel: 326-4806, fax: 326 1366.

BUDGET: **Arcadia Hotel**, 515 Proes St., PO Box 26 104, tel: 326-9311, fax: 326-1067. **Panorama**, 706 Arcadia Street, Arcadia, tel: 344-3010. **Eureka**

Hotel, 579 Church St, Arcadia, tel: 44-4261.

SURROUNDINGS: *MODERATE:* **Town Lodge Midrand**, corner Becker rund and Le Roux Ave, Waterfall Park, PO Box 5622, Halfway House, Midrand 1685, tel: 315-6047, fax: 315-6004. **Midrand Protea Hotel**, 14th St. Noordwyk, Ext. 20, PO Box 1840, Halfway House 1685, tel: 011/318-1868, fax: 318-2429.

Restaurants

Chagall's at Toulouse, Fountains Valley, tel: 341-7511 (excellent; closed Sun.). **Chez Patrice**, Riviera Galleries, 97 Soutpansberg Road, tel: 329-4028 (excellent; closed Sun & Mon). **La Madeleine**, 258 Esselen St. Sunnyside, tel: 44-6076 (closed Sun & Mon). **Gerard Moerdyk**, 752 Part St., Arcadia, tel: 344-4856 (South African cuisine; closed Sun) **Allegro**, State Theatre, Church St., tel: 322-4678. **La Perla** (Swiss cuisine), Didacta Building, 211 Skinner St., tel: 322-2759 (closed Sun).

Museums and Sights

Transvaal Museum and **Geological Survey Museum**, Mon-Sat 9 am-5 pm, Sun 11 am-5 pm. **Melrose House**, Tue-Sat 10 am-5 pm, Sun 12-5 pm. **Paul Kruger House Museum**, Mon-Sat 8:30 am-4 pm, Sun 11 am-4 pm. **Pretoria Art Museum**, Tue-Sat 10 am-5 pm, Sun 1-6 pm, Wed 7:30-8 pm. Guided tours of the city theater every Wednesday. **Voortrekker Monument**, Mon-Sat 9 am-4:45 pm, Sun 11 am-4:45 pm. **Premier Diamond Mine**, tours Tue-Fri 9:30-11 am; participants must be over the age of 10.

Tourist Information

Tourist Rendevouz Travel Centre, corner Prinsloo and Vermeulen St., tel: 323-1222, 313-7694 or 313-7980.

Weather forecast: tel: 21-9621.

SUN CITY

Telephone / fax area code 01465, postal code 0316. The airline Sun Air flies regularly from here to Johannesburg, Durban and Cape Town.

Accommodations

LUXURY: **The Palace of the Lost City**, PO Box 308, tel: 01465/7-3000, fax: 7-3111; **Sun City Hotel**, PO Box 2, tel: 2-1000, fax: 2-1470; **The Cascades**, PO Box 7, tel: 2-1000, fax: 7545. *MODERATE:* **The Cabanas**, PO Box 3, tel: 2-100, fax: 2-1590. Pilanesberg National Park, The Reservation Officer, Pilanesberg National Park, PO Box 1201, Mogwase 0302, tel: 01 465/5-5356.

Tourist Information

Pilanesberg Tourist Office (Sun City), PO Box Sun City, Pilanesberg, tel: 01 465/21-359.

NORTHERN PROVINCE

FROM PIETERSBURG INTO THE LOWVELD

SOUTPANSBERG AND THE VENDA REGION

NORTHERN PROVINCE

South Africa's northernmost province borders on Botswana, Zimbabwe and Mozambique. Occupying 8.9% of the total area of South Africa, it has 12.6% of the population. Its landscape is a succession of basins and plateaus, interspersed with mountains and mountain ranges, and cut through with deep valleys. Toward the north, where the country is increasingly lower in altitude, the temperature increases and the rainfall – except in the mountains – decreases. 56% of the inhabitants speak Pedi, 22% Shangaan, and 12% Venda. This province has the highest rates of unemployment, illiteracy and birth in all of South Africa.

FROM PIETERSBURG TO THE LOWVELD

As you drive from Pretoria northwards on the N 1, there are a number of interesting sights along the way. In **Papatso**, a craft center 7.4 miles (12 km) past Hammanksraal, the work of black South African artists and craftsmen is displayed and

Preceding pages: Tomato harvest in Northern Transvaal. Left: Pietersburg – a pose of boredom, or simple midday languor.

sold; here, you can also visit a reconstructed Ndebele village with painted houses. **Warmbaths**, around 34 miles (55 km) further north, is a spa with abundant hot springs said to be particularly beneficial to sufferers of rheumatism. After the small town of Potgietersrus, a turnoff from the N 1 leads 7 miles (11.5 km) to the massive limestone cave of **Makapansgat**. The cave entrance lies in a fissured gorge overgrown with euphorbia, aloes and trees. Excavations, as well as archaeological and paleontological research conducted on this site, have yielded important findings from the Paleolithic Age and prehistoric bones. You can only visit the cave, however, with the special permission of the Bernard Price Institute of the University of Witwatersrand.

Pietersburg (162 miles/261 km from Pretoria), founded in 1886 by Voortrekkers, sits on an open, grassy plateau 4,186 feet (1,280 m) above sea level. The provisional capital of the province is a bustling, modern place with wide, tree-lined streets. Six miles (9 km) to the southeast on the R 37 is the open-air museum **Bakone Malapa**, which includes an information center and a traditional North Sotho kraal; this group also sells specimens of its artisan work, produced with their traditional skill.

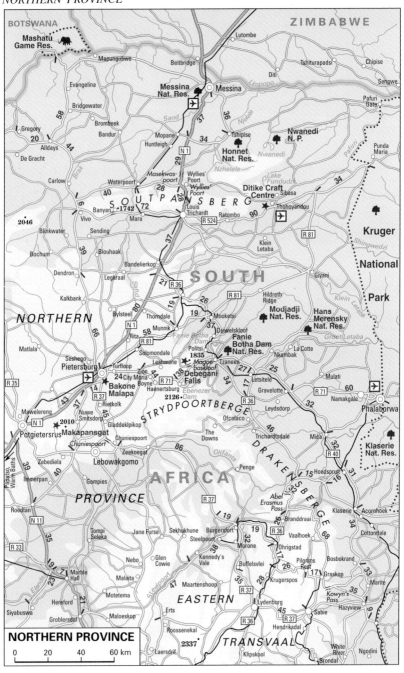

NORTHERN PROVINCE

| 0 | 20 | 40 | 60 km |

Pietersburg is a popular stopping place for travelers en route to the east and the north. A particularly attractive route leads from here via Tzaneen to the Phalaborwa Gate of Kruger Park. Take the R 71 east out of Pietersburg: after 16 miles (25 km), you will pass the modern buildings of the University of the North in **Turfloop**, which was the largest black university in South Africa when it opened in 1970, and now has approximately 16,000 students. Six miles (10 km) further on is **Zion City Moria**, the center of the Zion Christian Church, one of the largest independent black churches. Millions of the faithful gather here every Easter.

In **Haenertsburg**, at the foot of the 7,282-foot (2,227 m) mountain Wolkberg, the road forks. The R 528 leads directly to Tzaneen through the valley of the **Letaba** River, which has been dammed east of Haenertsburg to form the reservoir of the **Ebenezer Dam**, and from which the district takes its name. The R 71, after approximately 6 miles (10 km), goes up through the **Magoebaskloof**, one of the most magnificent gorges in South Africa, and into the lowveld, thereby crossing the Great Escarpment and ascending some 370 feet (600 m) in only 3.7 miles (6 km). Atop the pass, you can branch off for a highly recommended detour of about 6 miles (10 km) by turning left onto an unpaved road. Steep and somewhat bumpy in places, this route nonetheless rewards the traveler with lush, subtropical vegetation, waterfalls, cascades and splendid views. In the summer, however, it can be hot, humid, and also foggy. After 8 miles (13 km), a turn-off to the left leads to the **Debegeni Falls**; if you turn right, another 2 miles (3 km) will bring you back onto the R 71, which will take you the remaining 9 miles (14 km) to Tzaneen. As the drive

Above: Traditional North Sotho kraal in the Bakone Malapa open-air museum.

through the Letaba Valley is also extremely lovely, it's worth making a round trip, if not a day trip, from Pietersburg to enjoy it.

Tzaneen is an attractive destination in its own right. Nine miles (15 km) to the south is the **Coach House**, surrounded by lush greenery in the midst of forests, lemon, tea, and cotton plantations; the establishment, which has several times been awarded the title of best country hotel in South Africa, is an inviting place to tarry. In the nearby **New Agatha State Forest** are remains of the original jungle-like forest.

Duiwelskloof, 13 miles (21 km) north of Tzaneen, is an equally rewarding destination. On the way, set in pinewoods, is the **Fanie Botha Dam Nature Reserve**, a picturesque reservoir ideal for bird-watchers and anglers. A further attraction is the large **Modjadji Nature Reserve** to the northeast, 1,500 acres (600 hectares) in area. Thanks to strict conservation regulations, a unique wood with Modjadji cycads (breadfruit trees) has been

preserved in its original form. This tree (*Encephalartos transvenosus*), one of the largest of the 29 types of cycads, grows to a height of 16 to 26 feet (5-8 m), sometimes even reaching heights of 42 feet (13 m); the fruit can weigh up to 75 pounds (34 kg). It is one of the oldest plants in the world and was widespread at the time of the dinosaurs, 50 to 60 million years ago. The protected area is located 18 miles (28.6 km) northeast of Duiwelskloof in the territory of the Lobedu, a North Sotho tribe. Modjadji is home to the current successor of the legendary Rain Queen, a princess who fled here with a few followers in the 16th century, bringing with her the secret of rain-making, which has been handed down to her successors. The figure of the Rain Queen was the inspiration for Henry Rider Haggard's novel *She*, published in 1887. The

Above: Sable antelope in the Hans Merensky Nature Reserve. Right: There are many legends associated with the baobab (monkey-bread tree).

cycad forest is approximately a mile (2 km) from the queen's kraal.

If you go east out of Tzaneen on the R71, a turnoff after 19 miles (30 km) will lead you northeast to the **Hans Merensky Nature Reserve**, named for a famous geologist of German descent who played an important part in the discovery of the country's natural mineral resources and the development of mining in nearby Phalaborwa. The park contains a wide variety of birds; since 1954, these have been joined by a wealth of wild animals, which have gradually been resettled here. A reconstructed Tsonga kraal here has been set up as an open-air museum, and an attractive spa and holiday center has grown up around a nearby hot spring.

The town of **Phalaborwa**, 68 miles (110 km) southeast of Tzaneen, originated as a result of a nearby volcanic chimney. Its rich mineral reserves, including phosphates and the most abundant deposit of vermiculite in the world, are mined using open-cast methods. In places, the large mining and industrial

areas look like lunar landscapes, partly because of the sulphur, which is a by-product of the significant copper extraction that takes place here, and is used to make sulfuric acid. Next to this, the town, which was not founded until 1957, looks surprisingly green and attractive; and the mining companies have built extensive recreational and leisure facilities. About 2 miles (3 km) east of town is the entrance to the central part of Kruger National Park.

SOUTPANSBERG AND THE VENDA REGION

North of Pietersburg, the N 1 gradually descends, leaves the plateau and, after going 37 miles (60 km) through a landscape of scattered granite kuppies and large euphorbias, crosses the Tropic of Capricorn, which is marked by a stele on the left-hand side of the road; a plaque explains its meaning. **Louis Trichardt**, some 30 miles (50 km) further on and 3,090 feet (945 m) above sea level in a

rich and fertile agricultural area at the foot of the **Soutpansberg** mountain range, is a good center for excursions and hikes. The Soutpansberg, 80 miles (130 km) long and up to 5,673 feet (1,735 m) high, takes its name from a large salt pan at its western end, which is fed by a powerful salt spring; it has supplied the population with salt since prehistoric times. The fertile plateau that runs along the range's crest has attracted settlers since time immemorial. The heavy annual rainfall (up to 80 inches / 2,000 mm) has been conducive to the substantial reforestation of the area with evergreens, eucalyptus and acacias.

After Louis Trichardt, the N 1 slowly climbs into the densely forested mountains. On the left after 2.5 miles (4 km) is the entrance to **Clouds End**, a comfortable hotel in a splendid, spacious garden setting. After crossing the pass (4,983 feet/1,524 m above sea level), the road descends to the fertile central valley of the Soutpansberg chain. The road through the pass known as **Wyllie's**

Poort, a dramatic narrow gorge with steep rocky cliffs and yellow lichens patterning the dark stone, was destroyed by a landslide in 1958. Traffic now goes through the two **Verwoerd Tunnels**, (808 feet/247 m and 1,494 feet/457 m long), which were opened in 1961. From a lay-by on the left side of the road between the two tunnels, you can see part of the old pass road and its wild and spectacular surroundings.

North of the Soutpansberg range, the gently undulating savanna becomes increasingly dry; evergreen mopane trees and baobabs dominate the landscape. The baobab or monkey bread tree (*adansonia digita*) reaches a height of only 33-49 feet (10-15 m), but the circumference of its trunk can be as much as 91 feet (28 m). With modern methods of estimating age, it has been established that a baobab with a trunk 16 feet (5 m) in diameter is around 1,000 years old. The branches that grow out of the thick trunk are relatively few in number and short; this has the effect, when the tree has lost its leaves, of making the crown look more like the roots. The trunk can store moisture up to 400%: in dry periods, elephants bore holes in the trunks and eat the moist wood. The bell-shaped, wax-like white blossoms, measuring about 8 inches (20 cm) in diameter and with an unpleasant smell, appear between October and December, but last for only 24 hours; they are pollinated by bats and bushbabies (nocturnal lemurs). The flesh of the 6- to 8-inch-long (15-20 cm) fruit is edible and very rich in vitamin C. There are many African legends about the baobab; in South Africa it is a protected species.

At a road junction some 22 miles (35 km) north of the Verwoerd Tunnels, the R 525 leads off right to the **Honnet Nature Reserve**. This also includes the hot mineral spring **Tshipise**, which emerges from the ground at 150° F (65° C), and

Right: Typical village in the Venda region.

which the Venda have held sacred for centuries. The spa here, which is frequented by rheumatism sufferers, is a green oasis in the dry bushveld, with acacias, flamboyants, frangipanis and bougainvilleas. There's also a hotel and a few miles away are the luxurious Greater Kudu Lodges. 64 miles (103 km) farther east is the Pafuri Gate of Kruger Park.

23 miles (37 km) north on the R 525 (also on the N 1) is **Messina**, South Africa's northernmost town, 1,962 feet (600 m) above sea level. Its name is derived from the Bantu word for copper (*musina*), which is found in the area along with iron ore, magnesite and graphite. The extraction and smelting of iron ore, in particular, began here a long time ago; the whites did not start mining until after the Boer War. The town, which currently has around 15,000 inhabitants, was not built until 1907, when the road through the Soutpansberg was completed. The hot climate (mean annual temperature 85° F / 29° C) makes the town a picture in spring, with flowering flamboyant and coral trees, bougainvilleas, impala lilies and other blossoms.

The **Messina Nature Reserve** was created in 1980 in order to protect the area's many baobab trees. No one knows exactly how many of these primeval trees there are here, but one of them is 82 feet (25 m) high and 62 feet (19 m) in circumference. Experts have estimated that the reserve has more than 350 different types of trees and shrubs, but not all of them have yet been identified. In addition to giraffes, antelopes are the most common animals (kudu, eland and sable antelopes, among others). To visit this reserve you must apply for permission beforehand.

This area has many rock paintings and other evidence of the culture of earlier inhabitants. **Mapungubwe**, perched on a steep rocky hill and only accessible through a single narrow cleft, was once a natural fortress and the center of Mapungubwe culture (1050-1200), of which ar-

chaeologists have found abundant evidence, including artifacts of gold. The site has been a national landmark since 1984. 10 miles (16 km) north of Messina, the N 1 crosses the 1,540-foot (471 m) **Beit Bridge**, built in 1929, over the Limpopo to Zimbabwe.

Shortly after the second Verwoerd Tunnel, a good road leads off to the right and runs past lush green tea plantations through the Venda region to Thohoyandou. The Venda, an ethnically homogeneous Bantu people with related tribes in Zimbabwe, have been here since the end of the 17th century. From 1979-94 their homeland was "independent," but only recognized as such by South Africa. Many of them still live in traditional villages and they have preserved much of their original culture. Their language, which does not, like other Bantu languages, have any subgroups, was not written down until the beginning of this century, when it began to be transcribed by missionaries from the Berlin Missionary Society. It is closer to languages such as Swahili which are spoken in Zimbabwe and East Africa.

The Venda and the Lemba who live among them, an isolated group of people with their own distinct language and origins, are skilled wood-carvers, basket-weavers, metalworkers and potters. Of the numerous complex initiation rites, which can take months, the best known is the "snake dance" which is performed at one of the ceremonies (*domba*) for the girls. The subsistence economy which is still widely practiced (people grow their own produce – corn, millet, peanuts, vegetables and citrus fruits – and keep small numbers of sheep and goats) is slowly declining in favor of the cultivation of market produce. The subtropical, frost-free climate with an annual rainfall of 60 inches (1,500 mm), most of which falls in the summer, and the very fertile soils are ideal for the cultivation of tea, coffee, bananas, papayas and other fruit, which are also exported. There are mineral resources (coal, copper, zinc), but very little mining is done.

If you take the R 524, which leads along the southern foot of the Soutpansberg to the Venda region, you'll come, 39 miles (63 km) from Louis Trichardt, to the **Ditike Craft Center**, where the beautiful arts and crafts of the Venda are exhibited and sold. The **tourist office** here, where you can obtain the usual information, brochures and maps, is the starting point for half- or full-day excursions in small buses or Land Rovers (a minimum of three persons) and guided walks; to get to know the country properly and learn something about Venda culture, it's worth hiring a trained guide. After about 2 miles (3 km), a turnoff on the left from the R 524 leads to the former capital **Thohoyandou** (1.2 miles / 2 km) and the neighboring town of **Sibasa**, with government buildings, shops, impressive modern university architecture and the Venda Sun Hotel. Near the national stadium is a cultural history museum.

Above: Venda women selling fruits of the region.

The Venda region, which is still largely unaffected by tourism, has attractive, varied scenery with subtropical flora, numerous rivers, hot springs and waterfalls. There are historic sites such as the ruins of Datsa, the first early center of Venda culture, and many places associated with the Venda's abundant myths and legends such as the holy lake, **Lake Funduzi**, formed in some remote age by a landslide (permission to visit must be obtained beforehand). Around 40 miles (65 km) north of Thohoyandou (and more easily accessible from Tshipise) is **Nwanedi National Park**. On the shores of one of the two reservoirs in the park – a paradise for anglers! – is the **Nwanedi Resort** with comfortable chalets and a restaurant. If African solitude in a magnificent landscape (with every imaginable creature comfort, including a warm swimming pool) is what you want, **Sagole Spa**, approximately 30 miles (50 km) to the east, is the ideal place. From here, the road continues further east to the Pafuri Gate of Kruger Park.

NORTHERN PROVINCE
Transportation

Bus: Of the cross-country bus lines that run from Johannesburg to Harare (7 1/2 hours; Mon, Wed and Fri), Translux stops in Potgietersrus, Pietersburg, Louis Trichardt, Messina, Greyhound (Sun-Fri) in Pietersburg and Beitbridge.

Train: There are a number of rail connections between Johannesburg and Messina/Beitbridge (Bosvelder; daily; 14 1/2 hrs.) via Pietersburg and Louis Trichardt, continuing on to **Zimbabwe** (Bulawayo and Harare).

Air: From Johannesburg, Airlink flies to Pietersburg, Tzaneen and Phalaborwa, Interair to Messina and (also from Durban) Phalaborwa/Nelspruit, Theron Airways to Pietersburg and Thohoyandou (from Lanseria).

FROM PIETERSBURG INTO THE LOWVELD
Accommodations

WARMBATHS 0480: *MODERATE:* **Mabula Game Lodge** (lots of game, including the "Big Five"), Private Bag X 1665, tel: 01 533/616, fax: 733. **Aventura Warmbaths**, PO Box 75, tel: 014/736-2200, fax: 736-4712. *BUDGET:* **New White House Hotel**, 46 Voortrekker Rd, tel: 01 533/2404.

POTGIETERSRUS 0600: *MODERATE:* **Protea Park Hotel**, 1 Beitel St., PO Box 1551, tel: 0154/3101, fax: 6842. *BUDGET:* **Fiesta Park Motel**, PO Box 616, tel: 0154/5641.

PIETERSBURG 0700: *MODERATE:* **The Ranch**, Great North Road (on the N 1), PO Box 77, tel: 01 521/5377, fax: 7-5377. **Holiday Inn Garden Court**, Vorster St., PO Box 784, tel: 0152/291-2030, fax: 291-3150. *BUDGET:* **Great North Road Hotel**, 47 Landros Maré St., PO Box 139, tel: 01 521/7-1031.

MAGOBAESKLOOF 0730: *MODERATE:* **Magoebaskloof**, PO Box 1, tel: 015 276/4276, fax: 4280. **Troutwaters Inn**, Road R71, PO Magoebaskloof, tel. and fax: 015276/4245. *BUDGET:* **Magoebaskloof Holiday Resort**, PO Box 838, Tzaneen 0850, tel: 01 523/5633, fax: 5992.

TZANEEN 0850: *MODERATE:* **Coach House**, Old Coach Road, Agatha, PO Box 544, tel: 0152/307-3641, fax: 307-1466. **Karos Tzaneen**, D. Joubert Street, tel. and fax: 0152/307-3140.

DUIWELSKLOOF 0835: *MODERATE:* **Imp Inn Hotel**, Botha St, PO Box 17, tel: 01523/9253, fax: 9892.

PHALABORWA 1390: *MODERATE:* **Impala Inn**, 52 Essenhout Street, PO Box 139, tel: 01 524/5681, fax: 8-5234. **Lantana Lodge** (also holiday cottages), corner Kiatt and Hall St., PO Box 786,

tel: 01 524/8-5855, fax: 8-5193. *BUDGET:* **Andrew Motel**, Mila Rd, PO Box 330, tel: 01 524/2351.

Sights
Bakone Malapa Museum, 5.5 mi/9 km SE of Pietersburg, open daily 8:30 am-12:30, 1:30-3:30 pm.

Tourist Information
SATOUR, Pietersburg 0700, corner Vorster/Landdros Maré St., PO Box 2814, tel: 0152/295-3025, fax: 291-2654. **Department of Forestry**, Private Bag 2413, Louis Trichardt 0920, tel: 01551/5-1152 (permits for Magoebaeskloof hikes). **Letaba Tourism**, PO Box 129, Haenertsburg 0730, tel. and fax: 015276/4307. **Tzaneen** Tourist Office, PO Box 24, Tzaneen 0850, tel: 0152/307-1411, fax: 390-1507.
Phalaborwa Ass'n for Tourism, PO Box 1408, Phalaborwa 1390, tel: 01524/8-5860, fax: 8-5870

SOUTPANSBERG AND LAND OF THE VENDA
Accommodations

LOUIS TRICHARDT 0920: *MODERATE:* **Bergwater Hotel**, 5 Rissik St, PO Box 503, tel. and fax: 015/516-0262. **Clouds End** (2 mi/3 km N), Great North Road, Private Bag X 2409, tel: 015/517-7021, fax: 517-7187. *BUDGET:* **Mountain View Hotel** (5.5 mi/9 km N), PO Box 146, tel: 015/517-7031, fax: 9806. **Punch Bowl** (7 mi/11 km N), Great North Road, PO Box 226, tel: 015/517-7088

TSHIPISE 0901: *MODERATE:* **Aventura Tshipise**, PO Box 4, tel: 015 539/624, fax: 724. **Greater Kuduland Game Lodges** (with full board or self-catering), tel: 015 539/720, fax: 808; reservations: Sites of Africa, Johannesburg, tel: 2711/883-4345, fax: 2556.

MESSINA 0900: *MODERATE:* **Kates Hope Game Lodge**, Farm Mt. 21, District Messina, PO Box 2720, Cresta 2118, tel: 011/476-6217, fax: 678-0732. *BUDGET:* **Impala Lily Motel**, National Road, PO Box 392, tel: 01 553/4-0127.

VENDA: *MODERATE:* **Venda Sun**, PO Box 766, Sibasa 0970, tel: 059/2-1011, fax: 2-13657. **Nwanedi Resort**, Nwande National Park, reservations through Selected Hotels (Pty) Ltd., PO Box 98 146, Sloane Park 2152, tel: 015 539-723.

Tourist Information
Soutpansberg Tourism Association, PO Box 1385, Louis Trichardt 0920, tel: 015 539/720, fax 808. **Department of Forestry**, Private Bag 2413, Louis Trichardt 0920, tel: 01 551/5-1152 (permits for Soutpansberg hiking trails). **Tourist Information**, Main St., Messina 9000, tel: 01553/4-0211. **Venda Tourist**, Private Bag 5045, Thohoyandou, tel: 0159/4-1577, fax: 4-1408.

The **Beitbridge border crossing** to Zimbabwe is open daily 6 am-8 pm.

EASTERN TRANSVAAL

INTO THE LOWVELD

THE PANORAMA ROUTE

KRUGER NATIONAL PARK

PRIVATE GAME RESERVES

EASTERN TRANSVAAL

The second-smallest province of South Africa, occupying only 6.7% of the total land area, ranks fourth in terms of economic power. This is due to Eastern Transvaal's highly developed agriculture, a field which employs more than 20% of the province's working population. The average income here is three times as high as it is in, for example, Northern Transvaal. Of the approximately 2.84 million inhabitants, 40% speak Siswati and 28% Zulu. The provisional capital is Nelspruit. Most of the province is highveld and the climate is correspondingly moderate; in the lowveld, however, east of the Great Escarpment, it maintains a subtropical warmth and humidity.

INTO THE LOWVELD

To reach Eastern Transvaal from Johannesburg, get onto Market Street; this becomes the R 24, which runs into the motorway N 12 before leaving the city. This road passes first through the built-up, densely populated industrial area of the western province of Gauteng. East of

Preceding pages: Elephant herds like to bathe in the watering holes. Left: An impala eyes the photographer.

Witbank, it joins up with the N 4 motorway from Pretoria; this road runs parallel to the train tracks which, like the road, lead to the country's eastern border at Komatipoort. Because of its huge deposits of coal, which lie close to the surface of the earth in a seam 6.5-16 feet (2-5 m) thick, **Witbank** is the most important coal-mining center in the Republic of South Africa; the coal is mined in no fewer than 22 pits. In addition, vanadium is extracted in one of the largest plants in the world; there are also several large power plants both here and in the neighboring town of **Middelburg** (110 miles / 178 km from Johannesburg).

In Middelburg, the R 35 branches off to the north; about 5 miles (8 km) further on, you come to the former Fort Merensky. This was built in 1865 as a missionary station by Alexander Merensky (Berlin Missionary Society), father of the geologist Hans Merensky, who discovered a number of the country's main mineral resources. Today it is part of the **Botshabelo Open-Air Museum**, which includes a reconstructed Ndebele village. The **Loskop Dam Nature Reserve**, 28 miles (45 km) further north, is a splendidly isolated place in the midst of typical bushveld vegetation where many birds and wild animals have gradually been reintroduced.

65

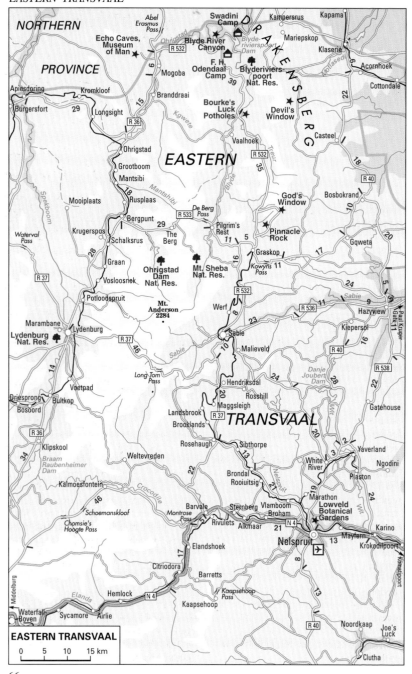

EASTERN TRANSVAAL

0   5   10   15 km

East of Middelburg, the N 4 gradually climbs to **Belfast**, almost 6,540 feet (2,000 m) above sea level, where the R 540 branches off north towards Lydenberg, 93 km (58 miles) away. The road runs along the foot of the Steenkampsberg range, where the highest mountain, **Die Berg**, measures 2,332 m (7,626 feet).

Near the N 4, 24 miles (39 km) to the east at **Waterval Boven** (old tunnel of the railway line to Mozambique) the Elands River drops 294 feet (90 m) over the edge of the Escarpment. The road leads on past Waterval Onder and into the lowveld to Nelspruit (57 miles / 92 km). 18 miles (30 km) on from Belfast, the R 36 branches off northwards from the N 4 and leads to **Lydenburg** (41 miles / 66 km), founded in 1849 by survivors of a devastating malaria epidemic; for eleven years, the town served as capital of a republic of the same name.

Moving east, the R 37 passes Sabie and then, by way of **Long Tom Pass** (7,027 feet/2,149 m at its highest point), crosses the Transvaal Drakensberg in 35 miles (57 km). The pass is named after a cannon that was used in the Boer War. The road follows an old Voortrekker route, established in 1871, which went from Lydenburg to Lourenço Marques (today Maputo, the capital of Mozambique). This route skirts the highest peak in the Transvaal Drakensberg, Mount Anderson (7,469 feet / 2,284 m); wending its winding way ever upward into the mountains, it commands splendid views of the wooded countryside. After 33 miles (53 km) it arrives at **Sabie**, situated on a terrace at an altitude of 3,926 feet (1,109 m). This important tourist resort is also a center of the timber industry and a major producer of paper and cellulose; from 1895 to 1950, it was also a gold-mining town.

Above: Woodsman near Sabie, a timbering center.

The R 536 follows an attractive scenic route east through the Sabie River valley to **Hazyview** in the lowveld (33 miles / 54 km); from here, you can also enter nearby Kruger Park (Numbi Gate and Paul Kruger Gate). The R 37 leads south from Sabie via White River to **Nelspruit** (38 miles/61 km), which is also on the N 4; today, it's the capital of the province of Eastern Transvaal. This attractive town set in the wide, fertile valley of Crocodile River, its luxuriant gardens full of flowers and its streets lined with jacarandas, flamboyants, palms and other trees, is the center of a major agricultural area producing mainly citrus fruits, lychees, avocados, mangos, bananas, nuts, vegetables, and tobacco, as well as other crops. The area is practically frost-free; in winter, it supplies the whole country with vegetables and fruit.

North of Nelspruit are the **Lowveld Botanical Gardens**: most of its 385 acres (154 hectares) is pure wilderness. At least 500 of the plant species here are indigenous to the Nelspruit region; 55

acres (22 hectares) are devoted to plants from all parts of the lowveld and the slopes of the Drakensberg. The airport is southwest of town. 38 miles (61 km) further on, the N 4 comes to the Malelane Gate of Kruger Park; after another 27 miles (44 km), it reaches **Komatipoort**, the border crossing into Mozambique.

THE PANORAMA ROUTE

Sabie is a good starting point for the **Panorama Route**, which has become increasingly popular with tourists. It covers a large section of the Transvaal Drakensberg, which, as the Great Escarpment, separates the highveld from the lowveld around 3,270 feet (1,000 m) below. Rivers have broken through the Escarpment, cutting deep gorges in the slopes and forming numerous waterfalls. The Precambrian rock, mostly dolomite and

Above: Old cemetery in the restored gold-diggers' town of Pilgrim's Rest. Right: The bizarre potholes in Bourke's Luck.

quartzite, is much older than that of the Drakensberg in Natal; in many places, it's covered with a multicolored array of lichens. The route leads through extensive reforested areas and areas still sporting their extremely varied original vegetation. From June to September, the weather is cool and dry, but frost can occur at any time; from September to April, during the summer rainy season, there is frequent fog. The best time for hiking is in April and May. Many organized tours, for example to Kruger Park, also follow the Panorama Route.

From Sabie, the R 532 runs north and meets the R 533 after approximately 15.5 miles (25 km). About 6 miles (10 km) to the west is the small village of **Pilgrim's Rest**, which has been designated a national landmark. In 1873, a prospector found gold in the small river of **Pilgrim's Creek** and decided to remain here and try his luck. A wild gold rush ensued, ultimately, after the findings had somewhat decreased, to be succeeded by a small mine, which remained in operation until

1972. Modern visitors can walk the streets of a lovingly restored turn-of-the-century gold-diggers' town, complete with houses, shops, a bank, the authentically reconstructed Royal Hotel, and a small museum.

About 9 miles (15 km) further west, a turn-off to the south leads to **Mount Sheba Nature Reserve**, which extends across a plateau 5,232 feet (1,600 m) up on the slopes of Mount Sheba (6,402 feet/1,958 m). Some of the original forest has been preserved; in addition to 100 species of tree, more than 1,000 different types of plant have been counted here, including a variety of orchids. The comfortable Mount Sheba Hotel, built at the end of the 1960s, adds to the area's attractions.

Back to the east: from **Graskop**, some 9-plus miles (15 km) from Pilgrim's Rest, the R 532 runs north along the edge of the Great Escarpment. Take the side turning about 2 miles (3 km) further on; this involves a small detour, but amply repays you with its splendid views of the lowveld. First of these is by **Pinnacle Rock**, a free-standing quartzite rock, which rises like a column from a densely wooded gorge; farther on, there's **God's Window**, a vantage point at a height of 1,829 m (5,981 feet), named because of the "divine" view it offers. This marks the end of the **Fanie Botha Hiking Trail,** which begins near Sabie (49 miles/79 km, 5 days), and is also the start of the **Blyde Rivierspoort Hiking Trail** (40 miles/65 km, 5 days), which is suitable even for people who are not seasoned hikers.

At the confluence of the Treur and Blyde Rivers (15 miles/24 km from Graskop), there used to be a small gold mine named "Bourke's Luck." The detritus and sand carried down by the water have worn bizarre "potholes" into the rocky walls of the deep river ravines. Paths and bridges lead to vantage points with views of **Bourke's Luck Potholes**, a popular tourist attraction because of their many different forms and colors, and a photographer's delight.

As it makes it way north to the Olifants River, the Blyde River has cut 2,289 feet (700 m) into the rock of the Great Escarpment: the **Blyde River Canyon**, the third-largest canyon in the world after the Grand Canyon in the U.S.A. and the Fish River Canyon in Namibia, is one of the most magnificent natural phenomena in South Africa. It is dominated by three similarly shaped rocks, the Three Rondavels. At its confluence with the Ohrigstad River, it's been dammed to create a splendid reservoir. The view out over the lichen-covered rocks, with the lake below and the vast lowveld spread out in the background, is overwhelmingly spectacular. The canyon is at the center of the **Blyderivierspoort Nature Reserve**, which extends over 56,667 acres (22,667 hectares). In addition to eagles, ospreys and white-necked cormorants, the bird life includes the South African turaco,

Above: Over the years, the Blyde River has cut a deep canyon into the cliffs of the Great Escarpment.

which inhabits the densely wooded areas, and the rare sacred ibis. Botanists can examine seven different types of heather and six types of protea, including the very rare *protea leatens*, which was only discovered here a few years ago. In the autumn and winter, the reserve glows with the vivid, coral-red blossoms of the mountain aloe (*aloe arborescens*).

The well-equipped **F.H. Odendaal Camp** lies close to the road (32 miles/51 km from Graskop), and another attractive camp, **Swadini**, has been established near the lake (accessible from the lowveld).

Where the R 532 meets the R 36 from Lydenburg, a little to the south, a small side road leads to **Echo Caves**, a series of stalactite caves in dolomite cliffs which extend for several miles. Archaeological findings from the Mesolithic and Neolithic periods are on display in the **Museum of Man**.

Moving north, the R 36 climbs 1,095 feet (335 m) to the top of the **Abel Erasmus Pass** (4,061 feet / 1,242 m), from where it descends again almost 2,615 feet (800 m) through a narrow gorge into the valley of the Olifants River. The end of the pass road is the 432-foot (132 m) **J.G. Strijdom Tunnel**; emerging from this tunnel into daylight, travelers find themselves in the vast lowveld, suddenly surrounded by a completely different vegetation. The R 36 continues north to Tzaneen (54 miles/88 km); you can get to Kruger Park by way of Klaserie (Orpen entrance, 55 miles/89 km) or Hoedspruit (Phalaborwa Gate, 65 miles/105 km).

KRUGER NATIONAL PARK

Hardly a visitor to South Africa neglects to visit the largest national park in the country, which is, in fact, one of the largest wildlife sanctuaries in the world. Located in the lowveld of Eastern and Northern Transvaal, the park runs from Crocodile River in the south to the Limpopo, the border river in the north, more than 215 miles (350 km) long and an average of 40 miles (65 km) across from east to west. With an area of 7,599 square miles (19,485 square kilometers), the park is only a little bit smaller than the state of Massachusetts. Largely flat, it rises to elevations of around 1,000 feet (300 m) and individual mountains (in the southwest 2,743 feet / 839 m high); in the east, the Lebombo mountains, which run along the border with Mozambique, reach altitudes of up to 1,625 feet (497 m). Under the surface, the dominant bed-rock is magmatic rock (rhyolite, basalt, and, in the western part, granite).

The climate is subtropical; summer is the rainy season, and there is more rain in the south than the north. The annual rainfall in the northern half, roughly as far as the Olifants River, is around 16 inches (400 mm), while in the south this average increases to as much as 28 inches (700 mm); the extreme northwest also has more rain. The quantity and frequency of precipitation however vary considerably,

as they do throughout the country. There are years when it is extremely dry, but also periods of above-average humidity. The rainy season usually begins in September/October and most of the rain falls in December, January and February; there is generally no rain at all in June, July and August. Temperatures in the summer occasionally rise above 104° F (40° C), the warmest months being December and January. The dry winter days are usually mild (around 68° F / 20° C); at night, however, it can be very cold, although frost is rare.

Seven large rivers flow across the park in an east-to-west direction; until recently, most of these had water in them all the year round. Agriculture and forestry in the lowveld has, however, meant an increase in the consumption of water; rapid population growth has contributed to the water shortage, as well as increasing the amount of pollutants within the rivers themselves.

The vegetation varies considerably, depending on the soil and the climate. The northern area, roughly between the Olifants and Limpopo rivers, is mopane country: in the western section, mainly in the form of large trees, as well as other varieties; in the east, as low, stunted bushes. In the area between Parfuri and the Limpopo, you can see impressive baobabs (monkey-bread trees); while in the southern part, marula, combretum, acacia and other trees alternate with spacious pastures. In some places, the rivers are lined with lush river forests comprised of a wide variety of trees.

Kruger Park, which began as the Sabie Game Reserve in 1898, has been open to the public since 1927. In the first year, only three vehicles took advantage of its presence; today, by contrast, it has more than half a million visitors a year. The park administration has built roughly 1,240 miles (2,000 km) of roads (approx. 435 miles / 700 km of them paved), accommodation (24 rest camps with 3,000

beds), and 13 picnic places. Since the animals can no longer migrate freely – the park was fenced off in the west in 1961 and in the east in 1974 – artificial water sources and more pastureland have had to be created.

Recently, by agreement with the owners of the adjacent private game reserves to the west, the fences separating these reserves from Kruger Park have begun to be removed. This means that the animals can once again move unimpeded over a larger area and find more water sources; in addition, they all come under the protection and reponsibility of the Kruger Park personnel. In order to maintain the ecological balance, a head count of all the animals in the park is undertaken every year; superfluous animals are moved to other reserves or culled. A large animal processing plant in Skukuza

Above: Peaceful coexistence in Kruger National Park. Right: Self-caterers cooking at Honey Guide Camp at the edge of Kruger Park.

used the meat to make biltong, a form of dried meat that's been popular in South Africa since the days of the Voortrekkers; bone meal is produced from the bones, and the hides are turned into leather. A staff of 1,500 takes care of the park, the animals and the visitors.

Routes to the park

From Johannesburg, you can reach the park's two southern entrances Malelane (432 km/268 miles) and Crocodile Bridge (497 km/308 miles) on National Route 4 (N 4), some of which is motorway; if you turn off in Nelspruit onto the N 4, you can reach Numbi Gate (254 miles/410 km) and Paul Kruger Gate (279 miles/450 km). The N 1 to Pietersburg via Tzaneen (337 miles / 544 km) will bring you to the Phalaborwa Gate, and the road from Louis Trichardt via Tohoyandu is the way to the Punda Maria Gate (approx. 590 km / 366 miles). If time permits, visitors coming from Nelspruit can combine a Kruger Park excur-

sion with a visit to Eastern Transvaal; those coming from Pietersburg can explore the Northern Province.

For travelers with limited time, Kruger Park can also be reached by air (there are airports in Phalaborwa, Skukuza and Nelspruit). Various companies offer tours to Kruger Park from Johannesburg or Durban with large buses (e.g. Springbok Atlas Safaris) or minibuses (up to 8 people, e.g. Welcome Tours). The price includes transport, accommodation and board. If you have limited time and are not used to observing animals and birds, or are not yet familiar with the flora and fauna of South Africa, it's advisable to take such a tour. The knowledgeable guides point out the wildlife and other sights en route; they also usually know the "right" places to look from long experience. With their help, visitors learn to tell the various types of antelope apart and distinguish crocodiles or hippos in the rivers from sandbanks and rocks. It is also much easier to see from a bus, which is usually also air-conditioned, than from a car. However, anyone with a bit more experience is still better off renting a car or Land Rover and driving out herself in search of the animals. Connoisseurs of the African wilderness find the northern, less developed and more natural part of the park particularly attractive.

Visiting Kruger National Park

The park is open all year round. Although every season has its own special attractions, the dry winter months, particularly July and August, are generally considered the best time to come, since observation of the animals is hindered least by the vegetation and they gather in great numbers at the watering holes. Spring and summer, on the other hand, are best for the lush, subtropical plant world. In these seasons, too, there are even more species of bird than usual, as the migratory birds from Europe are here for the winter, and there is a chance of seeing animals with their young. You should allow at least three days for a visit.

The roads connect the camps, lead to the best panoramic views and picnic places en route, and pass waterholes and drinking troughs. All the roads are well signposted. The speed limit is 31 mph (50 km/h), 25 mph (40 km/h) on gravel roads (speed checked by radar). It is strictly forbidden to get out, or even to lean out of an open window or roof. This regulation is for the protection of the visitors and the animals, which must not be disturbed – they are used to the vehicles – and of course must not be fed. There are heavy penalties for infringement of the rules. Only in the camps, at picnic sites and marked spots with panoramic views are you allowed to get out of your vehicle. The best idea is to buy one of the excellent maps at the gate, which contain plentiful information and are also obtainable in the camp shops.

The early hours of the morning and the late afternoon are the best time to drive

Above: Long-tailed monkey and lion, Kruger National Park.

round the park, since in the hot season animals retreat into the shade during the hottest part of the day; and, lying motionless, are usually hard to detect. Therefore, a siesta isn't a bad idea for visitors, as well as animals, during these hours.

Wilderness Trails

Anyone who wants closer contact with the wilderness can join one of the seven organized wilderness hikes, put together and led by an experienced gamekeeper and his assistant. For each of the hikes, which range from 5 to 9 miles (8 to 15 km) in length, there is a separate base camp. Special vehicles bring participants in from the assembly point to the camps; here, they spend two nights, and from here, they start each day's hike. Hikes are restricted to a maximum of 8 participants, who must be between 12 and 60 years of age. Equipment and food are provided. Since the trails are very popular, it is advisable to register well in advance (with the National Parks Board).

Driving through Kruger Park

Few visitors manage to drive the whole length of the park – there are dramatic differences between the northern and southern part – but it is also very rewarding to explore a specific area more thoroughly, whether large or small, using one camp as a base and observing nature at leisure. Breakfast and lunch can be taken at other camps. When planning your stay, it is important to take into consideration the vast distances involved. Even with the speed limit of 31 mph (50 km/h), you'll need a lot more time because you drive more slowly and make stops to watch the animals or to let them pass. If you reach the camp after it is closed you will have to pay a heavy fine.

Most visitors enter the park through the **Numbi Gate** or the **Paul Kruger Gate**, which is 7.4 miles (12 km) away from **Skukuza**, the largest camp: this is also the park's administrative center, and almost a small town in itself. Although the complex is very attractive, the size will not appeal to everyone (more than 600 beds). **Pretoriuskop**, the oldest of the camps, sits in a lovely park-like landscape somewhat higher up than the other camps; it's hence a little cooler, and this, together with its swimming pool, makes it especially popular in summer. As the surrounding vegetation is especially lush, a number of animals tend to gather here. With its modern chalets, **Berg-en-Dal**, a new camp in the extreme southwest, looks very different from the older camps; it also has a swimming pool.

Crocodile Bridge, a small camp in the southeast, lures visitors with the sight of hippos and crocodiles frolicking in the Crocodile River. **Lower Sabie**, a medium-sized camp, is splendidly located on the Sabie River. The constant water supply and lush vegetation here attract many animals. From here, it's 25 miles (40 km) north to the picnic place **Tshokwane** (which you can also reach on the

road from Skukuza), where you are allowed to get out of your car. Dominating the site is a giant sausage tree, with large, grayish-brown sausage-like fruit which can grow to more than a yard (1 m) in length and weigh around 22 pounds (10 kg). Some of the birds are very tame, especially the cape glossy starling with its shiny dark blue-green feathers and yellow button eyes.

Satara, 30 miles (48 km) east of **Orpen Gate**, is the second-largest camp and one of the most modern. If, instead of taking the main road to the north from Tshokwane, you drive east and then take the S 35 / S 37 north, you'll reach another picnic place near Nwanetsi, close to the Mozambique border (27 miles / 44 km). This is a worthwhile detour, particularly for photographers; late afternoon is the best time to enjoy the view out over the river from the top of a steep cliff. From

Above: The cape glossy starling and the hornbill seem oblivious to observers. Right: Evening in the Inyati Game Park.

here, it's another 13.6 miles (22 km) to Satara. The medium-sized **Olifants Camp** (which has huts, but no camping facilities) was also built fairly recently, in a unique cliffside setting 330 feet (100 m) above the Olifants River with a magnificent view of the lowveld. The African sunrises and sunsets are an unforgettable experience here. The outlook point on an outcrop of rock near the camp commands a view of many miles of river; with binoculars or a telescope, you can observe the abundant animal life on its shores.

To the north, the vegetation becomes noticeably sparser due to poorer soil and lower rainfall. Mopane trees are increasingly common here; when the sun is very hot they fold up their butterfly-shaped leaves – a favorite food of elephants – along the central rib, thus avoiding excessive evaporation. The black-and-yellow mopane worms that feed on the leaves are a popular local delicacy, dried or roasted.

Along the rivers, however, there is abundant vegetation. If it is not too dusty

or wet, take the gravel road along the Letaba River to Letaba. This detour is worthwhile for a sight of the Engelhard Dam, built across the river east of Letaba.

With its flowers and tall, shady trees, **Letaba**, on the main north-south road above the right-hand bank of a bend in the river, ranks as one of the most attractive camps in Kruger Park. On the road from **Phalaborwa Gate** to the east, 6 miles (10 km) from the gate, a Stone-Age tribal village has been reconstructed in the **Masorini Open Air Museum**.

Mopani, 46 miles (74 km) northeast of Phalaborwa Gate, the newest and most modern of the camps (with a swimming pool) is located on the shores of the Pioneer Dam, some 7.5 miles (12 km) south of the Tropic of Capricorn. There are no camping facilities here. 39 miles (63 km) farther north, you come to **Shingwedzi**, located on the river of the same name. It also has a swimming pool and is famous for its trees, its magnificent pink and white impala lilies, and numerous birds. The country around it has a decidedly

wilderness air, and an increasing number of baobabs; a majority of Kruger Park's leopards dwell in this region. The attractive little camp **Punda Maria**, 5 miles (8 km) from the gate of the same name, is the northernmost place to stay in the park. Rangers were once stationed here to guard against the notorious ivory poachers. The area north of here is densely wooded with mopane and baobab, mahogany, ebony, sycamore and other tree species.

The road from Punda Maria to the north leads through unspoilt countryside to **Pafuri**, a picnic place on the Luvuhu River. This area is a nature-lover's paradise with examples of various African ecological systems: wet areas and dry savanna, woods and open plains; rocks and sand, lava fields, deep gorges and high ridges of rock.

PRIVATE GAME RESERVES

On the western border of Kruger Park, between Phalaborwa and Paul Kruger

Gate, there are several private game reserves (Klaserie, Umbabat, Timbavati, Manyeleti and Sabi Sand). From the game lodges in these reserves, experienced, armed rangers leads tours through the bush, either on foot or in open Land Rovers, and sometimes even off the marked paths. In addition to conventional Land Rover trips, there are also night stalking excursions, on which you can observe, in the light of searchlights, nocturnal animals out hunting. Some of the lodges are very luxurious, such as **Mala Mala** in the Sabi Sand Reserve, the best known and most expensive, or **Ngala,** which belongs to the (private) Conservation Corporation in Timbavati Reserve: the straw-thatched rondavels are air-conditioned and surrounded by attractive gardens, and the catering is first-class.

Also in the Sabi Sand reserve are the two lodges Harry's and Kirkman's Camp, which are a little more basic and

Above: Animal watching from an open Land Rover.

not quite as expensive. The lodges further north, such as Inyati, Londolozi, Motswari, Mohlabetsi and Tanda Tula, are similarly equipped.

On the southern edge of Kruger Park is the **Malelane Sun Lodge**, a comfortable hotel from which you can undertake safaris either to private game reserves or Kruger Park.

From the south of Kruger Park (Malelane Gate or Crocodile Bridge Gate), you can get back to Johannesburg on the N 4; another alternative is the scenically attractive R 38 to Barberton, from where you can go on to a number of destinations (e.g. KwaZulu/Natal). If you are planning to make a (well worthwhile) detour to the kingdom of Swaziland, which is en route, there are border crossings at Josefsdal/Bulembu (25 miles / 40 km from Barberton), Jeppe's Reef/Matsamo (on the R 570, 27 miles / 43 km from the N 4 at Malelane Gate) and Border Gate/Mananga (on the R 571, 45 miles / 72 km from Crocodile Bridge Gate by way of Komatipoort).

EASTERN TRANSVAAL
Transportation

Bus: Greyhound buses run daily from Johannesburg/Pretoria to Nelspruit (about 5 hours).
Train: There are daily trains (Komati) from Johannesburg/Pretoria to Komatipoort (12 hrs., via Nelspruit).
Air: From Johannesburg and Durban, Airlink and Inter Air fly to Nelspruit and Phalaborwa; Comair runs from Johannesburg to Skukuza.

INTO THE LOWVELD
Accommodations

MIDDELBURG 1050: *MODERATE:* **Midway Inn**, Jan van Riebeeck St., PO Box 1240, tel: 0132/46-2081, fax: 46-1172. **Aventura Loskopdam**, Private Bag X1525, tel: 01 202/3075, fax 3916. *BUDGET:* **Olifants Hotel**, Presidents Rus, PO Box 638, tel: and fax: 0132/2-9114.
WATERFALL-BOVEN 1195: *MODERATE:* **Bergwaters Lodge** (near Waterval-Onder), PO Box 71, tel: 013 262/ ask for 103.
SABIE 1260: *MODERATE:* **Floreat Protea Hotel**, Old Lydenburg Road, PO Box 150, tel: 01 315/4-2160, fax: 42162.
LYDENBURG 1120: *BUDGET:* **Morgan's Hotel**, 14 Voortrekker St, PO Box 11, tel: 01 323/2165.
SABIE 1260: *MODERATE:* **Floreat Protea Hotel**, Old Lydenburg Road, PO Box 150, tel: 01 315/4-2160, fax: 4-2162. *BUDGET:* **Jock of the Bushveld Hostel** (youth hostel), Main Street, tel: 01 315/4-2178, fax: 4-3215.
HAZYVIEW 1242: *MODERATE:* **Sabi River Sun**, Main Sabi Road, PO Box 13, tel: 01 313/6-7311, fax: 6-7314. **Hazyview Protea Hotel**, Burgers Hall, PO Box 105, tel: 01 317/6-7332, fax: 6-7335. **Sanbonani Lowveld**, Paul Kruger Road, PO Box 112, tel: 01 317/6-7340, fax: 6-7703.
WHITE RIVER 1240: *MODERATE:* **Hotel The Winkler**, Old Numbi Rd, PO Box 12, tel: 01 311/3-2317, fax: 3-1393. **Karula Hotel**, Old Plaston Rd, PO Box 279, tel: 01 311/3-2277, fax: 5-0413.
NELSPRUIT 1200: *MODERATE:* **Hotel Promenade**, Louis Trichardt St. PO Box 4355, tel: 01 311/5-3000, fax: 2-5533. **Crocodile Country Inn** (12 mi/20 km W on the N 4), PO Box 496, Nelspruit, tel: 01 311/6-3040, fax: 6-4171. *BUDGET:* **Town Lodge**, corner Gen. Dan Plenaar and Koorsboom St., PO Box: 5555, tel: 01 311/4-1444, fax: 2258. **Intebane Youth Hostel**, Farm Sandford Eden, Main Rd, tel: 01 317/6-7636, fax: 6-7019.

Tourist Information

Nelspruit Publicity Association (also **SATOUR**), Shop 5, Promenade Centre, Louis Trichardt St. PO Box 5018, tel: 01 311/55-1988, fax: 55-1350.

White River Publicity Association, White River, tel: 01 311/5-1599.

PANORAMA ROUTE
Accommodations

PILGRIM'S REST 1290: *MODERATE:* Royal Hotel, PO Box 59, tel: 01 315/8-1100, fax: 8-1188. **Mount Sheba Hotel**, PO Box 100, tel: 01 315/8-1241, fax: 8-1241.
OHRIGSTAD 1122: **Aventura Blydepoort** (holiday town with quaint, rustic stone houses, near Blyde River Canyon), Private Bag 368, tel: and fax: 01 323/8-0155.
HOEDSPRUIT 1380: **Aventura Swadini** (holiday town), PO Box 281, tel: and fax: 01 528/3-5141. Central reservation service for Aventura holiday settlements: Central Reservations (from Europe: tel: 002712/346-2277, fax: 346-2293).

Tourist Information

Blyderivierspoort Nature Reserve, Private Bag X431, Graskop 1270, tel: 01 315/8-1216.

KRUGER PARK
Accommodations

You can reserve ahead for all camps through the National Parks Board in Pretoria.
Private Game Reserves: Lodges designated with (L) are luxury-class.
NEAR HAZYVIEW: **Mala Mala(L)**, **Kirkman's Camp (L)**, **Harry's Camp (L):** reservations: Rattray Reserves, PO Box 2575, Randburg 2125, tel: 011/789-2677, fax: 886-4382. **Londolozi Game Reserve (L)**, PO Box 1211, Sunninghill Park 2157, tel: 011/803-8421, fax: 803-1810. **Ngala Game Reserve (L)**, PO Box 1211, Sunninghill Park 2157, tel: 011/803-8421, fax: 803-1810.
NEAR HOEDSPRUIT: **Mohlabetsi Safari Lodge**, PO Box 1936, Nelspruit 1200, tel: 01 311/2-8183, fax: 2-6176. **Tanda Tula**, Country Lodge Marketing, PO BO 32, Constantia 7848, tel. 021/794-6500, fax: 794-7605. **Tshukudu Game Lodg**e, Box 289, Hoedspruit 1380, tel. and fax: 01528/3-2476.
MALELANE 1320: **Malelane Sun Lodge**, Riverside Farm, PO Box 392, tel: 01 313/3-0331, fax: 3-01455.- Located on the R 36 from Lydenburg to Tzaneen (in Northern Cape province) is the **Makutsi Safari Farm**, PO Box 598, Tzaneen 0850, tel: 015-2302/ ask for 2402, fax: 011/787-2651.

Border Crossings

Opening times, to Mozambique: Komatipoort/Lebombo (N 4) 7 am-8 pm; to Swaziland: Border Gate/ Mananga (R 571) 8 am-6 pm, Jeepe's Reef/Matsamo (R 570) and Josefsdal/Bulembu (S of Barberton) 8 am-4 pm, Oshoek/Ngwenya (N 17) 7 am-10 pm, Piet Retief (N 2)/Mahamba 7 am-10 pm, Golela/Lavumisa 7 am-10 pm).

KWAZULU / NATAL

DURBAN

COASTS AND BEACHES

ZULULAND AND

ITS GAME RESERVES

THE DRAKENSBERG

KWAZULU / NATAL

Bordering the Indian Ocean in the southeastern part of the country, the smallest province in South Africa has the second-highest population density: here 21% of all South Africans, of whom 80% speak Zulu, live in 7.5% of the country's total area. A referendum is going to be held to decide whether Pietermaritzburg or Ulundi becomes the capital. The proud, very tradition-conscious Zulus have managed to keep their region a monarchy (the only one in South Africa). The economy is based primarily on the cultivation of sugar cane, which not only covers the requirements of the region, but is also an important export. The north is an important mining area, primarily concentrating on coal and iron ore; while a large industrial complex has grown up around the harbor at Richards Bay.

A further important economic factor is tourism. Thanks to its beautiful, varied scenery, lush, subtropical vegetation, and a climate so mild that you can swim off the coast all year round, the province has become the most important vacation region in South Africa.

Preceding pages: Durban's "Golden Mile" with the amusement park. Left: A lunch-time game (Durban, in front of City Hall).

DURBAN

The largest city in the province, with some 3.5 million inhabitants, lies on a bay of the Indian Ocean which is a marvelous natural harbor. The bay was discovered by the Portuguese seafarer Vasco da Gama on Christmas Day (in Portuguese *Natal*), 1497. For three centuries, Port Natal was a refuge for an assortment of shipwrecked sailors and pirates, slave-traders and merchants. In 1824, white traders from the Cape Colony established a settlement here; it was they who gave it its present name, in 1835, after its British governor. The settlement was tolerated by the Zulus in the area, since it was useful for trade. In 1838, a group of Voortrekkers incorporated it into their short-lived Boer Republic of Natal, which became a British colony in 1843 after a siege by British troops. After this, Durban began its rise as a port city and the gateway to the interior of South Africa.

After Richards Bay and Saldanha, which mainly export raw materials, Durban is the most important port in South Africa with major industries. But the city is also the country's largest holiday resort, attracting 2 million visitors a year.

The spacious city with its wide streets still has something of an oriental atmos-

83

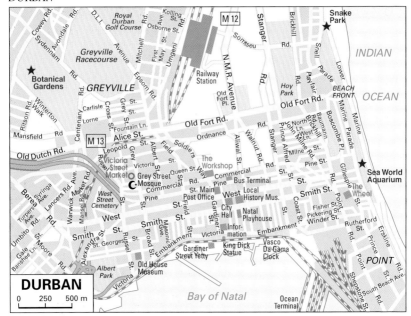

phere; only ten years ago almost half of the city's inhabitants were Indian. Today, however, the figure has now dropped to 16%, while the proportion of black residents has risen to 73%.

Once wooded, **Berea Ridge**, which dominates the city to the west, is today an attractive, densely built-up residential area with flourishing gardens. Visible from afar is the **Memorial Tower Building** of the university on the southwest end of the ridge; it commands a splendid view over the harbor and city (to get there, take the bus to Manor Garden or Howard College).

The main roads in the city are the two parallel one-way streets running roughly from east to west, **West Street** and **Smith Street**, lined with modern commercial high-rises interspersed with Victorian-style buildings or structures bearing a markedly Indian character. On Gardiner Street, which leads from Smith

Right: One of the many exotic beauties in Durban's Snake Park.

Street to the harbor, is the Tourist Office (Greater Durban Marketing Authority & Visitors Bureau); here, you can get all the information you need to explore the city, including a city map and plenty of brochures.

The **beachfront** area is probably the most important part of the city for most tourists, with its beautiful wide sandy beach, washed by the breakers of the Indian Ocean, stretching 5 miles (8 km) from the Blue Lagoon in the north down to The Point at the harbor entrance in the south. Alternate sections of the beach are reserved for swimmers and surfers; you can watch the latter from one of the long jetties which jut far out into the sea. **Marine Parade** (which turns into **Snell Parade** to the north), with its high-rise buildings, luxury hotels, holiday apartments and restaurants, is Durban's famous **Golden Mile**, of which South Africans are very proud. Between the hotels and the beach is a large, green, bustling, and colorful pedestrian area with an American-style amusement park.

In the **Snake Park** (Fitzsimon's Snake Park) at the end of the Golden Mile, you can see 80 of the 140 different types of snake that are found in South Africa. Opposite the junction of West Street and Marine Parade, the aquarium **Sea World** displays an array of splendidly colorful tropical fish, shellfish and crustaceans, and a fine collection of shells. The main attraction is a large pool containing sharks; you can watch these from the three tiers of galleries running around the pool. In the neighboring dolphinarium, a show featuring dolphins and fur seals is presented several times a day. Next to this, opposite the Balmoral Hotel, is a pavilion which houses a branch of the tourist office.

Not far from Sea World is the stand of the black rickshaw drivers – favorite models for visiting photographers, with their imaginative, brightly-colored costumes and headdresses and their splendidly decorated two-wheeled vehicles. The idea was brought back from Japan in 1893 by a sugar magnate. Rickshaws were extremely common here for a long time, but today, only a few drivers remain, basically as a tourist attraction. Because of the trademark Ferris wheel over the street, it's difficult to miss the ultra-modern shopping and entertainment center called **The Wheel**, located on nearby Gillespie Street; the complex contains around 140 shops and restaurants and 12 cinemas.

In the city center between Smith and West Street is **City Hall** with its large copper dome, built in 1910 and today a national landmark. In addition to the municipal offices and a library it also houses the excellent **Natural History Museum** and the **Durban Art Gallery**, the second-largest art museum in South Africa. In the neighboring building, once a courthouse, is the **Local History Museum**, which displays memorabilia from the early days of Natal and Zululand.

On Smith Street, opposite City Hall, is the **Natal Playhouse Complex** with five stages, which was built in 1986. The imposing building on the opposite side of

West Street, which served as city hall after its completion in 1886, and which has been the city's main post office since 1910, is a national landmark. A bronze plaque commemorates the speech Winston Churchill made from the steps of this building in 1899, after his escape from captivity during the Boer War.

Behind this building and to the north of it, is an edifice which was the main train station until 1980, and which is now going to be turned into an exhibition hall; the one-time station area has been expanded with buildings and facilities for trade fairs, exhibitions and congresses. A former train shed has been turned into an attractive shopping center, **The Workshop**; some of its shops are open on Saturdays and Sundays, and the complex also includes cinemas, bars and restaurants. The "Petite Suisse" café is an excel-

Above: The Indian spice stall in Victoria Street Market – a feast for nose and eye alike. Right: The Vasco da Gama Clock with its lavish Victorian ornamentation.

lent place to recover from the rigors of a shopping expedition with coffee and cake. Not far from the Workshop, between Commercial Road and Pine Street, is the **Bus Terminal**. Further to the east you reach Smith and Russell Street.

Compared to those of other large cities in South Africa, Durban's municipal bus system (Durban Transport Management Board, DTMB) is relatively easy to use. The DTMB's Mynah Shuttle Service is extremely useful for tourists; it links the southern beach area (South Beach Route) and the northern beach area (North Beach Route) via Smith Street (via West Street on the return route) with Albert Park.

From west Street turn right to Russell Street, past the large cemetery, to reach the **Victoria Street Market**. Although this is neither as large nor as splendid as the original, and renowned, Indian market, which burned down in 1972, and although it's today run primarily by blacks, this lively place still has something of an oriental atmosphere, and is still impressive, both for its ambience and for the wide variety of wares on offer. These include fruit and vegetables, and a panoply, varying greatly in terms of price and quality, of wicker- and brasswork, jewelry and silverware, woodcarving and souvenirs. There is an unbelievable range of curry mixtures, most of them with imaginative names. Equally foreign to most tourists, though perhaps less enticing, are the halls in which fish and in particular meat are sold.

The **Grey Street Mosque** on the corner of Queen Street and Grey Street ranks as the largest and most splendid mosque in the southern hemisphere; only around 20% of the Indians in South Africa, however, are Muslims. In Durban, 75% of the Indians are Hindus; their oldest, largest and most magnificent temple is on Somtseu Road.

Victoria Embankment commences on the southern side of **Albert Park**. This wide, busy street runs along the north side of the harbor basin, separated from it by a strip of green. Running down the west side of the harbor is Maydon Wharf with the large **Sugar Terminal**: its warehouse can store approximately 510,000 tons of sugar (register in advance if you'd like to visit). The deep-sea fishing fleet which berths here departs every morning at 6:30 a.m. from the **Fishing Jetty** at the end of Maydon Wharf.

The **Old House Museum** near Victoria Embankment is a typical residential house from the middle of the last century. In the middle of the green is the **Dick King Statue**, a monument commemorating a local teenager who fetched reinforcements to help the British out of a tight spot in the Boer War.

In the harbor is **Gardiner Street Jetty**, a point of departure for tours of the harbor and trips out to sea. Docked by the jetty is a ship which now serves as the **Natal Maritime Museum**. West of this, at the yacht mole, you can see yachts of every size and variety. The **Vasco da Gama Clock**, a lavishly decorated, bell-

shaped iron construction crowned with a clock, was presented by the Portuguese government in 1897 in memory of Vasco da Gama, the discoverer of Natal.

About a mile (2 km) north of the city center is the new train station. The **Greyville Race Course**, a little to the east of this, is the venue of the July Handicap, a major horse-racing and social event. The racecourse surrounds the golf course of the Royal Durban Golf Club. The beautiful **Botanic Gardens** further to the east on the edge of the Berea Ridge (also serviced by the Mynah Shuttle) are famous for their orchid house and the many different types of cycad, or palm ferns; including the particularly rare *encepahlartos woodii*.

On a rise to the north of this is the house of sugar magnate Sir Marshall Campbell. At the university are the Campbell Collections, which furnish the contents of the **Mashu Museum of Ethnology** and the **Killie Campbell Africana Library**, with old books and unpublished manuscripts on the history and ethnology of Zululand and Natal.

COASTS AND BEACHES

If you prefer small, quiet places to the hustle and bustle of the big city, you are sure to find something to your taste along the coasts around Durban – Dolphin Coast to the north, Sunshine Coast and Hibiscus Coast to the south – which have, moreover, plenty of facilities for vacationers.

Umhlanga Rocks (pronounced Umshlanga), only 11 miles (18 km) north of Durban, has in a few years grown from a small, sleepy coastal town into one of the most elegant and popular oceanside resorts, renowned in equal measure for its comfortable hotels, its fine cuisine including a variety of fish specialities, its lively and diverting nightlife, and, last but not least, for its beautiful long sandy beach, ideal for swimming, surfing and angling. In 1957, swimmers were attacked by sharks for the first time; as a result, protective nets around the beaches were introduced in 1962, and the **Natal Sharks Board** was founded for research purposes in 1964. The institute, on a hill above the town, is open to the public.

The beautiful stretch of coast which runs north from here to the Tugela estuary, called the **Dolphin Coast**, consists of some 55 miles (90 km) of sandy beach interspersed with a number of little rocky bays. The holiday resorts of Umdloti Beach, Ballito, Umhlali and Salt Rock, among others, are as yet less developed, and are therefore quieter and much cheaper than some of the more popular spots; they also have many different types of accommodation and sports facilities, including tidal swimming pools. In **Umhlali**, the available accommodations include a renowned Country House.

From Durban to the south, the N 2 is motorway as far as Hibberdene, although the old R 102, where it runs along the coast, is a more interesting route. Most of this southern coastal area, a region around 20 miles (30 km) wide with approximately 100 miles (160 km) of coast (down to Port Edward), is surrounded by a mile-wide strip of evergreen tropical forest with palms and banana trees; countless rivers and streams pool into lagoons before they finally empty into the sea, and these provide additional opportunities for boating and angling. In this area, one resort follows another, ranging from small and unassuming places where the houses are separated by rampant vegetation to large, built-up settlements fitted out with a complete array of sports and entertainment facilities.

The popularity of this holiday area with the South Africans is reflected in the accommodations available. Predominant are holiday apartments (flats, bungalows, and chalets), caravan parks and campsites; but most resorts also have a few small hotels (one or two stars). What all these towns have in common is the warm weather all year round and the sea, in which you can swim summer and winter. Shark nets ensure that the beaches are kept safe for swimmers; many beaches also have lifeguards on duty. Tidal swimming pools, tennis courts, squash and bowling facilities are to be found in most of the resorts, and there are well-kept, permanently green golf courses (18 holes) in, for example, Amanzimtoti, Umkomaas, Scottburgh, Port Shepstone, Southbroom and San Lameer.

Even if you are not an angler, the annual sardine migration in July is an exciting experience. Large shoals of sardines, which usually live in the cold water off the southern and southwestern coasts of the province of Western Cape, migrate to spawn in the warmer waters of the Benguela current. The current brings them close to the coast between Port St. John's (Wild Coast) and Durban, with numerous predatory fish, turtles and sea birds in their wake.

Right: The beaches in and around Durban are a surfer's paradise.

The rapidly growing town of **Aman-zimtoti**, 17 miles / 27 km from Durban, is still regarded as a residential suburb of Durban. Connoisseurs consider the golf course at **Umkomaas** (27 miles/44 km from Durban) to be one of the most beautiful on the South African coast. Above the southern shore of the Mzimkulu River estuary is **Port Shepstone** (74 miles/120 km from Durban), the oldest town and the administrative and trade center of this area. It dates back to 1882, when a group of more than 200 Norwegian settlers established a community here.

The railway line from Durban ends here, but connects with a narrow-gauge railway running west into the interior of the country; on certain days, this train takes on the name of **Banana Express** and carries tourists to Izotsha (1 1/2 hours) or Paddock (6 1/2 hours). The nostalgic train is pulled by a steam engine dating from 1939; but this ride isn't for steam-railway buffs alone. The tracks wind through the tropical vegetation of the coastal region, through hilltop banana and sugar-cane plantations, past waving (or begging) children and the relatively numerous Zulu settlements with their kraals, animals and small gardens. Tickets for this trip (including the return to Port Shepstone) must be reserved in advance.

This trip can easily be combined with a visit to the **Oribi Gorge Nature Reserve** (organized by private firms, such as Welcome Tours). A trip through the magnificent gorge of the Umzimkulwana River, 15 miles (24 km) long, 3 miles (5 km) wide and some 1,300 feet (400 m) deep, is an unforgettable experience for both nature-lovers and photographers. There is even an attractive tourist camp run by the Natal Park Board (fully equipped; bring your own food supplies)

Of course, you can also visit this impressive gorge on your own; to get there by car from Port Shepstone, follow the N 2 south. The road veers off to the west; after 6 miles (9.5 km), take the turn-off on the right, and after another 8 miles

cially attractive, and also quiet and well-kept, with a number of leisure facilities.

The south coast's largest and most popular holiday destination, **Margate**, presents quite a different picture. This resort (with 11,000 inhabitants) not only has a fine sandy beach, but also an enormous variety of entertainment facilities. If this is what you want, Margate will not disappoint you. During school holidays, there is regular air service to Johannesburg and daily buses to and from Durban. **Southbroom**, with its attractively-situated golf course, **Marina Beach**, which has a particularly wide sandy beach and **Port Edward** are the southernmost of the coastal holiday resorts.

The Umtamvuna River originally formed the border with Transkei; upriver is the unspoiled **Umtamvuna Nature Reserve** (8,093 acres / 3,237 hectares). There's plenty here to interest botanists; and birdwatchers can look out for nesting ospreys and vultures. On the other side of the river is the **Wild Coast Sun Casino** (with hotel) which is extremely popular; there's a daily bus to and from Durban. Along the rocky coast are limestone caves full of fossils; a little further south, you can spot gigantic fossilized trees at low tide in a spot known as the **Mzamba Fossil Beds**.

(12.6 km) you'll see the road leading to the Oribi Gorge Hotel (Fairacres Estate). This is private property, and you have to pay a small entrance fee for each vehicle; but you'll receive ample compensation with the magnificent views of the gorge. You can either take the same picturesque road back until it rejoins the N 2, or you can turn off left beforehand onto a road that crosses the reserve and then also joins up with the N 2.

South of Port Shepstone, the climate is better: the temperatures are not so high and the humidity is lower than it is further north. At **Uvongo**, there is a picturesque waterfall where the Ivungu River, shortly before its estuary, tumbles 75 feet (23 m) from its deep ravine into a lagoon. Uvongo has been joined up with St-Michaels-on-Sea and Manaba Beach. As the lush vegetation of this area has been protected for a long time, the holiday center that's grown up here is espe-

ZULULAND AND ITS NATURE RESERVES

The Zulus, the most numerous of the black groups in South Africa, are – like the Xhosa, Ndebele and Swazi – members of the Nguni language group. Traditionally, they are cattle herders who cultivate corn and vegetables for their own use, as well as millet, which they use to make their nourishing beer. Cattle are primarily a status symbol, and only marginally used for nutrition. Cattle were also the *lobola*, the traditional payment for a bride, which the family of the bridegroom had to pay the family of the bride

Above: Zulu women adorn themselves with caps and elaborate bead jewellery.

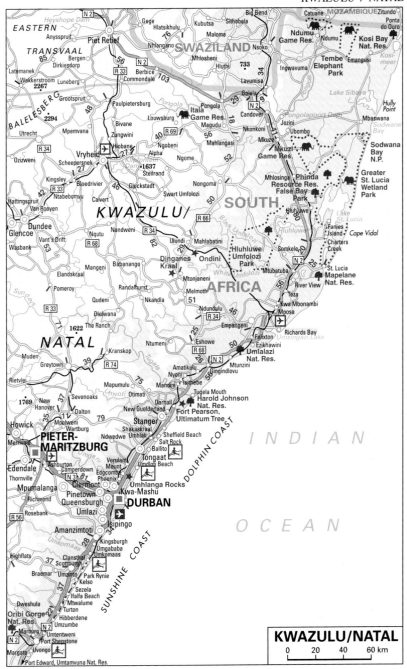

KWAZULU/NATAL

0   20   40   60 km

to compensate them for her loss; today, this payment is usually made in money. The traditional beehive-shaped, grass-thatched dwellings are increasingly being replaced by rondavels with cone-shaped roofs, or simple huts without any traditional features. Important objects for the men are spears and drums; for women, intricate headgear and creative beadwork in necklaces and other jewelry.

In their traditional religion, ancestor-worship plays a large part, as does the *sangoma*, the magician and medicine-man, who you can occasionally spot in his traditional costume. In addition, many belong to one of the largest syncretic Christian communities, the Nazareth Baptist Church; Isaiah Shembe, who founded it in 1911, is today revered as a prophet.

The Zulus only began to play a significant role in South African history at the beginning of the 19th century, when Shaka Zulu combined many small Nguni tribes to form an important, militarily strong nation. Although today the Zulus are scattered over the whole province and also live in many other areas of South Africa, their home was originally the area north of the lower reaches of the Tugela, which is still called Zululand and has many historic sites; here, too, is Ulundi, the possible future provincial capital and the seat of King Goodwill Zwelithini.

The road going north out of Durban (the R 102, which starts out as Umgeni Road, by the train station) passes through a landscape of rolling hills covered with a sea of green sugar cane extending as far as the eye can see, dotted here and there with the islands of isolated country homes or villages. After some 11 miles (18 km), a turn-off on the left leads to **Phoenix**, where Mahatma Gandhi, who came to South Africa in 1893, lived until 1914 on a farm he started himself. Nearby is KwaMashu, one of the largest black towns.

Above: Sugar-cane fields dominate the landscape in KwaZulu/Natal. Right: Model of a Zulu kraal in Shakaland.

92

The Hindu temple in **Mount Edgcombe**, built in 1899, was declared a national landmark in 1977. **Verulam**, the fourth-oldest European settlement in Natal, has been administered by Indians since 1967. The small industrial town of **Stanger** (45 miles / 72 km from Durban), where sugar and paper (from sugar-cane fibers) are produced, was founded in 1873, not far from the place where Shaka established his capital Dukuza in 1825 and where he was murdered in 1828. The white memorial stone over his tomb was erected in 1932.

About 12 miles (20 km) further on, the N 2 reaches the Tugela River. Shortly before the bridge, a small road leads east to the **Harold Johnson Nature Reserve**, an area with interesting coastal vegetation, including many orchids, It also includes the ruins of **Fort Pearson**, built in 1878 by the British, and the **Ultimatum Tree**, where, in 1878, the Zulu ruler Cetshwayo received a British ultimatum which triggered the war between the British and the Zulus at the beginning of 1879.

The other side of the bridge marks the start of **Zululand**, an attractive hilly region with lush, subtropical vegetation and numerous historical sites. Although it doesn't attract nearly as many tourists as Kruger Park or the Garden Route, it has a lot to offer, notably a number of very beautiful nature and game reserves. During the summer months (November to February), the heat, humidity and rain, especially in the coastal plain, can be very unpleasant; inland and higher up, the air is fresher.

At **Gingindlovu**, the R 68 branches off from the N 2 into the interior. It climbs 1,470 feet (450 m) in 16 miles (25 km) to the small, pretty town of **Eshowe**, where the Zulu ruler Cetshwayo built his kraal in 1860; he permitted a Norwegian missionary station to set up nearby. Under the dominion of the British, this became the administrative center of Zululand. The area played a large part in the Anglo-Zulu Wars; this period is documented in the **Zululand Historical Museum** in Fort Nonqai. Around 8 miles

93

(14 km) further on, a road branches off from the R 68 to **Shakaland**, a Zulu village which was built for the TV film "Shaka Zulu" and now functions as a living museum. The establishment providing comfortable accommodations in traditional Zulu huts is part of the Protea hotel chain.

About 16 miles (25 km) after Melmoth, the R 66 leads off to Ulundi; not far beyond this junction, a signpost marks the way to Dinganes Kraal. In 1828, Dingane, Shaka's half-brother and successor, established the large new capital of **Mgungundlovu**, comprised of around 2,000 huts, which were arranged in an oval kraal 150 acres (60 hectares) in area and inhabited by up to 10,000 people. In 1838, Dingane received the Boer leader Piet Retief here, signed a treaty with him, and then had him murdered. Mgungundlovu is currently being reconstructed as a museum.

Above: Angling in the surf near St. Lucia.
Right: Crocodiles in Lake Lucia.

Ulundi, capital of the Homeland KwaZulu until 1994, is dominated by the parliament building put up in 1984. The town developed around 2 miles (3 km) from the place where Cetschwayo founded his new capital after becoming king of the Zulus in 1873. In 1879, this capital was destroyed in the last battle of the war between the British and the Zulus, and the independence of the Zulu nation was at an end. **Ondini**, Cetschwayo's second royal kraal, is currently being restored, and the **KwaZulu Cultural Museum** has an interesting exhibition on the history and culture of the Zulus. Around 20 miles (32 km) further along the (unpaved) road is the western entrance to the Umfolozi Game Reserve.

Back to the N 2: about 11 miles (18 km) north of Gingindlovu, this road comes to the small coastal town of Mtunzini. To the east is the small **Umlazi Nature Reserve** (2,570 acres / 1,028 hectares), created primarily to preserve the unique dune forest and mangrove swamps of the coast. More and more, the

fields of sugar cane are giving way to large areas of forest planted with fast-growing eucalyptus trees and pines, used for the production of cellulose, paper and synthetic fibers.

Empangeni, founded in 1851 as a Norwegian missionary station, can also be reached directly from Ulundi on the R 34. Today the town is the center of Zululand's sugar industry, and has become an important road and railway junction through the development of **Richards Bay**, situated on a natural bay on the Indian Ocean coast with a deep-water harbor that was opened in 1976. In terms of volume, the coal loading equipment here is some of the largest in the world; there is also a large aluminium smelting works and a petrochemical industrial complex.

St. Lucia

Shortly after the bridge over the Umfolozi River, east of the road from **Mtuba-tuba**, leave the N 2 and follow the R 618 to St. Lucia. The place itself is part of the

Greater St. Lucia Wetland Park, one of the most magnificent nature reserves in South Africa, which was founded as long ago as 1897 and combines several areas round **Lake St. Lucia**. The lake is really a dammed-up estuary, which forms a lagoon 37 miles (60 km) long and 6 miles (10 km) wide but only about 6.5 feet (2 m) deep; it extends parallel to the coast, with a very narrow sea entry (St. Lucia Estuary). There is so much evaporation from the water's surface that, despite the heavy annual rainfall (some 40 inches / 1000 mm) and the streams flowing into the lake, it's sometimes hard to keep it filled, and the residual salt deposits pose a true threat to plant and animal life.

In its eastern part, the lake is marshy and overgrown with reeds; along its entire length and reaching to the coast are wooded dunes up to 400 feet (120 m) high. The mining of the precious titanium deposits here has given rise to much protest on ecological grounds. Given the watery nature of this natural paradise, it's

95

only natural that water animals – hippos and crocodiles – play a leading role; note that inflatable boats and swimming are forbidden! The lake is also populated with flocks of flamingos and pelicans, as well as ospreys, herons and other birds.

The fishing on the seashore, in the lake and the estuary is some of the best in the province; you can pick up the regulations regarding the number and size of fish you're allowed to catch in the park's administrative offices; you can also rent boats without engines. Between April and September there are Wilderness Trail hikes (details: Natal Parks Board).

To reach the southernmost part of the St. Lucia area, the **Mapelane Nature Reserve**, leave the N 2 near Kwa Mbonambi (14 miles / 23 km south of Mtubatuba) on a turn-off to the east; from Mtubatuba, the R 618 leads to **St. Lucia**

Above: a knob-billed duck in Hluhluwe Game Reserve. Right: Umfolozi and Hluhluwe were founded to protect the rhinos.

(15 miles / 24 km) and the **St. Lucia Game Reserve**, thence to Cape Vidal around 19 miles (30 km) farther north. If, instead, you continue on the N 2, you'll come, after 19 miles (30 km), to the road to Charters Creek and Fanies Island; **False Bay Park** can be reached from Hluluwe. All accommodation (camps, camping and caravan sites) must be booked in advance with the Natal Parks Board.

Hluhluwe

Hluhluwe (pronounced *shlushluway*), 35 miles (56 km) north of Mtubatuba, is a good base for various excursions; good places to stay here include the **Zululand Safari Lodge** and **Bushlands Game Lodge**, which also offer tours of the neighboring reserves. The main entrance of the Hluhluwe Game Reserve, **Memorial Gate**, is 11 miles (18 km) to the west; False Bay Park is 10 miles (16 km) to the east, and the Mkuzi Game Reserve is 37 miles (60 km) to the north.

The **Hluhluwe Game Reserve**, founded in 1897 and covering an area of 57,667 acres (23,067 hectares) is one of the best-known and most popular nature reserves in South Africa. It takes its name from the Zulu word for a thorny climbing plant common in the area, *dalbergia armata*, which belongs to the papilionaceae family. The attractive hilly country, 260-1,753 feet (80-536 m) above sea level, crisscrossed by the deep ravines of the Hluhluwe and other rivers, is thickly wooded on its northern heights and along its river banks; in other areas, the predominant vegetation is park-like savanna with brush and grassland. The most common animals are impala, nyala and buffalo, and there are also large numbers of wildebeests, kudus, zebras and giraffes. This is the best place to see white rhino; there are also a limited number of black rhino, a species threatened with extinction. Elephants were reintroduced here in 1981, and their numbers have risen noticeably.

You can get a good map of the park's 52 miles (84 km) of roads at the entrance; the speed limit is 25 mph (40 km/h). Experienced rangers lead guided trips in open Land Rovers and walking safaris. For reasonably-priced accommodation, try the expanded and renovated **Hilltop Camp** or the neighboring **Muntulu Bush Camp** (bring your own supplies) with a splendid view over the reserve to the Indian Ocean; some of this accommodation is in the luxury class (**Mtwazi Lodge**), and there's also a good restaurant, shops, and a gas station. The best time to come is during the dry winter months (May to September).

Umfolozi

The eastern entrance to the **Umfolozi Game Reserve**, which borders Hluhluwe to the southwest, is the Mabeni Gate, which you can reach on the N 2 from Mtubatuba; its southwestern entrance, Cengeni Gate, is accessible from Ulundi. Extending over 119,382 acres (47,753 hectares), it is the largest game reserve in the province. The reserve is named after two rivers which meet here, the Black and the White Umfolozi. It was founded, together with Hluhluwe, in 1897, primarily in order to protect the rhinos; as a result, this hilly bush area has the largest number of this still-endangered species. Since rhinos have no natural enemies, in order to maintain the ecological balance animals have been sold to other reserves and zoos all over the world. Umfolozi and Hluhuwe have more or less the same animals. 41 miles (67 km) of roads extend to around half of the area. You can stay in the camps at Mpila and Masinda; bring your own supplies.

Umfolozi has a long tradition of Wilderness Trails, organized hikes conducted from March to November in a special 60,000-acre (24,000-hectares) wilderness area under the leadership of an experienced, armed ranger; donkeys carry luggage and equipment. Since these hikes are very popular, it is advisable to reserve in advance.

The almost unspoiled area between Umfolozi and Hluhluwe, the **Corridor**, has recently been incorporated in the two reserves, so that **Hluhluwe Umfolozi Park**, with a total area of 240,000 acres (96,000 hectares), is now the third-largest game reserve in South Africa.

Sodwana Bay and Mkuzi

North of Hluhuwe, near Mhlosinga, an (unpaved) road, best negotiated in a four-wheel-drive vehicle, branches off to the northeast. It leads past the luxurious Game Lodge of the large **Phinda Resource Reserve** (containing the so-called "Big Five": lion, leopard, rhino, elephant and buffalo), which belongs to the Conservation Corporation, and on to **Sodwana Bay National Park** (1,032 acres / 413 hectares) by the Indian Ocean, a

Above: A "welcoming committee" awaits a tourist bus with sceptical curiosity. Right: Warthogs wallow in the mud (Mkuzi Game Reserve).

paradise for anglers and divers and very popular in the holiday season. Its attractions include coastal dune forests with silver oaks, wild fig trees and bird-of-paradise flowers, home to many different species of bird, as well as coral reefs and tidal pools. Observation tours are organized in December and January when the large leather-back turtles lay their eggs on the beach. The park has large campsites (with supermarkets) and chalets, which you can book with the Natal Parks Board. A little further to the north is the private **Rocktail Bay Lodge**, which was built under the supervision of ecologists and is wholly powered by solar energy.

The road to **Mkuzi Game Reserve** is a signposted turning off the N 2, 37 miles (60 km) from Hluhluwe. This game reserve, a little wilder and less visited than its neighbors, is located in the relatively flat, open countryside some 200-500 feet (60-150 m) above sea level between the Lebombo (also Ubombo) range in the west and the dense riverine

forest of the Mkuzi River in the east. From four observation huts at watering-holes, you can observe and photograph the animals and birds at close range (among the highlights are the weaver birds, which you can watch at work building their distinctive nests). Impalas, nyalas, warthogs and kudus are particularly numerous; the park is also home to giraffes, zebras and rhinos, hippos and crocodiles.

Plant-lovers will be enthralled by the variety of vegetation: wooded areas, in which there are large numbers of syca-mores, alternate with open, park-like countryside with wisteria, umbrella acacias and many other species. You can stay at the attractive Matuma Camp or a camp/caravan site. (For further information and registration for guided walks, contact the Natal Parks Board).

The area north of this is inhabited by various Nguni tribes, of which the Tembe is the largest. The Zulus didn't bother to differentiate between these peoples, calling them all Tonga; hence the area's orig-inal name of Tongaland. Today, how-ever, it's generally known as Maputaland after the Usutu River on its northern bor-der, which becomes the Maputo in Mo-zambique, whence it flows into the In-dian Ocean. In the Cretaceous period, the ocean reached to the foot of the Lebombo range; as it withdrew, it left a sandy plain behind it. In summer, the rivers fre-quently flood and the numerous flat pans are transformed into small lakes, a habitat for the area's many fish, birds, hippos and crocodiles. The coastal area extend-ing up north to the border, with its high dunes and a strip of coastal forest, is part of the St. Lucia Marine Reserve, which also extends 3.4 miles (5.6 km) out to sea from the low-water mark.

Ndumu and Tembe

At Nkonkni, about 7 miles (11 km) north of Mkuze, a road branches off from the N 2 and leads to Jozini, which has spectacular views of the large reservoir created on the Pongola River (**Pongola-**

poort Dam). This lake is the nucleus of one of the largest irrigation plants of South Africa. 52 miles (84 km) further on are the village of Ndumu and the boundary of the **Ndumu Game Reserve**, (291 miles / 470 km from Durban, measuring 25,292 acres / 10,117 hectares in area); from here, it's another 5 miles (8 km) to the rather basic camp (bring your own food and drink; equipment provided). Up to Ndumu, the road is paved. This remote area, which borders Mozambique in the north, is perhaps the most beautiful of the KwaZulu/Natal reserves; people tend to describe it exclusively in superlatives.

The reserve is densely wooded, especially along the rivers. Both the extraordinary variety of species (more than 200) and the size and beauty of the individual trees, including wild fig, marula, sycamore and fever trees, are unrivalled any-

Above: Coming home from work in the fields. Above right: Zulu rondavel at the foot of the Lebombo range. Right: The leopard's spotted coat is a perfect camouflage.

where else in South Africa. The approximately 400 different types of bird include tropical birds at the southernmost limit of their range as well as many water birds. The animals (various kinds of antelope, bush pigs, rhinos and cheetahs), are usually hard to spot in the dense undergrowth; all the more interesting, then, the hippos and crocodiles in the rivers and numerous little lakes caused by floods. The park organizes Land Rover excursions and walks, both accompanied by rangers. Recently built and notably comfortable, the **Ndumu Wilderness Camp** (with a restaurant), a joint venture of the local KwaZulu authority and a private entrepreneur, is billed as a special project designed to enable the local people to benefit from the income generated by tourists. Camping and caravans are not allowed.

Further east (in Sihangwane), a turn-off from the road from Jozini leads to the 75,000-acre (30,000-hectare) **Tembe Elephant Park**. Accommodation is provided in four two-bed tents, and there are organized Land Rover trips with a ranger. Still further east is **Kosi Bay Nature Reserve** (25,000 acres / 10,000 hectares). This consists of a system of four interconnected freshwater lakes, joined to the sea in the north by a narrow estuary. The park's attractions include the mangrove coast, with all the varieties of mangrove to be found in southern Africa; coral reefs; the breeding grounds of the endangered giant leatherback turtles, which can weigh up to 880 pounds (400 kg); and many different species of bird. Ndumu, Tembe and Kosi Bay are administered by the KwaZulu Department of Nature Conservation.

Itala Game Reserve

If, 8 km (5 miles) north of Nkonkoni, you take the R 69 which branches off to the west and drive 53 miles (85 km) to Louwsburg (the first 21 miles / 34 km of the road are unpaved), you'll leave Zululand and reach the little-known **Itala Game Reserve**. This reserve, set up in 1972 by the Natal Parks Board, is bordered on the north by the Pongola River and consists of 74,127 acres (29,651 hectares) of bushveld (up to 4,728 feet/ 1,446 m above sea level). The attractive mountainous area is home to elephants, leopards, giraffes, cheetahs, rhinos and many different antelopes, as well as 400 species of bird. Accommodation is provided at the luxurious **Ntschondwe Camp,** with chalets (also for self-catering) plus a restaurant, shop and swimming pool. Overnight stays, wilderness trails and night safaris must be booked in advance with the Natal Parks Board.

THE DRAKENSBERG

In the west of KwaZulu/Natal, South Africa's Great Escarpment rises to its highest altitudes along the Lesotho border. The Zulus called this mountain range *Quathlamba*, the "wall of upward-point-

ing spears," because of its serrated appearance. The same jagged edge reminded Voortrekkers of the back of a dragon which was said to live in the rugged country, prompting them to name the range "Drakensberg," or Dragon Mountain.

Seen from the east, the escarpment resembles a virtually sheer wall, its almost horizontal upper edge broken by a mere handful of ridges and protruding peaks. Highest point is Champagne Castle at an altitude of 11,040 feet (3,376 m) above sea level. Between Bushman's Nek in the south and Royal Natal National Park in the north there is only one dependable road, Sani Pass, within a stretch of about 400 miles (250 km). Nonetheless, this very section is one of South Africa's most important vacation regions.

Geology enthusiasts will be impressed by the tremendously massive, still-untouched layers of the Karoo Formation, which are visible here; these have piled up throughout southern Africa since the Paleozoic era. The deposits are covered

by a layer of basalt which once extended to the coast of Natal. This layer, up to 4,580 feet (1,400 m) thick, has survived only in the Drakensberg and Lesotho; the basalt continues to be eroded away by the combined effects of water and wind.

The foothills in front of the escarpment – Little Berg, 4,900-5,885 feet (1,500-1,800 m) above sea level – consist of remains of the basalt layer and sedimentary rocks (sandstone, slate and clay), some of them brightly colored; in valleys and ravines, their layers contrast notably with the dark basalt. Bushmen dwelt in many of the caves here, something attested to in the countless rock paintings they left behind them (mainly depictions of hunting scenes). Streams and rivers have carved out spectacular gorges, and form picturesque waterfalls of varying sizes.

There are stark contrasts in the weather, too, especially in summer, when daytime temperatures can range from 59° F to

Above: The Drakensberg Mountains – ideal for hiking.

91° F (15° C-33° C). In the afternoons, magnificent cloud formations can herald heavy thunderstorms; although these are short, they cause sharp drops in temperatures, and their torrential cloudbursts can swell streams and rivers so as to render them wholly impassable. Such rainstorms account for 50% of the annual rainfall of 39-66 inches (1,000-1,700 mm), 85% of which occurs between October and March. In the summer, places at high altitudes can be shrouded in sudden mist. During the winter months (April/May to September), the days are generally sunny, with daytime temperatures sometimes rising above 68° F (20° C); at night, however, they fall rapidly below freezing point. At this season, the air is fresh and there is very little rain, but snow may fall at higher altitudes.

Due to the predominance of grass, the mountains seem to be covered with a green carpet in the summer. In fact, the region's flora is extremely varied. In the alpine zone, above 9,156 feet (2,800 m), there is a low undergrowth of heather, everlasting flowers and strawflowers, while the zone below 6,540 feet (2,000 m) sports grasses, sclerophyllus, evergreens and proteas. In valleys and ravines, there are some thickly forested areas with mountain cypress, tree fern, and yellow-wood. In addition, some 800 types of flowering plants occur here, including 63 varieties of orchid.

The animal kingdom includes 12 types of antelope alone; occasionally, you can also see leopards, jackals and baboons, and smaller animals as the klipspringer antelope are even easier to spot. Of the numerous birds in the area, two remark-able species are the rare bearded vulture – with a wingspan of about 10 feet (3 m) – and the black eagle.

Tranquil and unspoiled, this magnifi-cent area is ideal for mountain hikes (gentle walks to strenuous treks). The na-ture reserves provide information and maps; for guided tours consult the Natal Parks Board. It goes without saying that sturdy shoes are a must.

The main road to the Drakensberg is the N 3 from Durban to Johannesburg, which is a freeway for much of its length. Minor roads branch off from this to the tourist resorts, which are not generally connected to one another. Several nar-rower roads following the course of the mountains offer scenic views of the es-carpment, but few are paved, which makes them hazardous in wet weather. They are likewise best avoided after dark.

Pietermaritzburg

Driving from Durban to Pietermaritz-burg on the N 3 you pass through a charming area, which, by virtue of its many gently undulating hills, has been christened **Valley of 1000 Hills**. These were created by the gradual realignment of the escarpment since the Paleozoic era. This exposed the ancient granite of the original mountain chain, which was then eroded down by the winding Umgeni

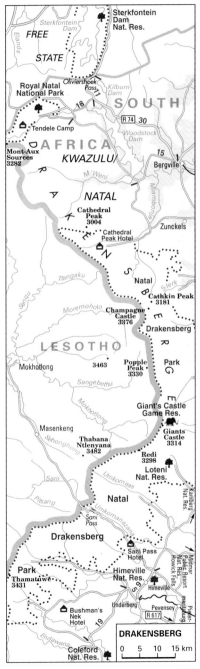

river and its tributaries and worn away to its present rounded form. Towering over the area is the **Natal Table Mountain**, 2,963 feet (906 m) above sea level, which commands spectacular views across the region as far as the Indian Ocean and the Drakensberg. From Botha's Hill, north of the N 3 on the R 103, you can reach **Phe-Zulu**, a Zulu village with traditional huts which is open to the public.

Pietermaritzburg, founded in 1838 by the Voortrekkers, was named after leaders Piet Retief and Gert Maritz. In 1843, the British annexed the town, and made it the capital of their colony Natal in 1856. The town still reflects the former English presence, in part because of its many red-brick buildings from the Victorian era. With a population of 250,000, it is Natal's administrative and industrial

Above: A black eagle keeps an eye out for prey. Right: There are caves with Bushman cave paintings in the Drakensberg, as well as reconstructions in the Natal Museum in Pietermaritzburg.

center, as well as home to part of its university; and is under consideration as a possible capital of the province. PMB is characterized by wide streets, splendid parks renowned for their azaleas, and a wealth of historical buildings.

These include **City Hall** (1900) with its 154-foot (47 m) bell-tower, reputedly the largest brick building south of the Equator. On its first floor is the **Tatham Art Gallery**, housing paintings, graphics and sculptures by 19th- and early 20th-century English and French artists. **St. Peter's Church**, an Anglican church consecrated in 1857, boasts stained-glass windows which once graced an English pre-Reformation abbey. Bishop Colenso (1814-83), the first prelate of the diocese of Natal, is interred in front of the altar. He was excommunicated and removed from office for attempting to establish friendly relations with the Zulus, but later rehabilitated after appealing to a British court. The **Old Voortrekker House** (1847), with its yellowwood ceiling and tiled floors, is the only remaining build-

ing from the city's beginnings. The **Natal Museum** on Loop Street has various interesting displays on cultural and natural history, including a life-size reconstruction of a Drakensberg cave, complete with rock paintings. Not quite 2 miles (3 km) southwest of the town are the **Natal Botanic Gardens**. The Natal Parks Board has its office in Queen Elizabeth Park, close to the N 3; while the tourist information office is in **Churchill Square**, the former marketplace.

In the **Midmar Public Resort Nature Reserve** (7,025 acres / 2,844 hectares), the Umgeni river has been dammed up to form a large lake (4,555 acres / 1,822 hectares); this reserve includes facilities for water sports and camping. Northeast of the dam and the N 3, the Umgeni river cascades 311 feet (95 m) over a ledge of dolerite to form the **Howick Falls**.

Underberg and Sani Pass

South of Howick near Merrivale, the R 617 branches off towards **Underberg** and **Himeville**. Both resorts lie in a fertile, intensely-cultivated arable area in the foothills at an altitude of 5,101 feet (1,560 m); behind them, the Drakensberg form an impressive backdrop. The numerous options for vacationers include the **Coleford Nature Reserve** (accommodation available) or the **Himeville Nature Reserve** (with campsite). From Himeville, tourists can reach the **Sani Pass**, 9,398 feet (2,874 m) above sea level, along a partially unpaved road. Located at the foot of the pass is the **Sani Pass Hotel**, a luxurious hotel with a pool, golf-course, tennis courts and horseback riding. The hotel organizes tours (four-wheel drive vehicles only) via the Sani Pass some 9 miles (14 km) away, to Lesotho, at the foot of the 11,386-foot (3,482 m) Thabana Ntlenyana (remember your passport!).

To reach the **Loteni Nature Reserve** and **Kamberg Nature Reserve** (with accommodation), take the R103 from Howick to Nottingham Road, after which you continue west.

Giant's Castle Game Reserve

To visit **Giant's Castle Game Reserve**, at 85,556 acres (34,638 hectares) the largest in the Drakensberg region, leave the N 3 in Estcourt. What is arguably the most impressive section of the Drakensberg escarpment extends from Champagne Castle (11,040 feet/ 3,376 m) in the north to Giant's Castle (10,837 feet / 3,314 m) in the south, and consists of a continuous basalt wall 22 miles (35 km) long, forming a backdrop to the plateau on which the reserve is located. The lovely camp here, which includes "Giant's Lodge" (luxurious accommodation for 7 people), does not have a restaurant; but there is a cook who will prepare meals if you bring your own provisions. (Note that there are no shops for miles around!) The camp is set in a flower garden, and you can watch the

Above: Howick Falls (Umgeni River). Right: Clouds move over the Drakensberg – portent of approaching storm?

birds practically from your "back door." There's a special "Lammergeyer Hide" from which to observe the nesting of this rare bearded vulture. A herd of eland also makes its home here.

You don't need to have had extensive mountain climbing experience to embark on a trek along one of the marked trails (varying degrees of difficulty), but you should, for safety reasons, report longer excursions. Another option is to join a ranger-led hike. Bushman rock paintings can be seen in many caves; the most accessible and interesting are **Main Caves** (with some 546 paintings), less than 1 1/2 miles (2 km) from the camp.

Horses can be hired from **Hillside Camp**, a simple camp about 19 miles (30 km) from the main camp. **Injasuti Camp** is of particular interest to the nature lover. It lies 4,807 feet (1,470 m) above sea level in a deep and densely-wooded river valley, overshadowed by Champagne Castle and Cathkin Peak. A hiking trail leads to **Battle Cave**, which contains 750 Bushman paintings.

Cathedral Peak

Some 15 miles (25 km) on from Winterton after the turnoff from the N 3, you come to **Cathedral Peak Hotel**, situated 4,741 feet (1,450 m) above sea level. Aside from its fantastic panorama, it also offers a wide variety of leisure activities. The 3-mile-long (5.5 km) **Ndedema Gorge** is well-known among rock painting experts; in the Sebayeni caves alone there are 4,000 exquisite rock paintings, many of them in several colors. The oldest ones were executed between 970 and 1230 AD, the more recent ones from 1720-1820. (The hotel provides information on rock-painting tours.)

Royal Natal National Park

One of the highlights in the Drakensberg area is the **Royal Natal National**

Park, opened in 1916 and now extending over 19,992 acres (8,094 hectares). It received its name after a visit by the British Royal Family in 1947. The park is 42 miles (68 km) from Harrismith on the R 615, or 58 miles (93 km) from Winterton/Bergville on the R 74 from the south (exit from the N 3 in Frere).

The most spectacular part is the **amphitheater**, which is impressive even from a distance. As there are no foothills here, the arcing basalt wall rises directly some 5,886 feet (1,800 m) from a base 3,989 feet (1,220 m) above sea level. It is flanked in the east by the 9,964-foot (3,047 m) Eastern Buttress and in the west by the 10,350-foot (3,165 m) Sentinel. The plateau which adjoins it to the south is overshadowed by the even higher form of **Mont-aux-Sources** (10,732 feet / 3,282 m), from which the whole formation takes its name. Five rivers have their sources here, including the Tugela and the Khubedu, one of the source rivers of the Orange. **Tendele Camp**, attractively located on a hillside

5,167 feet (1,580 m) above sea level, has both a restaurant and groceries (advance booking advisable). Another lodging option is the Karos Mont-aux-Sources Hotel in front of the park entrance.

Anyone who wants to walk though the almost 9-mile (14 km) long **Tugela Gorge** should allow a whole day for the trip. Half of the walk presents no problems; in the narrow, wooded gorge, you have to cross the river several times, negotiating gravel, but this is only difficult when the river is in flood. A tunnel some 196 feet (60 m) long can be avoided by using a rope ladder. The reward for your efforts: a magnificent view of the wall of the amphitheater over which the Tugela crashes some 2,779 feet (850 m) in several spectacular waterfalls, the largest single fall being 598 feet (183 m).

Carrying on towards Johannesburg, you can traverse the escarpment either over the **Van Reenen Pass**, 5,494 feet (1,680 m) (N 3), or the equally charming **Oliviershoek Pass**, 5,690 feet (1,740 m) above sea level (R 615).

107

KWAZULU/NATAL
Transportation

Bus: Greyhound and Translux run regular buses from Durban (via Pietermaritzburg, 1 hr.) to Johannesburg (7-8 hours), Umtata/East London/Port Elizabeth (about 13 hours), Bloemfontein/Kimberley/Upington (15 1/2 hours) and Cape Town (about 20 hours). Buses leave from and arrive at the main train station. There are also buses to Umhlanga Rock, Margate and the Wild Coast Casino.

Train: There are daily trains between Durban and Johannesburg with Trans Natal (13 hours), while Trans Oranje runs between Durban and Cape Town (about 36 hours).

Air: Durban is serviced by the international airlines LTU and British Airways; domestic lines include SAA, Airlink (Nelspruit, Port Elizabeth, Umtata, Bloemfontein), Comair (Johannesburg and Cape Town), Phoenix Airways (Johannesburg), Transkei Airways (Umtata). There's a regular bus service (tel: 031/42-6111) between the airport, 8.5 mi/14 km S of town, and the SAA Terminal at the corner of Aliwal/Smith Sts.

Central Reservation Service
for holiday accommodations

Natal Parks Board, PO Box: 622, Pietermaritzburg 3200, tel: 033/147-1981, fax: 147-1980. **Coastal Holiday Letting**, PO Box 11, Ballito 4420, tel: 0322/6-2155, fax: 6-1122. **Beach Holidays**, PO Box 855 Margate 4275, tel: 03 931/2-2543, fax: 7-3753. **Umhlanga Flat Services**, Chartwell Centre, Umhlanga Rocks 4320, tel: 031/ 561-1511, fax: 561-4210.

DURBAN

Telephone and fax area code: 031, postal code: 4000

Excursions

Tours of the city, Shakaland, Valley of 1000 Hills, Wild Coast Casino, and other destinations are organized by **U-Tour Coach Company**, The Marine Building, 22 Gardiner St. (buses also depart from here), as well as by **Venture Tours and Safaris**, Shop 4 Nedbank Circle, corner West and Point Rd. For ocean and harbor tours: **Sarie Marais**, PO Box 3805, tel: 305-4022.

Accommodations

TOWN: *LUXURY:* **Royal Hotel**, 267 Smith St., PO Box 1041, tel: 304-0331, fax: 307-6884. *MODERATE:* **City Lodge**, corner Brickhill and Old Fort Rds., PO Box 10 842. tel: 32-1447, fax: 32-1483. *BUDGET:* **Le Plaza**, 9 Bad St., tel: 301-2591. N of the Greyville Race Course: **Tekweni International Youth Hostel**, 169 Ninth Ave. Morningside, tel: 303-1433.

BEACH FRONT: *LUXURY:* **Elangeni Sun**, 63 Snell Parade, PO Box 4094, tel: 37-1321, fax: 32-

5527. *MODERATE:* **Edward Hotel**, Marine Parade, PO Box 105, tel: 37-3681, fax: 32-1692. **Holiday Inn Garden Court**, 73 Marine Parade, PO Box 10 199, Marine Parade 4056, tel: 37-2231, fax: 37-4640. *BUDGET:* **Balmoral**, 125 Marine Parade, PO Box 10 935, Marine Parade 4056, tel: 37-4392.

Restaurants

Throughout the city, specialties are seafood and, above all, Indian curries. Notable among the hotel restaurants and other eateries, in all price categories and of varying quality, along the Marine Parade is the **Edwards** (with several restaurants). On Gillespie Street, not far from the Marine Parade, Italian food is offered at **Aldo's** (No.15; tel: 37-0900; closed Sun) and **Villa d'Este** (No.29; tel: 37-0264), **The Lighthouse** (in **The Wheel**, tel: 37-8978) specializes in seafood. Famous for its curries and British atmosphere is the **Queens Tavern** of **The Middle East Indian & Dining Club**, 16 Stamford Hill Road, NE of the Greyville Race Course. tel: 309-4017.

Museums and Sights

Snake Park, open daily 9 am-4:30 pm. **Sea World**, open daily 9 am-9 pm; for hours of tours and feeding times, call 37-4079. **Durban Art Gallery**, Mon-Sat 8:30 am-5 pm, Thu 8:30 am-7 pm, Sun 11 am-5 pm. **Durban Natural Science Museum**, **Local History Museum** and **Old House Museum**, Mon-Fri 8:30 am-5 pm, Sun 11 am-5 pm. **Sugar Terminal**, tours and registration: tel: 301-0331. **Natal Maritime Museum**, Mon-Fri 8:30 am-4:30 pm, Sun 11 am-4 pm. **Botanic Garden**, daily 7:30 am-5:30 pm, orchid house, 9:30 am-12:30, 2-5 pm. **Campbell Collections of the University of Natal**, 220 Marriott Rd., (Mynah Bus to Musgrave or Marriott Rd.; registration: tel: 28-5311, fax: 16-2051). **Durban African Art Centre**, 8 Guildhall Arcade, 35 Gardiner St. (sales exhibition for Zulu art and artisan work), tel: 304-7915, fax: 304-4949.

Tourist Information

Greater Durban Marketing Authority, Information Office, in the building The Marine, 22 Gardiner St., tel: 304-4934, fax: 304-6196; also Beach Office, tel: 32-2608, and Airport Office, tel: 42-0400.

SATOUR, Shop 1, in the same building as the information office, tel: 304-7144, fax: 305-6693. **Automobile Association**, AA House, 33 St. Georges Street, tel: 305-5677.

COASTS AND BEACHES
Accommodations

UMHLANGA ROCKS 4320 *LUXURY:* **Beverley Hills Sun**, 54 Lighthouse Rd., PO Box 71, tel:

031/561-2211, fax: 561-3711. *MODERATE:* **Oyster Box Hotel**, 2 Lighthouse Rd., PO Box 22, tel: 031/561-2233, fax: 561-4072. Edge of the Sea, Lagoon Drive, PO Box 20, tel: 031/561-1341, fax: 561-4072.
UMHLALI 4390: *MODERATE:* **Shortens Country House** (Silver), Compensation Rd., PO Box 499, tel: 0322/7-1144, fax: 7-1144.
AMAZIMTOTI 4125: *BUDGET:* **Beach Hotel**, PO Box 24, tel: 031/903-5328, fax: 903-5328.
SCOTTBURGH 4180: *MODERATE:* **Cutty Sark Protea Hotel,** Beachfront, tel: 0323/2-1230, fax: 2197.
PORT SHEPSTONE 4240: *MODERATE:* **Bedford Inn**, 64 Colley St., tel: 0391/2-1085, fax: 82-4238.
RAMSGATE 4285: *MODERATE:* **Crayfish Inn**, Marine Drive, tel: 03 931/4410, fax: 7-9521.
PORT EDWARD 4295: *LUXURY:* **Wild Coast Sun Hotel**, PO Box 23, tel: 0471/5-9111, fax: 5-2778.

Sights
Natal Sharks Board, viewings Tue, Wed, Thu, the first Sun of the month, three times daily. **Banana Express**, departs from Port Shepstone Thu 10 am, Sun 11 am; additional runs during school holidays: tel: 03 931/7-6443.

Tourist Information
Umhlanga Publicity Association (headquarters at Lagoon Drive), Private Bag X4 Umhlanga Rocks 4320, tel: 031/561-4257, fax: 561-1417. **Hibiscus Coast Resorts Association**, Bendigo Caravan Park, PO Box 91, Anerley 4230, tel: 0391/8-3451. **Margate Publicity Association**, Main Beach, PO Box 25, Margate 4275, tel: 03 931/2-2322, fax: 1886.

ZULULAND AND GAME RESERVES
Accommodations
ESHOWE 3815 *MODERATE:* **Royal Hotel**, 9 Osborn Rd., PO Box 24, tel: and fax: 0354/4-1117. **Shakaland**, PO Box 103, tel: 03 546/912, fax: 824.
ULUNDI 3838: **Ulundi Holiday Inn**, PO Box 91, tel: 0358/2-1121, fax: 2-1721.
RICHARD'S BAY 3900: *MODERATE:* **Karos Bayshore Inn**, PO Box 51, tel: 0351/3-1246, fax: 3-2335.
MTUBATUBA 3935 *BUDGET:* **Sundowner Hotel**, PO Box 473, tel: 035/550-0153.
HLUHLUWE 3960 *MODERATE:* **Zululand Safari Lodge**, PO Box 16, tel: 03 562/63, fax: 193. **Bushlands Game Lodge**, PO Box 79, tel: 03 562/144, fax: 176. *LUXURY:* **Phinda Resource Reserve**, PO Box 1211, Sunninghill Park 2175, tel: 011/803-8421, fax: 803-1810.
MKUZE 3965: *LUXURY:* **Ghost Mountain Inn**, PO Box 18, tel: 03586/12. Reservations **Ndumo Safari Camp** and **Rocktail Bay Lodge**: Wilderness Safaris, PO Box 651 171, Benmore 2010, tel:

011/884-1458, fax: 883-6255. Registration for Ndumu Game Reserve, Tembe Elephant Reserve and Kosi Bay Nature Reserve: **KwaZulu Dept of Nature Conservation**, Private Bag X9024, Pietermaritzburg 3201, tel: 0331/94-6696, fax: 42-1948.

Museums and Sights
Zululand Historical Museum, Nongqai Rd., PO Box 37, Eshowe 3815, daily 10 am-5 pm. **Mgungundlovu Museum**, daily 8 am-5 pm. **Ondini Cultural-Historical Museum**, PO Box 523, Ulundi 3838, tel: 0358/79-1854.

Tourist Information
Eshowe Publicity Association, PO Box 24, Eshowe 3815, tel: 0354/4-1117. **St. Lucia**, corner Katonkel and McKenzie St, PO Box 120, St. Lucia 3936, tel: 035/590-1143, fax: 5901-1330; **KwaZulu Monuments Council**, Ondini, tel: 0358/79-1854. **Maputaland Travel and Information**, PO Box 103, Mkuze 3965, tel: and fax: 035/573-1120.

DRAKENSBERG
Accommodations
PIETERMARITZBURG 3200: *MODERATE:* **Imperial Hotel**, 224 Loop St., PO Box 140, tel: 0331/42-6551, fax: 429796. **Summer Place Youth Hostel** 85 Pietermaritz St., tel: 0331/94-5785, fax: 45-6731.
UNDERBERG 4500: *MODERATE:* **Drakensberg Gardens**, reservations PO Box 10 305, Marine Parade 4056, tel. and fax: 033/701-1355. *BUDGET:* **Underberg**, Main Rd., PO Box 28, tel: 033 712/ ask for 22.
HIMEVILLE 4585: *MODERATE:* **Sani Pass Hotel**, Sani Pass Rd., PO Box 44, Himeville 4585, tel. and fax: 033/701-1435.
WINTERTON 3340: *MODERATE:* **Drakensberg Sun**, Cathkin Park, PO Box 335, tel: 036/468-1000, fax: 468-1224. **Cathedral Peak Hotel**, PO Winterton, tel. and fax: 036/488-1888.
MONT-AUX-SOURCES 3353: *MODERATE:* **Karos Mont-aux-Sources Hotel**, Private Bag X1, tel. and fax: 036/438-6230.
BERGVILLE 3350: *MODERATE:* **Little Switzerland Resort**, Private Bag X1661, Bergville 3350, tel. and fax: 036/438-6220. *BUDGET:* **Hotel Walter**, PO Box 12, tel: 036/448-1022, fax: 448-1562.

Museums
PIETERMARITZBURG: **Tatham Art Gallery**, Tue-Sat 10 am-6 pm. **Natal Museum**, Mon-Sat 9 am-4:30 pm, Sun 2-5 pm.

Tourist Information
Pietermaritzburg Publicity Association, 177 Commercial Rd., PO Box 25, tel: 45-1348, fax: 94-3535. **Automobile Association (AA)**, Brasforth House, 191 Commercial Rd., Pietermaritzburg, tel: 42-0571. **Drakensberg Publicity Association**, PO Box 12, Bergville 3350, tel: 036/448-1557, fax: 448-1562.

EASTERN CAPE

LAND OF THE XHOSA
EAST LONDON
GRAHAMSTOWN
PORT ELIZABETH
NATIONAL PARKS FOR
ELEPHANTS AND MOUNTAIN
ZEBRAS
THE GREAT KAROO

EASTERN CAPE

The province of Eastern Cape covers 13.9% of South Africa's territory and is home to 16.4% of its population, but accounts for a mere 7.4% of the gross domestic product. Infant mortality is at its highest here, and life expectancy at its lowest. Poverty is most rife in the former homelands of Transkei and Ciskei. Traditionally, this has been an agricultural region devoted to sheep and cattle-raising, but in the regions further east where the rainfall is higher, forage cereal is grown, while pineapple is cultivated in the coastal areas. Sprawling industrial conurbations have developed around Port Elizabeth/Uitenhage and, to a lesser extent, around East London. The province's capital is to be either Bisho or King William's Town.

Sandwiched between KwaZulu/Natal and Western Cape, the province contains a spectrum of diverse ecological zones. This is because of the varied climate: regions with year-round precipitation give way to areas with a single rainy season in summer. As a result, the vegetation changes from Mediterranean (fynbos) to

Preceding pages: Typical "Koppies" in the Great Karoo. Left: A Xhosa woman wearing traditional turban-like headdress.

a more African type (grass and bushveld, with wooded valleys). Historically, this was the place where members of two separate cultures first met, then clashed, and ultimately engaged in long and bloody battles: the Boers, later joined by white British and German settlers, and the Xhosa, the southernmost tribe of the Bantu people.

LAND OF THE XHOSA

The Xhosa people's main territories derived their names from the Great Kei River. Two homelands were created: "trans-Kei," on the other side of the Kei, and "cis-Kei," this side of the Kei. Between the two ran the thin corridor of Cape Province. Though both Ciskei and Transkei were granted independence in 1976 and 1981 respectively, their status went unrecognized outside of South Africa. Since 1994, however, the two states have been a part of the Republic of South Africa, forming a portion of the Eastern Cape province.

Numerically, the Xhosa, comprising several different tribes of Bantu peoples, and belonging to the Nguni language group, are the second-largest tribe in South Africa. The first group came from the North in the 17th century and came into contact with the Hotttentots; they

113

subsequently took over many of the clicking sounds from the Hottentots' language into their own. Today, Xhosa (of which there are several dialects) is one of the official languages of South Africa; it's spoken by 85% of the province's inhabitants, although by only 16% of the residents in the province of Western Cape.

Towards the end of the 18th century, when the Xhosa began to look for new grazing land, they clashed with white settlers advancing northwards. After a number of serious border wars, first with the Boers and then with the English, the area was incorporated into the British Cape Colony. The entire region, particularly the former Ciskei homeland, is littered with memorials to the *Frontier Wars*. However, the Xhosa themselves also indulged in bitter infighting.

In addition, thousands died as a result of the visions of a Xhosa girl named Nongqawuse. She prophesied that on February 18, 1857, two blood-red suns would rise, a cyclone would sweep the whites into the sea, cattle would multiply, crops would yield rich harvests, and fallen warriors would come back to life. However, for this to happen, the ancestral spirits required everyone to sacrifice all of their cattle and crops as a sign of faith. Unfortunately, most Xhosa complied with this demand. In the ensuing catastrophe, population figures in the affected areas dropped from roughly 105,000 to 37,000. Tens of thousands of people died of starvation, and countless more fled to the Cape Colony in the hopes of eking out a living there. The British left the traditional structure of the province unchanged and allowed most of the tribal chiefs to stay in office.

Today, many Xhosa live in and around industrial and urban centers, where they gradually lose contact with the traditional culture which has managed to prevail, at least in part, in the original Xhosa territories. All Xhosa tribes have in common

the shape and arrangement of their round dwelling huts, or *rondavels*, which are generally made of stone, clay bricks and clay. These rondavels are whitewashed and have conical grass roofs; their doors always point east. Near the huts, which are widely scattered over an open area, often on hillsides, is the kraal. These days, you often see small vegetable gardens here as well, usually fenced in to protect them from the village's numerous little black pigs, which roam about at will. But the land is not otherwise divided, as it is deemed to be the common property of everyone.

Today most of the Xhosa wear modern clothing, though one sometimes sees an older woman in the traditional orange

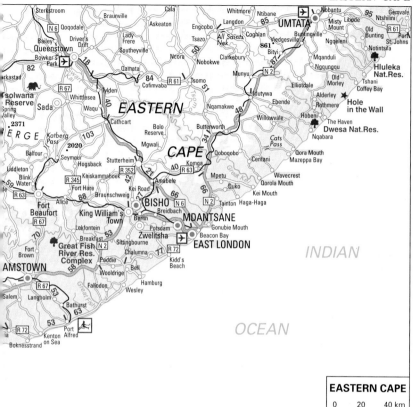

clothing, with the intricate turban-like hat, smoking a long-stemmed pipe – the status symbol of married women.

Because of the ongoing population explosion, the land has been overgrazed for a long time; one result is severe soil erosion (*dongas*). Despite the relatively good conditions for agriculture, moreover, the land simply can't produce enough to feed the expanding population; as a result, many Xhosa go as migratory laborers to areas with a better economy.

Wild Coast

The coastline of the former **Transkei**, known as the "wild coast," is one of South Africa's most beautiful. There are steep, craggy cliffs and gentle green hilltops, small remote bays and magnificent stretches of wide sandy beaches; and this is the southernmost area in which you'll find mangrove swamps. This piece of unspoiled nature is a true El Dorado for anyone with an interest in geology or botany, as well as for bird-watchers, artists and photographers – and, last but not least, for anglers, thanks to the many estuaries in the area.

Umtata, the former capital of Transkei, lies about 2,290 feet (700 m) above sea level on the Umtata River and the N 2, a freeway running parallel to the coast which crosses the entire area. Originally founded as a mission station in 1879, Umtata expanded rapidly; today, it has

115

some 120,000 inhabitants. City Hall and the former parliament building (*Bunga*) both date back to the colonial period. On the southern edge of town stands the impressive complex of buildings that comprises the university, founded in 1977. About a mile (2 km) northwest of town as you head towards Queenstown are Izandia Pottery, where those with a taste for handicrafts can purchase stoneware, and **Hilmond Weavers**, which sells handwoven mohair products.

All along the N 2, roads branch off leading to the various coastal resorts; except for the roads to Port St. Johns and Coffee Bay, however, most of these are unpaved. This is reason enough to drive carefully; motorists should, moreover, be aware that the cattle in this area are not fenced in and roam around free, and that the children here are likewise unaccustomed to traffic and may be careless. The

Above: The former homeland of Transkei is one of South Africa's poorest regions. Right: The beach at Port St. John's.

roads are particularly bad in wet weather, and wholly unsuitable for caravans and mobile homes.

Port St. Johns, 56 miles (91 km) east of Umtata, is the northernmost and probably the most popular resort on the Wild Coast. It lies at the mouth of the Umzimbuvu River, which flows here into the Indian Ocean between two dramatic, towering cliff faces up to 1,175 feet (360 m) high. The weather is ideal the whole year round; ocean swimming is possible even in the winter. The lush, subtropical vegetation, including palms, banana trees, and other tropical and subtropical fruit trees, extends down to the coast. So dense is this vegetation that it not only tends to seal the resort off from the outside world, but isolates nearly every hour from its neighbor. Indeed, the place has retained its original, unspoiled character while catering to tourists with golf, bowling and tennis facilities.

The comfortable bungalow complex **Umngazi** is reached on a turn-off from the R 61 just before St. Johns and conti-

nuing 7 miles (11 km) south. Situated near a river mouth roughly 100 yards from the coast in a quiet, secluded spot, the hotel is surrounded by unspoiled country, with sea and river, forests, grassy hillsides, and rich vegetation.

Further south along the coast is **Coffee Bay**, which you reach on a turnoff from the N 2 at Viedgesville. It allegedly derives its name from one of the many ships which was wrecked off this rocky coast (hence the term "Wild Coast"); this particular ship was carrying coffee beans, which were washed up onto the shore. Built on a rocky incline, the **Ocean View** hotel commands a panoramic view out across the small bay and its broad sandy beach. Though the golf course can't boast a smooth English-type green, it makes up for this with a marvelous view over part of the coast. Take the time to stroll out to **Hole in the Wall**, an outcropping of rock in the sea just offshore; the continual pounding of the sea has worn a large hole in the middle of it, through which the waves roll. Walking

along the coast, you'll encounter a number of rivers: to avoid time-consuming detours when you want to cross one, simply avail yourself of the assistance of one of the many children standing about (they will usually offer it themselves in any case). The other coastal resorts – Qora Mouth, Wavecrest, Qolora Mouth, and others – are equally charming, but less accessible due to the poor roads.

Vacationers wishing to visit the former homeland of **Ciskei**, the other home of the Xhosa, can take the N 2 from East London 39 miles (63 km) to **King William's Town**. While its population numbres only 23,000, it is the area's commercial and industrial center, although Bisho was the capital of Ciskei and neighboring Mdantsane has a much larger population. The town, which developed from a mission station founded in 1826, became the capital of the newly-established colony British Kaffraria. The **South African Missionary Museum**, located in a former mission church, gives a good general impression of the life and work

117

of missionaries of various faiths. One of the most comprehensive collections of African mammals is on display in the **Kaffrarian Museum** (founded in 1884). One of the more unusual exhibits is Huberta, the hippopotamus (now stuffed) who made headlines when she traveled of her own volition from the Natal coast to here in 1930 – a distance of some 500 miles (800 km).

From this town, you can travel out on the R 63 for day trips into the relatively unspoiled interior. Two roads to the north lead through magnificent scenery: after 14 miles (22 km), the R 345 to **Stutterheim**; after a further 25 miles (40 km) or so (just after Alice), the R 352 to **Hogsback**, a popular resort 2,309 feet (706 m) above sea level in the Amatola Mountains. Not far from the little town of Alice on the R 63 is the university of **Fort Hare**. Founded in 1916 as a college for

Above: Hippos in the Great Fish River Reserve Complex. Right: Harvesting pineapples, East London.

blacks and run as a branch of the UNISA (University of South Africa) since 1923, it was granted independent university status in 1970. Not only did Nelson Mandela begin his law studies here; other notable students have included Archbishop Desmond Tutu, Robert Mugabe, the Prime Minister of Zimbabwe, and Kenneth Kaunda, President of Zambia.

In Fort Beaufort the R 67 branches off to the north after 14 miles (23 km); continuing northwards, you come to the Katberg Hotel at the foot of the **Katberg Pass,** 5,886 feet (1,800 m) above sea level in the Winterberg range – an area rich in forest and ideal for hiking. On a clear day, there are some incredible views as you drive over the pass, but in wet weather or snow, the road is hard going.

Founded in 1979, the **Tsolwana Game Park,** 25 miles (40 km) further north, covers an area of 21,056 acres (8,500 hectares), and is home to white rhinoceros, giraffes, mountain zebras and antelopes; it has, furthermore, as yet managed to avoid being stormed by hordes of tourists. Accommodation is available in three fully-serviced lodges (Lilyfontein, with pool; Otterford, with tennis court; and Indwe). You can also go on guided hikes or drive out in Land Rovers to look for big game.

South of Alice, three nature and wild-life reserves on both sides of the Great Fish River have been incorporated into the **Great Fish River Reserve Complex** (112,500 acres / 45,000 hectares). A number of animals which had become extinct here have been successfully reintroduced to this area of dense bushveld vegetation, and there are once again hippos in the river. In the eastern section, in the **Double Drift Game Reserve**, lodges and chalets are available.

EAST LONDON, GRAHAMSTOWN, PORT ELIZABETH

East London

This port which developed at the mouth of Buffalo River in 1848 is the only river port in the country of any economic significance. Predominant exports from here are such agricultural products as corn, pineapples, wool and citrus fruits. Industry has grown up on the west bank of the river. East London is the meeting point for two major roads: the N 6 from the north from Bloemfontein and the N 2 from the northeast from Kwa-Zulu/Natal and from the west from Cape Town.

The city's main thoroughfare, **Oxford Street**, some 3 miles (5 km) long, is also the main shopping district, with a number of important offices and facilities. It branches off to the north from the R 72, whilch leads on to the west along the coast. The second street which crosses it, Terminus Road, leads to the **main train station**; here, you'll also find the **Air Terminus** of South African Airways. A little further north on the main street

stands **City Hall**; the **Visitors' Bureau** is just around the corner in Argyle Street, and the **Main Post Office** is on the next corner, on North Street. The **Ann Bryant Art Gallery** is in an attractive house dating from 1905 near the end of Oxford Street. Most of the works on display are by South African artists.

The **East London Museum** is not far away at the end of Oxford Street (or the beginning if you come from the N 2), and owes its fame to a fish named *coelacanth*. It belongs to the genus *Latimeria chalumnae* and its characteristic fleshy, limblike pectoral fins covered in scales point to a former amphibious existence. Experts who knew of the fish only from fossil remains assumed it had been extinct for 50 million years, so when a live one was caught near East London, it caused great excitement among scientists. The ethnology section features exhibits illustrating the traditional life of the nearby Bantu tribes, while the history section concentrates on the history of the German settlers. There's also a **German**

119

Settlers' Memorial located on the esplanade, which runs along the shore for about a mile (2 km). In the nearby **aquarium,** visitors can admire 400 aquatic animals, including seals, sharks, penguins and sea lions. There are some beautiful beaches north of the Buffalo River estuary.

East London is a good base from which to visit the surrounding area. To the east, you can reach the resorts on the Wild Coast on the N 2, which comes to Umtata after 143 miles (231 km). To the north, the N 6 brings you to Aliwal North after 229 miles (369 km); while the coastal and scenic R 72 leads westward to **Port Alfred**. Located on a lagoon on Kowie River, this extremely attractive and idyllic resort with 250,000 inhabitants is the center of the *Sunshine Coast* and a main pineapple-growing area. It combines beautiful beaches, high dunes,

Above: In Grahamstown. Right: The sleeping habits of days gone by – inside Castle Hill Museum, Port Elizabeth.

pleasant accommodation, one of the country's most beautiful golf courses, diving and surfing, hiking, and finally fishing, canoeing and boating on the Kowie River. There are two luxury hotels (Sun Chain) in attractive settings east of Port Alfred: the Fish River Sun at the mouth of the Great Fish River, 17 miles (27 km) away; and the Mpekweni Sun, 24 miles (38 km) away, or 623 miles (1,005 km) from East London. Both have excellent sports facilities; Fish River Sun also has a casino. Traveling northwest on the R 67 from Port Alfred, you reach Grahamstown after 35 miles (56 km).

Grahamstown

Grahamstown is the capital of "settler country." Founded in 1812 as a military outpost, it has been the scene of many bitter and bloody clashes between blacks and whites, of which there are many reminders throughout the region. Today, however, this university town is known above all as a cultural center famous for

its many schools, notably Rhodes University. The population of 55,000 has more than 40 churches to choose from; towering over the city center is the Anglican **Bishop's Cathedral** in Town Square, begun in 1824, and with a tower some 150 feet (45.75 m) high. All that remains of the Drostdy, the old magistrate's building, is the door, which now forms the entrance to the university. A few of the small, picturesque early **Settlers' Houses** have been restored and proclaimed national landmarks (on Artificer's Square).

The **Botanic Gardens**, laid out in 1850, are among the oldest in South Africa. The **Albany Museum's** main collections concentrate on natural history exhibits; historical and cultural history collections are found in the **Settlers' Memorial Museum**. Forming a backdrop to the town, **Gunfire Hill** offers a fine lookout from **Fort Selwyn**, a star-shaped fort built in 1835. In 1974, a memorial was built here for the settlers of 1820 (**1820 Settlers' Monument**),

together with a conference center and theater. This is the location of the annual **National Festival of Arts**, the largest cultural event in southern Africa. The site is surrounded by a **Wild Flower Reserve** which not only features wild plants from the Eastern Cape province, but also a genuine English garden, complete with lavender, forget-me-nots, English roses, and other typical flowers.

Some 45 miles (72 km) before Port Elizabeth, the private **Shamwari Game Reserve** is well worth a visit. Situated on the Bushman River between Alicedale and Paterson, it has a luxurious lodge, swimming pool, tennis court, excellent service and guided game-viewing (leopards, hippos, antelopes etc.) in a Land Rover or on foot.

Port Elizabeth

Port Elizabeth lies on the west coast of Algoa Bay, where Portuguese sailors first arrived as early as the 15th century. In 1799, the British set up a fort and a small garrison here, at the mouth of the Baakens River. In 1820, after 4,000 British settlers landed, the settlement was named for the wife of Sir Rufane Donkin (the British governor), Elizabeth, who died at an early age. Today, Port Elizabeth is the country's fifth-largest city, has the fourth-largest harbor, and is both a university town and an industrial center: it and Uitenhage, 23 miles (37 km) to the north and home to Volkswagen, form the center of the South African automobile industry. Port Elizabeth's population is estimated at around 1 million. In recent years, the country's economic problems have increased poverty and violence here, as well. Nonetheless, Port Elizabeth continues to promote itself as "the friendly city." The British have left an ineradicable mark here, with Victorian buildings standing easily alongside modern high-rises, but the progressive freeway system cuts through the city center in a brutal fashion.

By contrast, the area's miles of magnificent beaches seem untouched by the hectic pace of city life. The sea is a pleasant 70°-77° F (21°-25° C) all year round, and surfers can enjoy some great breakers. Fishing enthusiasts will have many an opportunity to indulge in their passion; deep-sea fishing tours also operate on the weekends. And you can sail at any time of year. This makes Port Elizabeth a popular holiday resort for South Africans; as it gets busy during school vacations, it may hold less attraction for Europeans then. Still, it remains a good point of departure for trips along the Garden Route or into the Great Karoo.

The historical heart of the city, the marketplace with **City Hall**, is situated on a narrow strip of land between the coast and Main Street. In front of City Hall there is a reconstruction of the stone cross that Bartolomeu Dias erected when

Right: Memorial to the horses that "fell" in the Boer War, Port Elizabeth.

he first landed in Algoa Bay. City buses leave from the underground **Bus Station** under the Norwich Union building. The **White House** in Fleming Street, once home to the port authority, is one of the few examples of Art Nouveau architecture in South Africa. At the harbor entrance – cut off from the city by the ghastly freeway – stands the **Campanile** or bell tower, a plain square-shaped brick building built in 1923 as a memorial to the first settlers. Those with the energy to climb the spiral stairway's 204 steps to the lookout are rewarded by a fantastic view over the bay and the city. The 21 bells of the tower's carillon ring out three times a day. The **main railway station** is just to the north of the tower.

A steep hill behind Main Street leads to **Donkin Reserve,** a lawn area with flower beds and a stone pyramid which is a memorial to Elizabeth Donkin; her husband willed that the area be kept open and not built upon for all time. The lighthouse, built in 1881, has housed the tourist office since 1994. The reserve is flanked by some fine Victorian architecture: **Donkin Street** to the north, for example, has a number of terraced houses from the period. The houses are all still in use – the local SATOUR office is located in number 21-23 – and all have historic landmark status. So, too, does the neo-Gothic **Old Grey Institute** (built 1859 and still a place of learning today) on Belmont Terrace, at one end of the reserve, as well as another relic of the British colonial period, the Hotel Edward, a charming old-fashioned house with a friendly, cozy atmosphere, commanding great views of the lower part of the city and the harbor.

Opposite Donkin Street, at the lower end of White Road, is the country's oldest **Opera House** still in use, which is also the oldest intact Victorian theater (built in 1892). The city's oldest extant residence, **No. 7 Castle Hill Museum** is today a cultural history museum. From

Fort Frederick (1799) on Belmont Terrace, there's a view of the Baaken River mouth and the southern part of the city.

Largest and oldest park in the city is **St. George's Park**, located in the west of the city center. The **King George VI Gallery** at the park entrance exhibits collections of British and South African art as well as oriental porcelain and miniatures. Not far away, on the corner of Cape and Russell Roads, there is a strange, perhaps unique memorial that was put up in 1905 to commemorate the horses that died in the Boer War. The memorial shows a horse whose rider is kneeling down to give it water.

If you follow the road along Algoa Bay (M 4) to the southeast, you'll pass **Humewood Station,** once the starting point of the **Apple Express**, a train pulled by a steam locomotive (to the joy of steam buffs) which transported fruit from the Langkloof valley to the harbor. Today the train occasionally transports tourists during the high season. Not far from here is the airport. City buses operate to the two

nearby beaches of **King's Beach** and **Humewood Beach**; there is also bus service to the city's special attraction, the **Port Elizabeth Museum** (on Humewood's Beach Road), which incorporates an **oceanarium** and **snake park**. Apart from a large variety of fish and other sea creatures, there are also performing dolphins (two performances daily). The adjoining snake park is world-famous for its serum research and extraction; the daily demonstrations for park visitors are extremely informative. The **Tropical House,** which is part of the snake park, is unique in South Africa: tropical birds and reptiles live here amid dense, tropical vegetation. The **museum** itself has displays on cultural history.

NATIONAL PARKS FOR ELEPHANTS AND MOUNTAIN ZEBRAS

There are three national parks within reasonable distance of Port Elizabeth. Traveling north out of the city on the R 102

(continuation of Main Street), you'll come, after a few miles, to the R 335, which brings you, after a total of 45 miles (72 km), to **Addo Elephant National Park**. The park extends over and protects an area of 36,442 acres (14,754 hectares) covered with dense, tangled evergreen valley bushveld. It was here, towards the end of the last century, that the few remaining survivors of what had once been large elephant herds in the Cape Province retreated. As they were proving extremely destructive to the efforts of farmers in the region's intensely cultivated farmland, the farmers started shooting them at will. To protect the survivors, the National Park was founded in 1931; originally eleven, their ranks have steadily swelled to reach, today, some 200 in number.

Above: The Malachite hummingbird, here in Addo Elephant National Park, is a veritable gem. Right: Once nearly extinct, mountain zebras have built up their numbers once again in Mountain Zebra National Park.

The black rhinoceros, once native to the area, was extinct by 1853, but in 1961 seven rhinos were brought from Kenya to re-establish a colony. A few of the buffalo which once dwelt in large herds in the Cape Province survived in the park and have adapted to the scarcity of grazing land by changing over to a diet of foliage.

As the dense vegetation makes the animals difficult to see, the best place to view them is at the water-holes. The park authorities organize night-time excursions on which you can see not only elephants and the rhinos and buffalo which keep out of sight in the daytime, but also nocturnal creatures, including mongoose, aardvark, porcupines, genets, eland, and bushbok. There are attractive walks and a biotope from which elephants, buffalo and rhinos are excluded. The rest camp is complete with pool and restaurant and offers accommodation in 24 well-equipped chalets.

North of this park is **Zuurberg National Park,** created in 1984. Situated

some 820-3,170 feet (250-970 m) above sea level, it now covers an area of 74,100 acres (30,000 hectares), but tourists can only enter a part of this. To date, there are only two entrances: one in the east section, 10 miles (16 km) north of the entrance to Addo Park on the R 335; the other in the west section, which you reach by taking the R 335 south from Kirkwood, then the R 336 west. Overnight accommodation (for 6 persons) is also available for park visitors, but must be booked through the warden in Addo. The latter also issues permits for the many walks in the area.

This grandiose scenery with its rugged mountains and deep valleys is of particular interest to botany enthusiasts, since the park boasts five different types of vegetation: fynbos, valley bushveld (each covering about a third of the total area), grassland, African mountain forestland and mountain fynbos. Occurring in various combinations, these intermingle to form an intricate patchwork. The park is already home to countless birds (including eagles), antelopes and mountain zebra, and there are plans to reintroduce a number of other animals which were once native to the area.

Leaving the Addo Elephant National Park and following the R 342 first north, and then east, you come, after 17 miles (27 km), to the N 10, which leads north up through the (partly irrigated) fertile valley of the Great Fish River. Just after Cradock, the R 61 branches off to the left; from here, keep an eye out for a small road leading off to the left toward **Mountain Zebra National Park**. It's located in mountainous country at the eastern edge of the Great Karoo, where the highest mountain is the Spitskop, 6,399 feet (1,957 m) above sea level. As the summers are very hot here and winters very cold, the best time to visit is from March to May.

The park was set up in 1937 with a mare and 5 stallions, to protect one of the mammals most threatened with extinction, namely the mountain zebra. Today, over 200 of these zebras live in the park

alongside antelopes, baboons, ostriches and jackals. There is a 23-mile (37 km) network of gravel roads and walking trails through the typical Karoo landscape with its koppies, ridges and plateaus of dolerite. The unique vegetation differs from the less mountainous areas of the Karoo in that there are more trees, such as wild olive, sumac and sweet thorn, as well as succulents, shrubs and many flowering plants, most of which blossom in April. There is also a rest camp here with 18 chalets, pool, restaurant, shop and gas station.

THE GREAT KAROO

Port Elizabeth is an point of departure for excursions into the Great Karoo and a visit to Graaff-Reinet. You leave the city on the N 75 (the continuation of Main Street), which leads to **Uitenhage**.

*Above: The stark beauty of the Great Karoo.
Right: Cactuses predominate in the Great Karoo's flora.*

Founded in 1804, the city now has more than 200,000 inhabitants. Not only is it home to the car industry (notably Volkswagen) and its supplier industries, but it also has a large railway repair shop. Built in 1875, the train station, complete with its original, Victorian-era appointments, has been converted into a railway museum.

North of the city, the R 75 passes through the Kleinwinterhoek Mountains (here still part of the Cape range). From their heights, you can see the seemingly endless vista of the Great Karoo spread out before you.

A person crossing the **Great Karoo** along the main route between Cape Town and Johannesburg for the first time, either by train or by car, could be forgiven for initially finding this solitary, endless, unrelieved expanse of sparsely vegetated semi-desert boring. But anyone who has a sense for the unique beauties of this very African landscape – which Olive Schreiner described so vividly in her novel *An African Farm* – and who's willing to venture off the time-honored tourist routes, will come away with unforgettable impressions.

The semi-desert region of the Great Karoo, situated some 1,960-4,250 feet (600-1,300 m) above sea level, covers more than a quarter of South Africa's total land area. Below the earth's surface were massive, horizontal layers of sedimentary rock; from the center of the earth, molten material thrust up into these layers and then itself solidified. Over the years, the extreme erosion effected by the region's periodic heavy rains washed out the softer rocks, and thanks to the greater resistance of the harder upper layers (largely dolerite, a coarse-grained basalt), molded the remaining stone into the distinctive forms characteristic of this area: *koppies, dykes, silks* and tables.

The region is subject to extreme temperature swings, both during the day and from season to season. The low rainfall, up to 11.7 inches (300 mm) annually and dropping off from east to west, occurs mostly in February and March, usually during storms, but some years there is no rain whatsoever. The sparse vegetation consists of low woody shrubs with a sprinkling of succulents (aloes, euphorbias, mesems stapelia and cactus, which are not indigenous). When it does rain, this barren region is transformed into a carpet of amazingly varied flowers.

The few settlements in the area are oases requiring irrigation. Catchment basins have been installed at some of the rivers which are most prone to drying up. Windmills, which pump water up out of the depths, are also a characteristic feature of the region. The latter also supply water for the large herds of cattle which form the economic mainstay of the area. Merino sheep and angora goats thrive well here, but require enormous grazing areas which are fenced in along the roadside. The large nomadic herds of deer which were once common here were almost wiped out in the 18th and 19th cen-

turies, but today you can occasionally see springbok, impalas and other antelopes. Since the air is extremely dry, it is also extraordinarily clear. At midday, contours appear harsh; in the bright, shimmering light, you often see mirages, or fata morganas; and you may occasionally sight a cyclone or tornado. But early in the morning, in the late afternoon, and in the early evening, the softer light, longer shadows and deepening colors confer a new fascination upon the landscape. And the light falling on the gathering clouds of an approaching storm creates an even more spectacular image.

Graaff-Reinet

Lying like an oasis in the barren landscape, 2,456 feet (751 m) above sea level in a cleft in the magnificent Sneeuberg Mountains, is the town of Graaff-Reinet, named for the Cape governor van der Graaff and his wife Reinet. In 1786, this governor chose a site on a defensible bend of the Sundays River to be the ad-

ministrative headquarters of the recently-created fourth district in the restless border country. Overshadowing the town to the southwest is the imposing **Spandau Kop,** a typical example of a Karoo koppie. Today, Graaf-Reinet is a commercial and trading center with approximately 35,000 inhabitants.

Leading into town from the south, the main street, Church Street, features, at its northern end, the neo-Gothic **Grootkerk** (Dutch Reformed Church), built in 1866. Behind the church is City Hall and, on a hill, the powder magazine of 1831. Many of the charming, well-preserved houses from various bygone eras have been declared national landmarks. Strolling through the wide, tree-lined streets, and drinking in the atmosphere, you might have the impression you're in an open-air museum.

Above: Parsonage Street with the Reinet House in the town of Graaf-Reinet. Right: Jagged rocks in the lonely "Valley of Desolation."

On Parsonage Street, which runs east from Church Street, there is a row of painstakingly restored houses which are true architectural gems. **Reinet House**, at the end of the street, is undoubtedly one of the best examples of Cape Dutch architecture; built in 1812 as a parsonage, it today accommodates the Cultural Museum, containing an exquisite collection of furniture from the 18th and early 19th centuries. The **grapevine** planted here in 1870 is thought to be one of the oldest in the world. It still bears grapes, but part of the vine stock had to be removed several years ago because of a fungus. The building of the **John Rupert Little Theater** was originally the church of the London Missionary Society. The **Hester Rupert Art Museum** (originally the mission of the Dutch Reformed Church) exhibits works of art by contemporary South African artists.

In 1977, the former drostdy (local administrator's office), built in 1806 and since beautifully restored, was converted into the beautiful, stylish, and comfort-

128

able **Drostdy Hotel**. In the cobbled street of **Stretch's Court,** behind the hotel, the cottages originally built for laborers now form part of the hotel complex. The hotel is well worth a look, even if you don't plan to stay there. On the corner of Church and Somerset Streets, the Old Library now houses a **museum**, in which you can see, as well as a fossil collection from the Karoo, a collection of clothing from the period around 1800.

Virtually surrounding the town is the **Karoo Nature Reserve**, created in 1975 mainly to protect the unique flora indigenous to this region. Extending over 39,520 acres (16,000 hectares), it encompasses the **Van Ryneveld Pass Dam** north of town on the Sundays River. Another, even more impressive section of the reserve is the **Valley of Desolation**, which was declared a national landmark in 1935. It lies west of the city; to get there, take a turn-off from the R 63 near the dam. Footpaths lead from the parking lot to the various lookout points commanding vistas of this phenomenon of nature. Over millions of years, erosion has formed deep crevices in the rocky plateau of dolerite-covered layers of sediment, creating stacks and towers of rock up to 390 feet (120 m) high. The stones are also rich in fossils, making this area a lucrative hunting-ground for paleontologists. Looking out south and west across the bare expanse of plain that is the Karoo, east over Graaff-Reinet in the arm of the Sundays River, and north to the Sneeuberg Mountains, which form part of the Great Escarpment, is an unforgettable experience.

To the north, the R 63 rejoins the N 1.

If you wish to experience the vast open spaces and solitude of the Great Karoo, take the N 9 / R 61 to Beaufort West. In a drive of 130 miles (209 km), you pass through a single settlement, the little village of Aberdeen, after 35 miles (56 km).

Beaufort West

Lying just within the province of Western Cape, **Beaufort West**, founded

129

in 1820, today numbers around 250,000 inhabitants. A veritable transportation hub, lying on the N 1 and the Cape Town-Johannesburg railway line, it is a center for the merino sheep-breeding in the surrounding area. Though the town is situated in an extremely dry region, irrigation plants were installed here early, turning it into a veritable oasis. The streets are lined with pear trees which blossom through September and October, adding to the town's charm. The average temperature in January is 90° F (32° C); in July, 64°F (18° C). The average annual rainfall is a low 9 inches (233 mm).

Karoo National Park was created in 1979 northwest of the town on a plain at the edge of the Nuweveld Mountains, 2,698-6,249 feet (825-1,911 m) above sea level. Extending over 81,510 acres (33,000 hectares), the park protects the unique flora, fauna and fossils of the Great Karoo. Much of the game which lived here in large numbers at the beginning of the last century has been resettled in the reserve: springbok, kudus, klipspringer, mountain reedbock, duiker, and the like. In addition, many smaller animals live here, including 5 species of turtle and the largest number of black eagles in South Africa.

The short (0.25 mi/400 m) walk of **Fossil Trail** leads the visitor through a large section of the earth's history and documents the development of creatures over millions of years. The most fascinating exhibits are fossils of creatures which were probably precursors to mammals, the *therapsida*. Some fossils prepared by staff from the South African Museum are displayed in glass cabinets, and information on them is available. Incidentally, fossils are protected as national monuments, and anyone found taking them would be severely punished. The half-mile (800 m) **Bossie Trail** is also very informative, and gives you an idea of the area's fascinating flora. Accommodation is available in a rest camp.

EASTERN CAPE
Transportation

Bus: Greyhound, Translux or Mainliner operate regular buses along a number of routes in all directions to and from Port Elizabeth and East London (Cape Town, Johannesburg, Durban). These bus lines also service Umtata, Graaff-Reinet, Grahamstown, Swellendam, Mosselbay, Oudtshoorn, Knysna, Plettenberg Bay, and others. The trip from Johannesburg to Port Elizabeth takes 13-14 hours (overnight); from Cape Town to Port Elizabeth (Translux and Mainliner, day and night buses), 10-12 hrs.; from Durban to Port Elizabeth (Greyhound and Translux, daytime buses) about 13 hours.

Train: Daily trains run between Johannesburg and East London (via Bloemfontein; 20 hrs.)

Air: SAA has regular service to and from the Port Elizabeth and East London airports (each is about 6 mi/10 km from the city center, and can only be reached by taxi or rental car). Airlink also connects Port Elizabeth and East London with Bloemfontein, Johannesburg, Umtata and Durban; Cape Atlantic runs to Cape Town, Oudtshoorn, Plettenberg Bay.

LAND OF THE XHOSA
Accommodations

WILD COAST: *LUXURY:* **Wild Coast Sun**, see Port Edward, KwaZulu/Natal. **Wild Coast Holiday Reservations**, tel: 0431/5-8003, fax: 5-8007. *MODERATE:* **Umtata Protea Hotel**, PO Box 111, Umtata 5100, tel: 0471/2-5654, fax: 31-0083. **Holiday Inn Garden Court**, PO Box 334, Umtata 5100, tel: 0471/37-0181, fax: 37-0191. **Second Beach Holiday Resort**, Port St. Johns, tel: 0457/44-1245. **Umngazi River Bungalows**, PO Box 75, tel: 0471/22370. **Ocean View Hotel**, Coffee Bay, tel: 0471/37-0254, fax: 5-3344.

KING WILLIAM'S TOWN 5600: *MODERATE:* **Amatola Sun Bisho**, PO Box 1274, tel: 0401/9-1111, fax: 9-1330. **Grosvenor Lodge**, 48 Taylor St. PO Box 61, tel: 0433/2-1440, fax: 2-4772. **HOGSBACK** 5721: *MODERATE:* **Hogsback Inn**, PO Box 63, tel: 045/642, ask for 6, fax: ask for 15. **KATBERG**: *MODERATE:* **Katberg Protea Hotel**, PO Box 665, tel. and fax: 0404/3-1151. **Tsolwana Game Reserve** and **Great Fish River Game Reserve** (Double Drift Lodge), registration: tel: 0401/95-2115, fax: 9-2756.

Museums

KING WILLIAM'S TOWN: **Kaffrarian Museum**, Albert Rd., Mon-Fri 9-12:45, 2-5 pm, Sat 9 am-12:45, Sun 3:30-5 pm. **South African Missionary Museum**, Berkeley St., Mon-Fri 9-12:45, 2-5 pm.

Tourist Information

Transkei Tourism, Private Bag X5029, Umtata 5100, tel: 0471/31-2885, fax: 31-2887. **Contour**,

PO Box 467, King William's Town 5600, tel: 0401/95-2115, fax: 9-7562.

EAST LONDON

Telephone and fax area code: 0431, postal code: 5200

Accommodations

MODERATE: **Kennaway Protea Hotel**, Esplanade, PO Box 583, tel: 2-5531, fax: 2-1326. **Holiday Inn Garden Court**, corner John Baillie and Moore St., PO Box 1255, tel: 2-7260, fax: 43-7360. *BUDGET:* **Hotel Majestic** (near city and beach), 21 Orient Rd., PO Box 18027, Quigney 5211. **Port Rex Youth Hostel**, 128 Moore St. Eastern Beach, tel: 2-3423. **PORT ALFRED** 6170: *LUXURY:* **Mpekweni Sun**, PO Box 2060, tel: 0405/66-1026, fax: 66-1040. *MODERATE:* **Fish River Sun**, PO Box 232, tel: 0405/66-1101, fax: 66-1115.
BUDGET: **Kowie Grand Hotel**, corner Grand/ Princess Ave, PO Box 1, Kowie West 6171, tel: 0464/4-1150, fax: 4-3769.

Museums

East London Museum, Mon-Fri and Sun 8:30 am-5 pm, Sat 9:30 am-12. **Ann Bryant Art Gallery**, Mon-Fri 9:30 am-5 pm, Sat and Sun 2-5 pm.

Tourist Information

Greater East London Publicity Association, Old Library Building, Argyle St., PO Box 511, tel: 26015. **Automobile Association**, AA House, Fleet St., tel: 2-1271.

GRAHAMSTOWN

Telephone and fax area code: 0461, postal code: 6400

Accommodations

MODERATE: **Cathcart Arms Hotel**, 5 West St., PO Box 6043, tel: and fax: 2-7111. **Graham Protea Hotel**, 123 High St., PO Box 316, tel: 2-2324, fax: 2-2424. **The Settlers Inn**, N 2 Highway, PO Box 219, tel: 2-7313, fax: 2-4951.
LUXURY: **Shamwari Game Reserve**, reservations: PO Box 7814, Newton Park 6055, tel: 042/851-1196, fax: 851-1224.

Museums

All museums are open Tue-Fri 9:30 am-5 pm, Sat and Sun 2-5 pm.

Tourist Information

Grahamstown Publicity Association, 63 High Street, tel: 2-3241, fax: 2-9488.

PORT ELIZABETH

Telephone and fax area code: 041, postal code: 6000

Accommodations

MODERATE: **Holiday Inn Garden Court - King's Beach**, La Roche Drive, PO Box 13 100, Port Elizabeth 6013, tel: 52-3720, fax: 55-5754.

City Lodge, corner Beach and Lodge Rd., Summerstrand, Port Elizabeth 6013, tel: 56-3322, fax: 56-3374. **Marine Protea Hotel**, PO Box 501, tel: 53-2101, fax: 53-2076. (All conveniently located near the airport, beach and oceanarium). **The Edward Hotel**, Belmont Terrace, P.O.Box 319, tel. and fax: 56-2056 (near the city center). **Bed'n Breakfast** (also for Graaff-Reinet and Beaufort West), 112 Church Road, Port Elizabeth, tel. and fax: 041/51-3611.

Museums and Sights

Campanile can be climbed Mon, Tue, Thu, Fri 9 am-1 pm, 2-4 pm, Wed and Sat 8:30 am-12:30. **No.7 Castle Hill Museum**, Sun and Mon 2-5 pm, Tue-Sat 10 am-1 and 2-5 pm. **King George VI Art Gallery**, Mon-Sat 9 am-4:30 pm, Sun 2-4:30 pm. **Port Elizabeth Museum** with **Oceanarium** and **Snake Park**, daily 9 am-1, 2-5 pm, dolphin shows 11 am and 3 pm, demonstrations in the Snake Park daily at 10 am, 12:15, 2:30 and 4:15 pm.

Tourist Information

Port Elizabeth Publicity Association, PO Box 357, tel: 52-1315, fax: 55-2564. **Eastern Cape Tourism Board**, PO Box 1161, tel: 55-7761, fax: 55-4975. **SATOUR**, 21-23 Donkin Street, PO Box 1161, tel: 55-7761, fax: 55-4975. **Automobile Association (AA)**, 2 Granville Road, Greenacres, tel: 34-1313.

National Parks for Mountain Zebras and Elephants

Registration for the National Parks and accommodations: National Parks Board, Pretoria.

THE GREAT KAROO

Accommodations

GRAAFF-REINET 6280: *MODERATE:* **Drostdy Hotel**, 30 Church St., PO Box 400, tel: 0491/2-2161, fax: 2-4582. **Karoopark Guesthouse & Cottages**, 81 Caledon St., PO Box 388, tel: 0491/2-2557, fax: 2-5730.
BEAUFORT WEST 6970: *MODERATE:* **Oasis Hotel**, 66 Donkin St., PO Box 115, tel. and fax: 0201/3221. **Vine Lodge** (youth hostel), 23 Meintjies St., tel: 0201/5-1055. **Karoo National Park:** registration and accommodation: National Parks Board.

Museums

Reinet House and **Old Library Museum**, Mon-Fri 9 am-12, 3-5 pm, Sat 9 am-12, Sun 10 am-12. **Hester Rupert Art Museum**, Mon-Fri 10 am-12, 3-5 pm, Sat and Sun 10 am-12.

Tourist Information

Graaff-Reinet Publicity Association, corner Church and Somerset Str., PO Box 153, Graaff-Reinet 6280, tel: 0491/2-4248.
Central Karoo Information, PO Box 56, Beaufort West 6970, tel: 0201/5-3001, fax 3675.

WESTERN CAPE

**GARDEN ROUTE
OUTSHOORN, LITTLE KAROO
THE WINELANDS
SOUTHWEST COAST, FALSE
BAY
CAPE TOWN
THE CAPE PENINSULA**

WESTERN CAPE

The province of Western Cape, South Africa's fourth-largest province, encompasses the country's southwest. It comprises 10.6% of its area, but only 8.9% of its population, which in turn account for 13.2% of the gross domestic product. Some 63% of its inhabitants – mostly coloreds – speak Afrikaans, 20% English and 16% Xhosa. Thanks to the relatively good economic situation here, the unemployment rate is the lowest in the country at 13%. Industry (especially textiles) centers mainly in the urban area around Cape Town. The region's agriculture specializes in specialty products: wine, citrus fruits, apples and vegetables are cultivated. The Swartland around Malmesbury is the country's most important wheat-growing area.

Cape Town and the Garden Route are tourist highlights that few visitors to South Africa would be willing to miss. The region's landscape is dominated by the Cape ranges, rugged, crenellated chains of mountains running almost parallel to the coast, and includes a section of the Great Karoo. Nestled within the Cape range are long valleys such as the Little Karoo, Langkloof, the Hex River Valley, and large basins such as Ceres or Elgin. Highest mountain in the region is the Seweweeks Mountain in the Swartberg range, with an altitude of 7,606 feet (2,326 m) above sea level.

For the first settlers the hard sandstone of the Cape mountains, with their deep ravines, or kloofs, represented an almost insurmountable obstacle; today, these mountains have been conquered with a number of excellent roads, some of which include grandiose mountain passes. In the valleys and basins, summers are hot and winters cool and rainy; at higher elevations, there is occasionally snow, but it seldom stays on the ground for long. The west coast is cool and extremely dry; the south coast, with its mild oceanic climate, gets rain all year round. In the interior, the climate becomes progressively drier and warmer towards the west and north, and there are greater variations within the daytime and annual temperatures.

GARDEN ROUTE

The most famous route in South Africa, featured on every tour operator's program, extends along the coast of the

Preceding pages: View of Cape Town and Table Mountain from the waterfront. Left: Flowering proteas – an explosion of Cape-region color

135

Indian Ocean roughly from Mossel Bay in the west to the mouth of the Storms River in the east. Before the dramatic, hazy blue backdrop of the steep cliffs of the Cape range lies a coastal region rife with charming bays, clean sandy beaches, rocky cliffs, lagoons, and rivers running through deep gorges, all blanketed with lush, colorful vegetation interspersed with tracts of indigenous forest. The climate is kind the whole year round, with average temperatures of 68° F (20° C) and long hours of sunshine; the annual 35 inches (900 mm) of rainfall is spread over the whole year, and occurs mainly at night. The Indian Ocean is warm enough to swim in at any time of year. The region's countless rivers, flowing down from the mountains and swollen with mountain rain, are largely free of bilharzia and therefore ideal for swimming, canoeing or fishing. And furthermore, there are a wide range of different resort towns throughout the area, which offer activities and accommodation to suit every taste.

For most South Africans this stretch of permanently lush greenery is a veritable Garden of Eden in comparison with the barren land of the adjacent Great Karoo and the seasonal dryness in the rest of the country. This means that the area is particularly busy with local traffic in December and January, a period that overseas visitors might prefer to avoid.

Many tourists fly in to the airport in Port Elizabeth in the Eastern Cape province, and depart from here for their drive along the Garden Route. From the airport, it's easy to reach the N 2, which is identical with the Garden Route for most of the way. **Van Stadens Wild Flower Reserve and Bird Sanctuary**, some 19 miles (30 km) away, is best visited in the spring. This reserve features rare plants of the eastern Cape fynbos zone, including a variety of proteas. The bridge over the Van Stadens River Gorge is one of the longest concrete suspension bridges

in the world; its largest span measures 647 feet (198 m) (total length: 1,144 feet/350 m).

A turn-off onto the R 102 brings you to **St. Francis Bay**, where the beautiful beaches offer some of the best surfing conditions in the world. This is especially true of **Jeffreys Bay**, where the broad sands are also a treasure trove for shell collectors. Passing Humansdorp, you rejoin the N 2 some 11 miles (18 km) further on. If you continue on this road for another 22 miles (36 km), you can make an interesting detour by turning off onto the R 402 and following it north past Kareedouw to the **Langkloof Valley**. Typical of the Cape range, this long valley extends for 149 miles (240 km) in an east-west direction, flanked by high mountain ranges to the north and south. Irrigated by the waters of rivers which flow all year round (not always the case in the variable climate of South Africa), the valley resembles a giant orchard; in fact, it is, after the Western Cape province, the second-largest fruit-growing re-

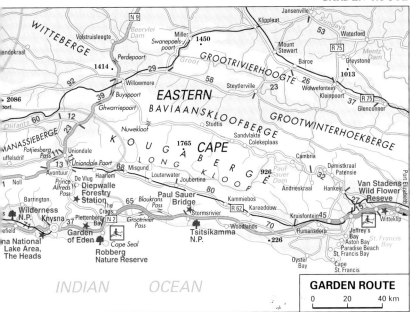

GARDEN ROUTE

0   20   40 km

INDIAN   OCEAN

gion in South Africa. In September and October it is transformed into a mass of blossom. During the harvest season, in addition to countless trucks, the steam train *Apple Express* transports the fresh fruit and vegetables to Port Elizabeth.

The N 2 crosses the 425-foot-deep (130 m) Storms River Gorge on the **Paul Sauer Bridge**, which consists of a single span 628 feet (192 m) long. If you want to stop off for an overnight pause or meal, turn left shortly after the bridge into the little village of Storms River; here, the **Tsitsikamma Forest Inn** is a comfortable, very quiet and reasonably-priced hotel serving good food. Some 2 miles (4 km) further along the N 2, a road leads south for 4 miles (6 km) to the entrance of **Tsitsikamma National Park**. From here, it's another mile or so (2 km) to the camp **Storms River Mouth**, which has fully-equipped accommodations (cottages, chalets, holiday apartments), as well as a restaurant, a shop, and a campsite. This National Park, established in 1964, protects a strip of coast about 50

miles (80 km) long, and includes approximately 3 miles (5.5 km) of sea, beyond the beach and surf line. In 1987, the area was enlarged with the addition of the Vasselot Section on the mouth of the Groot River (with campsite, but without a restaurant).

The sea bed drops off sharply from the coast, meaning that there is no shallow shelf to break the force of the surf; the sea here, therefore, is seldom calm. Low tide exposes craggy and creviced rocks; these form tide pools where you can see a colorful variety of marine life: corals, sea urchins, mussels, and their ilk.

Because rain falls here all year round (the annual average is 47 inches/1,200 mm; May and October are the wettest months, and June and July the driest), the vegetation is lush. The steep coast is blanketed with rich forest, famous for its yellowwood trees up to 800 years old and reaching heights of 165 feet (50 m), interspersed with ferns and flowers. Because of the humidity here, the fynbos vegetation in this area is different from that in

137

the southwestern Cape region. In addition to a number of varieties of heather and proteas, there are also a multitude of lilies and orchids. The forest is inhabited by baboons, klipspringers and various small antelopes. A range of different birds live in the forested areas and on the cliffs; while beyond the breakers you can sometimes sight whales and dolphins. In this park, visitors are free to move about as they wish and explore this fascinating environment at their own pace.

Among the numerous marked walking trails here is the first and finest of all in South Africa's entire network: **Otter Trail**. You should allow 5 days to walk these 25 miles (41 km) between the Storms and Groot Rivers (accommodation en route), to allow yourself enough time and energy truly to appreciate this gorgeous coastal area and the unique

Above: Tsitsikamma National Park is home to many varieties of heather. Right: The otter lent its name to "Otter Trail" in Tsitsikamma National Park.

diversity of nature it has to offer. The walk is hugely popular, so advance booking is a must; some people reserve up to a year beforehand.

The Tsitsikamma region, named for the Hottentot word meaning "clear water," was long considered impassable until Thomas Bain, South Africa's most famous road builder, took the task in hand in 1868; not until 1885 was it possible to drive along the stretch to Humansdorp. Along this road, today part of the R 102, are two spectacular passes, **Bloukrans Pass** and **Groot River Pass**. A quicker route is the N 2, which negotiates the gorge of the Bloukrans River, 883 feet (270 m) deep, via a bridge 1,504 feet (460 m) long, but it's less interesting and you have to pay a toll; the former road, although it's about 4 miles (7 km) longer, is definitely to be recommended.

Plettenberg Bay, today undoubtedly the most popular resort on the Garden Route, lies on a lovely sweeping bay; which the Portuguese, when they first landed here in 1576, christened "Bahia Formosa," or beautiful bay. In 1788, Governor Joachim van Plettenberg laid a stone here and took possession of the bay, which received his name, for the Dutch East India Company. Today, the town of Plettenberg Bay offers visitors a range of holiday leisure activities and excursions. The rocky island in the middle of the bay (separated from the mainland by a river, but linked to it by a causeway) was called "Beacon Island" after a beacon for ships that had been set up here back in 1772. A Nowegian whaling company had a base here from 1912-20. The island also boasts a luxurious hotel which dominates the bay, opened in 1973. Even more appealing are the 12 miles (20 km) of lovely, sandy beach extending along both sides of the island. The sea is very calm here, especially northeast of Beacon Island, making the beaches ideal for youngsters, and the water temperature is between 66° and 73° F (19° and 23° C).

To the south and west of Beacon Island, a beach of fine sand extends down to the southern point of **Robberg Nature Reserve**; this is the the quieter part of the bay, where one can still find solitude. The reserve itself, a rocky peninsuala 4 miles (6 km) long, is well worth a visit. From July through September, whales from the Antarctic come to this protected bay to calve. With its combination of unspoiled countryside and great tranquility, this area is not easily forgotten.

On the slopes of the Outeniqua Mountains between Plettenberg Bay and Knysna extends **Knysna Forest**, the largest remaining tract of original natural forest in South Africa. The indigenous tree species here were once highly valued for their wood, particularly for furniture and ships, and commercial logging was responsible for the area's wealth; today, however, these species are protected by law. A few of the stinkwood and yellow-wood trees are thought to be around 600-800 years old. Pines, eucalyptus and some species of acacia have been planted in among the remaining indigenous trees. Another section of indigenous forest is protected in the **Garden of Eden**, 10 miles (16 km) from Plettenberg Bay, which you can reach from a parking lot on the N 2; a short circular walking trail lets you gain an impression of the area.

Another interesting place nearby is the **Diepwalle Forestry Station**; after 6 miles (10 km) further on the N 2, turn onto the R 339 and continue for another 12 miles (20 km). Here, you can collect a permit to hike the circular trail named Elephant Walk, which is well marked and not particularly strenuous; unfortunately, your chances of sighting one of the few remaining free-ranging Knysna elephants en route are slim. **Prince Alfred's Pass**, built in 1897 and largely unpaved, snakes its way up to an altitude of 3,417 feet (1,045 m) above sea level through the Outeniqua Mountains and reaching Avontuur in the Langkloof Valley, 50

miles (81 km) from the N 2 (and 72 miles/116 km from Oudtshoorn). Though crossing this pass requires a bit more time, the spectacular landscape makes it well worth the effort.

Knysna (the "k" is silent) is attractively situated on the northern bank of a lagoon covering 4,445 acres (1,800 hectares). Its history begins with George Rex, a British immigrant who settled here in 1804 and has since become a quasi-legendary local figure; he is counted the founder of the town, which was not officially established until 1825.

The Dutch East India Company had already set up a logging station here in 1776 to take advantage of the surrounding forests, and the lagoon developed into an important harbor; its significance, however, declined when the railway line was opened in 1928, and it was closed altogether in 1953. Two islands in the lagoon are each joined to the mainland by a causeway. The lagoon's sea mouth is flanked by two towering cliffs of reddish sandstone overgrown with lichens,

139

known as **the Heads**. The salt content in the water of the lagoon is diluted by the constant influx of water from the Knysna River. This creates a unique ecosystem which has, since 1992, been protected by the National Parks Board as the **Knysna National Lake Area**.

Situated in a varied landscape on one of the most attractive sections of the Garden Route, the town is a popular holiday destination, and provides an ideal base for trips and excursions. Countless furniture stores purvey objects made of the wood of the indigenous trees; stinkwood is the most valuable. This tree derives its name from the somewhat unpleasant smell of the freshly-sawn wood, which varies in color from grayish-yellow through brown to near-black. One reason this wood sells for such incredible prices at the annual auction (1982 saw the rec-

Above: Sunrise over the lagoon in Knysna.
Right: The Bartholomieu Dias Museum in Mossel Bay transports you into a world of seafaring history.

ord price of 9,600 rand for a cubic meter) is that the trees must be at least 200 years old before they can be felled and worked into furniture.

Wilderness National Park (6,175 acres/2,500 hectares), established in 1985 and administered by the National Parks Board, encompasses a series of lakes, former lagoons separated from the coast by a narrow strip of dunes along a stretch of 17 miles (28 km). This chain does not include Groenvlei, south of the N 2, which is not linked to the sea and is therefore virtually a fresh-water lake. The estuary of Swartvlei, the largest of the lakes, runs into the sea near the little town of Sedgefield. The other three lakes, Rondevlei, Langvlei and Eilandvlei, are connected to the sea by the alluvial plains of the Duiwe and Touws rivers. The area abounds in bird life, especially waterfowl. This lovely, tranquil area, with plenty to offer enthusiasts of water sports and fishing, is a popular resort (self-catering accommodation in the Wilderness Camp; no restaurant).

Wilderness, a small resort full of flowers, is a popular stopover on the Garden Route. It offers a range of attractive accommodation, including facilities for mobile homes. As it continues on to George, the N 2 passes a bridge spanning the deep gorge of Kaaiman's River just before the river mouth. Photographers often wait here for the **Choo-Tjoe**, the steam train which runs from George to Knysna and back, and crosses a railway bridge nearby. From the train, you have marvelous views of stretches of scenery you can't see from the road (the George to Knysna journey takes around 3 hours). As the trip is extremely popular, you have to arrive early in order to secure a window seat.

Founded in 1811, the town of **George**, named after the British king George III, is scenically situated 5 miles (8 km) from the coast on a plateau 739 feet (226 m) above sea level. Numbering some 50,000 inhabitants, this garden town, its broad streets lined with old oaks, is a popular retirement community. The golf course is considered to be one of the most beautiful in the country on account of its location and surroundings. Not far away is the only hop-growing area in South Africa. The airport is about 6 miles (10 km) southwest of town. Most visitors to George also make excursions out to Oudtshoorn and the Little Karoo.

It was in **Mossel Bay,** 41 miles (66 km) west of George, that explorer Bartolomeu Dias first set foot on South African soil in 1488 – 15 years before the first European ship put down anchor in Table Bay. To commemorate the 500th anniversary of his landing, the **Bartolomeu Dias Museum Complex** was opened in 1988. The next European here was Vasco da Gama, who landed in 1497. In 1500, a sailor left a message here by placing it inside a boot which he hung in a milkwood tree over a spring where sailors were wont to go for fresh water. The letter was later found and taken away by other sailors. Over the years, it gradually became a custom to deliver messages through this tree. The tree still exists, with a mailbox

141

at its foot; any letters sent here are stamped with the postmark "Old Post Office Tree."

Mossel Bay, an autonomous town since 1848, derived its name from the large number of shellfish in the bay. Once a very popular resort, it has changed dramatically over the last few years, developing into an important industrial base. This change was fueled (literally) by the increase in offshore drilling for natural gas, which is then processed into fuel in a large refinery (Mossgas). As the plant lies outside of town, however, the latter has retained its character as a small harbor town.

OUDTSHOORN AND THE LITTLE KAROO

The Little Karoo, a broad plain 981 feet (300 m) above sea level, and bisected by the Olifants River, extends about 60

Above and right: Ostrich farming in Oudtshoorn in the Little Karoo.

miles (100 km) in a north-south direction and 185 miles (300 km) east to west. In the north, the Swartberg range divides it from the Great Karoo, while in the south the Langeberg range and the Outeniqua Mountains separate it from the Indian Ocean. The climate is cool and sunny in the winter; hot, but with low humidity, in summer. Rainfall is low, an annual average of 9 inches (230 mm) spread throughout the year. The fertile land is kept well irrigated by the many small rivers running down from the mountains, which carry water all year round. The main crops are grains, tobacco, fruit and wine, but above all lucerne, used to feed the ostriches for which Oudtshoorn is famous the world over, and which still constitute an important economic factor today.

Oudtshoorn, founded in 1847, not only lies at the center of the Little Karoo, but is also its largest and most important city, particularly in the field of tourism. Lawyer Cornelis Jacob Langenhoven, one of the most popular Afriakaans authors, lived in the **Arbeitsgenot**, today

a museum; it was Langenhoven who, in 1918, wrote the national anthem of white South Africans: *"Die Stern van Suid-Afrika."*

Completed in 1906, the green-domed **C. P. Nel Museum** exhibits historical artifacts, but is best known for its informative displays on various aspects of ostrich breeding, an industry favored here by the semi-arid climate. This field saw its heyday around 1880, when ostrich feathers were in vogue; in this period, more than 750,000 ostriches lived here, and 1,023,000 pounds (465, 000 kg) of feathers were exported in 1913 alone. In Oudtshoorn, you can still see some of the "feather palaces" built by the nouveau-riche ostrich barons during this period. There was a drastic drop in demand during and after World War I; but business has picked up again since. Today, ostrich breeding has developed into a well-organized industry; some 250,000 ostriches live here, and, as well as their feathers, meat, eggs, bones and leather are used and exported worldwide.

Three farms offering guided tours in several languages have become great tourist attractions. To reach the **Safari Show Farm**, follow the R 62 / R 328 east out of Oudtshoorn for 2 miles (4 km); its complex also includes Welgeluk, one of the most beautiful feather palaces. Some 4 miles (6 km) farther on is **Hoopers Highgate Ostrich Show Farm**; the guided tours here, which last around 2 hours, present a lot of interesting information about ostriches and the ostrich industry. After this, you can pick up souvenirs and ostrich-leather products in the adjoining stores. The third, **Cango Ostrich Farm,** lies on the north-bound R 328; off the same road, just after you leave Oudtshoorn, is **Cango Crocodile Ranch & Cheetahland**, where you can learn about crocodiles or observe cheetahs and other big cats in their outdoor enclosures, and, if you're lucky, even stroke a young cheetah.

The **Cango Caves** on the same road, 17 miles (28 km) from Oudtshoorn, are one of the area's highlights. This fasci-

nating system of calcite caves lies at the foot of the Swartberg Mountains. A stretch of about 2,615 feet (800 m) is open to the public, allowing you to admire the chambers and halls of bizarre, multicolored stalactite and stalagmite formations, illuminated to advantage. The acoustics are no less impressive.

The **Swartberg** range in the north of the Little Karoo is arguably one of the most impressive in South Africa. The mountains form a barrier 124 miles (200 km) long and up to 7,606 feet (2,326 m) high between the Great and Little Karoo: a seemingly endless chain of craggy summits, ridges and cliffs, broken by deep crevasses and gorges. The bizarre shapes of the layers of sandstone with their twists and folds, combined with their rich warmth of color – the red of glowing coals – is a remarkable sight. In the

Above: The Swartberg Pass is acclaimed as a remarkable feat of engineering. Right: The Kleinplasie Living Open Air Museum in Worcester.

winter, snow can occur at altitudes as low as 3,924 feet (1,200 m); most of the annual rainfall occurs in March and August. The flora embraces various members of the Cape fynbos zone – including proteas, everlasting flowers and heathers – as well as typical Karoo vegetation, such as shrubs, aloes and euphorbias.

Of the three passes which traverse the mountains, **Meiringspoort** is the furthest east, the lowest (2,241 feet/716 m) above sea level, and the busiest (R 29, Oudtshoorn-Beaufort West). The **Swartberg Pass** which is the highest at 5,127 feet (1,568 m) above sea level, is also the most spectacular, and acclaimed as an engineering masterpiece by the 19th-century father-son team of road builders, Andrew and Thomas Bain. Although the road, which reaches the top of the pass 8 miles (13 km) after Cango Caves, is largely unpaved, it's not difficult driving. Another 19 miles (31 km) past the pass, this road comes to **Prince Albert**, a town lying at the northern foot of the range, which is famous for its peaches and apricots. The comfortable Swartberg Hotel is a good place to stop over, particularly if you want to drive back along the road in the other direction and see the canyon-like section at the beginning of the road, with its magnificent palette of colors, in the light of morning.

Oudtshoorn, the Cango Caves and ostrich farms aside, the Little Karoo is still fairly untouched by tourism; yet it's quite impressive, and a worthwhile place to explore, particularly the **Little Karoo Wine Route**. A significant town in this field is **Calitzdorp**, which boasts two vineyards and a wine-growers' association; it's especially well-known for its port wines, which have won a number of awards. In the small, but cozy **Dorpshuis**, next to the church, you'll find good lodging with excellent service.

Some 17 miles (28 km) to the east on the R 62, a road leads north to **Seweweekspoort**, the third of the spectacular Swartberg passes. Though unpaved, the road is good; it has little gradient, merely winding its way 13 miles (21 km) through wild, multicolored mountains. If you're reluctant to negotiate the last, difficult stretch of road to Lainsburg on the N 1, you should at least drive along part of the road from the south and then return the same way (it's no problem to turn around here), rather than missing out on such spectacular scenery altogether.

From **Ladismith,** you have a number of options for a route out of the Little Karoo. You can join the N 1 in the north, or the N 2 in the south, both of them heavily traveled roads and probably the quickest route to Cape Town. If you'd rather encounter less traffic and more scenic beauty, you should opt for a somewhat longer route through the winelands and/or taking in the southwest coast.

THE WINELANDS

South African wines are produced in the north near the Orange River; in the

southwest in the Little Karoo; in Constantia on the Cape Peninsula, in Durbanville (north of Cape Town) and the adjacent Swartland to the north; and in the Olifants river valley. But the industry centers in the area around the towns Stellenbosch, Paarl and Franschhoek, which extends to the east and northeast to include the Breede (Robertson, Worcester) and Hex river valleys (Wellington and Tulbagh). All of these areas, with the exception of Orange River District, have established signposted wine routes leading to the vineyards; at many, visitors can taste and, of course, purchase the wines; and some even have restaurants. The tourist offices of the individual districts are happy to supply information on routes, opening times, and the like.

Breede River and Hex River Valley

To reach **Robertson** in the **Breede River Valley**, you can take the R 60 from the Little Karoo through Swellendam or the R 62 through Montagu and the pic-

turesque gorge of **Kogman's Kloof** (the route through which Europeans first entered the Little Karoo). Founded in 1853, the town at the southern foot of the Langeberg range is the center of the country's largest irrigated wine-growing area. The vineyards and wine growers' associations here specialize in dessert wines; breeding race-horses is another specialty.

Worcester, founded in 1820 and conveniently situated at the intersection of the R 60 and the N 1, has developed into the economic hub of the Breede River Valley. The valley, which is very wide at this point, is ringed by imposing mountains which reach heights of up to 6,504 feet (1,989 m) above sea level in the north, and form an impressive backdrop for the town, which today has around 70,000 inhabitants. A number of old

Above: Harvesting wine in the evening with the help of miners' lamps. Right: 18th-century residential houses make Tulbagh an architectural gem.

Cape Dutch buildings have been preserved, including the drosdty (built in 1825). The **Kleinplasie Living Open Air Museum** is a complete functioning 18th-century farm complex. The Worcester Wine District, the largest in the country, accounts for 25% of South Africa's total wine harvest. The KWV Brandy Cellar, the largest of its kind under one roof in the world, is open to the public. Also worth visiting is the **Karoo National Botanic Garden** located in the north of town at the foot of the Brandwag Mountain and relatively accessible from the N 1. The 284-acre (115 hectares) garden, a branch of the garden in Kirstenbosch, specializes in plants from the country's arid zones which do not thrive in Kirstenbosch due to the unfavorable climate.

East of the city, the **Hex River Valley,** 13.5 miles (22 km) long and up to 2.5 miles (4 km) wide, traversed by the main train line and the N 1, is among the most beautiful valleys in South Africa. After 1709, it was used primarily as grazing

land, until work started on building the main traffic thoroughfares and their passes in 1875. Along the broad valley's northern edge is the mighty wall of the Hex River Mountains (up to 7,354 feet/ 2,249 m above sea level); the valley itself gets adequate rain in winter, and can be irrigated with water from the Hex River in summer. It's developed into South Africa's most important grape-cultivating region; 65% of its harvest is exported. The majestic valley is especially lovely to behold in summer, when bunches of ripe grapes are suspended between the vines' green leaves; in autumn during the harvest; or in late autumn and early winter (June), when the leaves of the main varietal grown here, the Barlinka (imported from Algeria in 1909), turn a deep red.

In the **Hex River Valley Railway Pass,** one of the most spectacular in the world, the railway line (built in 1875) has to make up the difference in elevation between De Doorns (1,560 feet / 477 m above sea level) and Matroosberg (3,136 feet/959 m above sea level) within a distance of 15 miles (25 km), switchbacking around numerous curves to do so. Between 1948 and 1989, the route was shortened by 5 miles (8 km) through the addition of 4 tunnels, a total of 10 miles (16 km) in length; one is the longest railway tunnel in the country at 8 miles (13 km). Though this cut down on travel time and increased capacity, rail passengers were deprived of some of the magnificent scenery. The section in question can still be admired on the road toward the Great Karoo (N 1), which crosses the **Hex River Pass** at an altitude of 3,155 feet (965 m). Shortly after this, the R 46 leads off north to **Ceres**. Here, in a fertile basin ringed with mountains more than 6,540 feet (2,000 m) high, and scattered with reservoirs or "dams," is South Africa's leading center of fruit cultivation and fruit juice production. You can visit the fruit processing and packing plants; the well-to-do little city also offers hiking, mountain climbing, fishing, and the **Ceres Mountain Fynbos Reserve**.

147

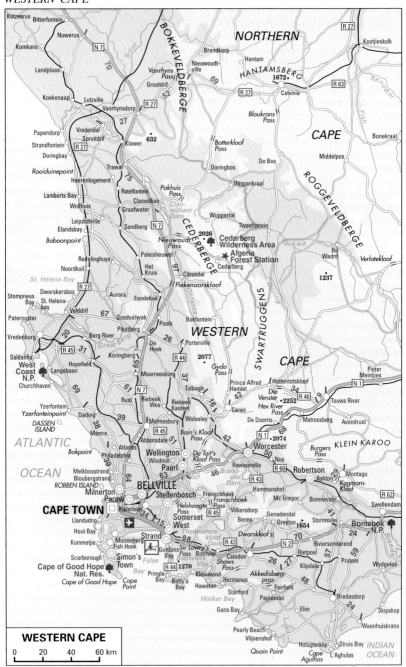

WESTERN CAPE

0   20   40   60 km

Tulbagh lies 22 miles (36 km) northwest. In 1969 an earthquake – a rare occurence in the area – destroyed much of the town. However, meticulous restoration has made Church Street with its 32 18th-century houses the largest single concentration of national landmarks in South Africa. The **Tulbagh Wine Cellars**, founded 1906, is the largest wine co-operative of its kind in South Africa; its two main customers are Great Britain and Sweden.

As they continue southwest to Wellington, the roads from Tulbagh and Ceres (R 46/R 303) traverse one of South Africa's most scenic passes, **Bain's Kloof Pass**. Built by Andrew Bain and first opened in 1853, the pass, 1,946 feet (595 m) above sea level and some 10 miles (16 km) long, commands breathtaking views. in all directions.

Wellington is the starting point for a small wine route and center of the country's dried-fruit industry. A few miles farther south is Paarl, which the N 1 also links directly to Worcester (31 miles/ 50 km). Rather than using the 2-mile (4 km) Huguenot Tunnel, completed in 1988, which shortens the journey by 7 miles (11 km), you should opt for another spectacular pass, **Du Toit's Kloof Pass** (finished in 1949), with its magnificent views of the Paarl Valley.

Just before Paarl, the R 101 branches off north to **Nederberg**, one of the leading Cape vineyards, which lies east of the Berg River on the edge of the Klein Drakenstein. The house was built in the Cape Dutch style in 1800 and has retained its original appearance. Nederberg's award-winning wines are exported all over the world. Since 1975, Sotheby's has held annual wine auctions here in February or March; South Africa's leading wine producers offer the best of their vintages, and the affair is at once a business and a social highlight.

Above: Girl Scout in Paarl.

Paarl

Second-largest city in the Western Cape Province, with 88,000 inhabitants and a significant industrial economy, Paarl is also the center of the Paarl Wine Route, the largest in the country with 17 participating vineyards. The city extends on either side of the Berg River across a broad, fertile valley. Towering over it to the west is **Paarl Mountain**, a massif which, with its three granite peaks (up to 2,384 feet / 729 m above sea level) stands out from the reddish folds of sandstone layers all around it. Under certain weather conditions, this granite glistens like pearls, whence the city's name (*paarl* is Afrikaans for pearl). Paarl was founded in 1720; the **Strooidakkerk** or thatched church, completed in 1805, is one of the oldest churches still in use in the country. It stands on **Main Street**, an oak-lined boulevard extending roughly 7 miles (11 km). On one of the intersecting streets, Pastorie Avenue, stands the **Oude Pastorie** or old vicarage, built in 1787; in

can wine-growers, and is said to have one of the largest wine cellars in the world. It represents around 5,000 producers and accounts for 70% of the country's wine export business.

Branching off the other side of Main Street, Jan Phillips Drive brings you to the **Afrikaans Language Monument (Taal Monument)**, which was erected to commemorate the establishment of Afrikaans as a language in its own right. This abstract construction of granite and concrete, officially dedicated in 1975, can be seen from quite a distance. In the adjoining **Paarl Mountain Nature Reserve** there are numerous scenic driving roads and hiking trails, interesting flora, and incredible views; on a clear day, you can see as far as Table Mountain. At the edge of town, Main Street becomes the R 45, which continues the 29 miles (47 km) on to Franschhoek.

1937, the building was restored and set up as a museum of cultural history. In the neighboring **Afrikaans Language Museum,** the development of Afrikaans is chronicled on the upper floor, while the lower floor contains the original furnishings of the former owner.

The **Grande Roche Hotel** is also near Main Street, in a unique location on the slopes of Paarl Mountain. A former wine-growing estate with Cape Dutch architecture, it's been converted into one of the best hotels in the country. Its excellent restaurant has received a number of awards.

A litttle further south, on the other side of Main Street, are the headquarters of the wine cooperative **KWV** (*Kooperatiewe Wijnbouwers Vereinigung*). Established in 1918, the cooperative is an umbrella organization for all South Afri-

Franschhoek

Passing first through the broad Berg River Valley, the road then follows the far narrower valley of the Franschhoek River, where the landscape takes on a new and much more dramatic character. You see more and more wineries along the road, most with French names such as La Motte or La Provence, on account of the French Huguenots who started settling in this fertile valley, together with Dutch and German immigrants, around 1688. The Huguenots adapted quickly and learned to speak Dutch. To commemorate the arrival of these early settlers, the **Huguenot Memorial** was erected in 1938. It stands at the end of Main Street, before the imposing backdrop of the Franschhoek Mountains; the nearby **Huguenot Museum** has displays devoted to the first Huguenot settlers and their descendants, as well as information about Huguenots the world over.

Most of the 15 vineyards on the **Franschhoek Wine Route** are open to

Above: Some 85% of South Africa's grapes are white. Right: Boschendal winery is one of the country's loveliest examples of Cape Dutch architecture.

the public. This area is also the center of production for South Africa's sparkling wine (*Méthode Champenoise, Méthode Cap classique*). Le Quartier Francais is a particularly attractive hotel with a wonderful ambience and a fine restaurant; Le Ballon Rouge is somewhat less expensive, but stylish and cozy, with fantastic food. Also highly popular is the Swiss Farm Excelsior hotel with its own vineyard; to get there, take the street that leads right at the Huguenot memorial. To the left, the R 45 rises steeply to the top of the **Franschhoek Pass**, from where there is a magnificent view out across the orchards, vineyards and the many catchment basins. The road continues to Theewaterskloof Dam; from here, you can reach the N 2 by driving southwest over the Vilijoens Pass and through Elgin.

If you go back 9 miles (15 km) on the R 45 from Franschhoek and take the R 310, which branches off the R 45 just after it crosses the Berg River, you come, on your left, to the **Boschendal** winery at the foot of Groot Drakenstein, which is on the Franschhoek Wine Route. The De Villiers family, Huguenots who had settled in the area in 1715, built the main house in 1812; it is considered to be one of the most beautiful Cape Dutch houses in South Africa. Following careful restoration, it is now furnished with objects dating back to the days of the Dutch East India Company; it was given national landmark status in 1976. Located in an adjacent building, the restaurant is only open at lunchtime, when it offers its famous lunch buffet; reservations are a must. For something a little less sophisticated, but equally attractive and of comparable quality, try "Boschendal's Pique-Nique" whose garden is a delight from November to the end of April. A new addition is "Le Café," recently opened in the former slave quarters, offering inexpensive snacks, sweets, and beverages. After negotiating **Helsooghte Pass**, 1,197 feet (366 m) above sea level, which commands splendid views, the road descends into the Eerste River valley and brings you to Stellenbosch.

Stellenbosch

This town is so charming that it makes you want to stay on and on; ideally, you should allow more than just a couple of hours for a visit when planning your itinerary. Unfortunately, organized bus tours from Cape Town which call on Stellenbosch fail to do it justice; but you can also reach the town from Cape Town on the local train. For car drivers who are hoping to escape the traffic congestion, chronic shortage of parking spaces, and rising crime rates associated with big cities, Stellenbosch, or one of the many-country hotels in the winelands, is an ideal base for a variety of excursions.

There are 50 wine producers lie on the Stellenbosch Wine Route. Of these, only 18 wineries and 5 co-operatives are open to the public; but at these, you can taste more than 280 different wines.

Above: Wine country near Stellenbosch.
Right: The old-style mom-and-pop store
Oom Samie se Winkel, Stellenbosch.

Simon van der Stel, the second governor of the Dutch East India Company in Cape Town, first explored the Eerst River Valley, 31 miles (50 km) east of Cape Town, in 1679. He was so impressed with the beauty of this green, sheltered, well-irrigated area, that he chose it as the site of a new settlement. The city which bears his name, the second-oldest and one of the loveliest in South Africa, has retained much of its original charm and character. Set in a marvelous landscape, the growing town featured broad streets planted with oaks and whitewashed, thatched houses. Despite three major fires, some of the original Cape Dutch houses with their rounded gables still stand today.

The most attractive buildings date from the period between 1775 and 1820; many of them are under landmark protection. In effect, Stellenbosch is an open-air museum, though there is nothing museum-like about it whatsoever; on the contrary, it is very much alive. Wine and fruit-growing dominate the economy; no other industries have settled here. The population has grown slowly and now stands at 56,000. The city's first magistrate was appointed back in 1682, and the first school was established a year later. The high school founded in 1859 grew into a college in 1866; since 1928, it has been one of the most acclaimed universities in the country, with, today, some 14,000 students.

Center of town is the **Braak**, or town square, a green which was originally used for parades and celebrations, and surrounded by some noteworthy buildings. **St. Mary's on the Braak** (built in 1852), a thatched Anglican church, lies on the north side of the green. The **Burgerhuis** on Bloemstreet, which runs along the west side, was built in 1797 as a private house; it's a fine example of Cape Dutch architecture. Off to the east leads Market Street where the Stellenbosch Tourist Bureau is located. Apart from the usual

advice and tips, this office offers a useful brochure entitled "Discover Stellenbosch on Foot."

South of the Burgerhuis is the **Krui-thuis**, built as a powder house in 1777, and today a military museum. On the southern edge of the Braak stands the **Rhenish Church**, built in 1823 primarily for slaves and coloreds, a new wing was added on in 1840.

A little further on, in Ryneveld Street, which is the next street on the right, is the entrance to the **Dorp Museum**. Armed with a brochure, you can explore this group of four carefully restored houses dating from between 1710 and 1850, each furnished in the style of its respective epoch. From the stark contrast between the small and very modest Schreuder House, built in 1709, and Grosvenor House, a two-storey patrician's house completed in 1803, you can see how extreme were the changes in lifestyle, furnishings and fashion within this span of time. Even the gardens of each house have been laid out in the style of its

day. The entire complex occupies an area of more than 16,350 feet (5,000 m).

The **Dutch Reformed Mother Church** in nearby Drostdy Street was built from 1717-22, but received its present form in 1863. Located on Van Riebeeck Street, the continuation of Plein Street, are the small but interesting botanic gardens of the university. The university buildings are located a bit father north, between Victoria Street and Merriman Avenue. At its southern end, Drostdy Street, runs into **Dorp Street**, a shady, tree-lined street (with gutters) which was once the main road to Cape Town. Whitewashed houses, some with finely-crafted gables, add to the charms of this shady street. You can also look around **Oom Samie se Winkel** – Uncle Samie's store, an old-fashioned shop – for a bargain, such as wine, which the store even ships to Europe.

On the corner of Dorp Street and Strand Road, **Libertas Parvas**, a building from the latter half of the 18th century which was restored in 1971 and is

now a national monument, houses the **Stellenryck Wijn Museum** (old furniture and wine-making paraphernalia) and the **Rembrandt van Rijn Art Gallery**, which displays works by South African artists.

On the eastern edge of town at the beginning of the Jonkershoek Valley is **Lanzerac**, a charming winery in a beautiful setting. Its main house, built in 1830, is a national monument, and the entire complex has been converted into one of the country's finest hotels. If you're not willing or able to stay there, you should try to at least have a meal there; it's well worth it (but book in advance).

Neethlingshof, an winery on the R 310 (which continues on to Cape Town as the M 12) is another fine example of Cape Dutch architecture; it was completed in 1692. It is open to the public and has a restaurant.

Above: A splendor of bloom in the Caledon Wild Flower Garden. Right: Cape Agulhas – South Africa's southernmost point.

Durbanville, at the center of the smallest of the wine routes, lies in Cape Town's northern catchment area. If you don't have enough time to visit the heart of the winelands, you can compensate with a number of attractive old wineries here. The **Hydro Rustenberg** is a must for the health-conscious; it offers the latest homeopathic remedies, lavish surroundings, and views of Table Mountain.

SOUTHWEST COAST AND FALSE BAY

Swellendam, established in 1747 as the Dutch East India Company's third settlement, after Cape Town and Stellenbosch, lies at the foot of the Langenberg range. The **Old Drostdy**, the country's only extant 18th-century drostdy, dates back, like many of the town's other buildings, to Swellendam's founding, and is an excellent example of Cape Dutch architecture. Now restored and a national monument, it houses a museum of cultural history.

On the Breede River, 4 miles (6 km) south of Swellendam, is the small but interesting **Bontebok National Park**. It was set up in 1931 to save the bontebok from extinction; since then, the local population of this unusual antelope has increased from an original 17 animals to around 200. Since the area is too small to sustain greater numbers, animals are also sent to other reserves. The park supports a great diversity of flora and birdlife. The only accommodation is a campsite.

If you'd like to visit the country's southernmost point, leave the N 2 at Stormsvlei, 21 miles (34 km) west of Swellendam, take the R 317 32 miles (52 km) south to Bredasdorp, and then get on the R 319, which will bring you the remaining 27 miles (43 km) to **Cape Agulhas**, the southernmost point of the African continent. Explorer Bartolomeu Dias was the first European to sight this point in 1488. Oceanologists recognize Cape Agulhas as the meeting point of the Atlantic and Indian Oceans. Even early sailors took note of the strange behavior of the compass here, and therefore dubbed it "Needle Cape." A radio transmitter and lighthouse here warn passing ships of possible perils, since the rocky plain with its low-lying hill system continues under the ocean, extending for a further 125 miles or so (200 km) as a flat, rocky bank. This area, known as the **Agulhas Bank**, is one of the richest fishing grounds in the world. From Bredasdorp, the R 316 leads southeast to **Arniston**, a picturesque fishing village popular with both artists and photographers, also known as **Waenhuiskrans**. Some of the fishermen's houses have been resored and are national monuments. There is an attractive, cozy hotel which serves fresh fish in its restaurant.

From Bredasdorp, the R 316 leads the 45 miles (72 km) back to the N 2, which it rejoins just by **Caledon**. This small town has 7 mineral springs containing iron, which yield 909,000 liters of water

a day; six of the springs are at temperatures of over 122° F (50° C). Another attraction is the **Caledon Wild Flower Garden** north of town, established in 1927 and extending over 529 acres (214 hectares); a big flower show is held here every September. About 19 miles (30 km) north of Caledon is **Genadental**, the oldest mission station in South Africa, founded by the Herrnhuter Missionary Society in 1793 (there was a first, failed attempt in 1737, but the station had to be abandoned in 1744). The village, surrounded by old oak trees, conveys an impression of what life must have been like in the Cape 150 years ago. It has 18 houses dating from the 18th century, and the whole village has been proclaimed a national monument.

The N 2 cuts through large wheat fields and enormous sheep-grazing areas. At Botrivier, the R 43 branches off to the south, and itself forks at Botriviervlei, 6 miles (9 km) further on. From here, the R 44 follows the coast southwest, while the R 43 leads south and east to **Hermanus** (which can also be reached on the R 326 from the Bredasdorp-Caledon road). This former fishing village is now a large town and popular resort extending for 5 miles (8 km) along the foot of the Kleinriviers Mountains and the coast of Walker Bay. Its attractive setting, kind climate, good hotels and extensive sport and leisure opportunities have made it a favorite holiday destination for South Africans; its population of 8,600 almost triples during the high season (mid-December to mid-January). The best time to visit is between January and May, when the bulk of the crowds are gone but the weather is still good. As winters are mild here (the average temperature is around 55° F / 13° C), it is also worth coming out of season. The town is a mixture of old--fashioned fishermen's houses and luxurious hotels.

The coast is largely rocky, but there are two good bathing beaches (Voelklip and Grotte) east of town. From June onwards, you can spot the whales that come here to calve; the best time to see the whales and their young is October. A town crier makes the latest whale information public. There are plans to open a whale museum behind the market place, run by a marine biologist, for the benefit of whale lovers, both amateur and professional. The old harbor around which the fishing village grew up was declared a national monument in 1970 and shortly thereafter proclaimed an open-air museum, the **Old Harbour Museum**. As in other coastal resorts, you can gett excellent fresh fish and seafood here; a speciality of the area is *Perlemoen*, a marine mollusc also known as abalone or haliotis, which must measure at least 4.4 inches (11.4 cm) when caught.

The Publicity Association office has a good supply of information on walks and trips starting in Hermanus. One attractive

route is Cliff Path, a 6-mile (10 km) trail along the cliffs that line they bay coast; also good for walkers is the **Fernkloof Nature Reserve** north of Hermanus, which extends over 3,572 acres (1,446 hectares) on the slopes of the Kleinrivier Mountains at altitudes of between 206-2,753 feet (63-842 m). There is a 31-mile (50 km) network of hiking trails with fantastic vantage points and rich vegetation (coastal and mountain fynbos). In an area of 6 square miles (15 square km) there are 1,001 varieties of flowering plants (New Zealand, to give a standard of comparison, has only 1,996 on 103,740 square miles / 266,000 sq. km, and Ireland 1,125 in an area of 27,300 square miles / 70,000 sq. km).

Past the Botriviervlei, the coastal road that leads along the foot of the jagged, blue-violet cliffs of the Cape range through a magnificent stretch of coast to the little resort of Kleinmond, the R 44, is one of the most scenically rewarding roads in South Africa. The **Kleinmond Coastal and Mountain Nature Reserve**, at the mouth of the Palmiet River, protects coastal and mountain fynbos with rare varieties of heather and protea; its hiking trails lead past rocky tidal pools.

Betty's Bay, the next coastal resort, consists almost entirely of private holiday homes (there are no tourist accommodations). Main highlight here is the **Harold Porter National Botanic Gardens**. Of a total of 467 acres (189 hectares), only 12 acres (5 hectares) are cultivated; the remaining land is occupied by the original, and protected, fynbos vegetation. Two rivers run through the area; while the 2,998-foot (917 m) peak of the Platberg towers over it. In the **Disa Kloof**, a deep, forested gorge, you can see the *Disa uniflora*, a particularly luxuriant red orchid which blooms in January. At first glance, the white sand of the dunes, which are farily common here, looks like snow.

Right: Sand and sea for the crowds at Muizenberg.

A detour of around 6 miles (10 km) leads left after the small resort Silver Sands and brings you to **Cape Hangklip** at the southern tip of False Bay's eastern border. The hotel there is simple (it was originally built as barracks for British soldiers in World War II), but the restaurant in the main building serves excellent food, such as crawfish or abalone. The solitude and tranquility are complete, and the view out across the wide expanse of False Bay to the jagged ridge of the Cape Peninsula and its southern tip is breathtaking, especially at sunset. Unforgettable, too, is the foaming surf crashing against the rocky coast, and, especially in spring, the sheer number and diversity of flowers and countless protea shrubs.

False Bay, an arm of the Indian Ocean some 19 miles (30 km) across, is located between the continent's two southern extremes, Cape Point and Cape Hangklip. It is thought to have got its name from early sailors who, traveling from the east, mistook Cape Hangklip for the Cape of Good Hope and often ran aground in the shallow bay. Between August and November, you can see whales along some sections of the coast. During the summer months, the prevailing southeasterly wind drive the warm waters of the Agulhas current from the Indian Ocean into the bay; during the main season water temperature is ideal at 72° F (22° C). During the winter months, the northwesterly winds blow this current outwards, and the colder waters of the Atlantic enter the bay, pulling the water temperature down to 59° F (15° C), but creating, at the same time, ideal surfing conditions. On the east coast, at the foot of the Hottentot Holland Mountains, **Gordon's Bay** and **Strand** are two popular resorts which unfortunately become overcrowded in the season and on Sundays. The former has a large yachting harbor (excellent restaurant), while Strand started out as a coastal suburb of Somerset West.

At Zandvlei, the M 5 turns north and leads 4 miles (6 km) to the **Rondevlei Nature Reserve**, primarily a waterfowl

157

sanctuary, which forms an enchanting oasis of calm in the shadow of the bustling city.

Muizenberg, in the northwest of the bay, was founded in 1743 as a military outpost on the way to Simonstown; today, it is a popular seaside resort. It became famous on account of Cecil Rhodes who bought a holiday villa here in 1899, and died there in 1902. In 1913, it was incorporated into Cape Town, some 16 miles (26 km) away. Freeways and a good train service make for good connections. Basically, Muizenberg consists of a not very attractive collection of hotels, holiday homes and apartments, but it does have a wonderful, wide, clean white sandy beach which slopes gradually into the sea and is therefore especially safe for bathing.

Above: Cape Town's sprawling slum areas attest to the desperate need for new housing. Right: The most striking view of Table Mountain is from the beach at Bloubergstrand.

North of the beach, which extends for 22 miles (35 km) along the entire north coast of False Bay, are broad, level expanses of sand which once formed part of the sea bed, known as the **Cape Flats**. During the days of the apartheid system, this flat dune area was developed after 1974 into Mitchell's Plain, a satellite town originally intended for 250,000 coloreds; but what actually tended to spring up, thanks to the ever-increasing, ever-accelerating migration of the rural population into urban areas, were enormous slum settlements such as Crossroads. Visiting these sites gives you a better idea of the problems that face the new South Africa; you can gain insight on one of the organized and generally knowledgable tours led through these areas. The best place to get more information is from a Cape Town agency such as Captours.

CAPE TOWN

Few cities in the world have such a grandiose and incomparable backdrop as

Cape Town (*Kaapstad* in Afrikaans). Situated at the foot of the magnificent, protective wall of Table Mountain, it is flanked by Lion's Head and Signal Head to the west and Devil's Peak to the east. On a clear day, you can see Table Mountain from the sea some 95 miles (150 km) away; for early sailors, it was thus an important landmark to help them navigate into Table Bay. In the mountain's shelter, a little base established to supply passing ships with provisions developed into today's flourishing urban center with more than 1.5 million residents. From the original settlement at the edge of Table Bay, Cape Town has spread around Signal Hill and along the coast up to Bakoven, and in the southeast as far as False Bay, taking in Cape Flats with their satellite cities of Mitchell's Plain, Khayelitsha, and the squatter settlement Crossroads.

The most attractive, most famous and most-photographed view of the city is that from **Bloubergstrand**, a small seaside resort 15 miles (25 km) north of Cape Town on the R 27 or M 5 toward Milnerton. But photographs can't compare with the real thing. The modern travesties wreaked upon cityscape fade into insignificance before the mighty side of Table Mountain; and the view is even more impressive if a strong southwesterly wind happens to be blowing, spreading a distinctive "tablecloth" of cloud over the mountain's top.

After landed here on April 6, 1652, Jan van Riebeeck's first act was to build a mud-walled fort and plant a vegetable garden. As trade and shipping increased, so did the importance of the supply base; even today, it continues to play a significant role for shipping traffic from America and Europe to Asia and Australia. Supertankers on the Cape route, which are too large to navigate the harbor's shallow waters, are supplied by helicopters offshore.

For a long time the history of Cape Town and the area around it was identical to that of South Africa. For the Boers who crossed the mountains to the interior of the country, Cape Town remained the "mother town" – a name still lovingly used today. Under the British, it was the capital of the British Cape Colony from 1806-1910. Since then, it has been the seat of Parliament for the republic. During the six months that Parliament is in session, the government also moves from Pretoria to Cape Town. Economically, the town proves its importance with headquarters of legion banks, insurance companies, businesses and industries; and Cape Town is also an important cultural center, with its university, theaters, opera house and symphony orchestra.

The long years of British supremacy in the Cape have somewhat obscured the region's Dutch roots; even the city's liberal tradition is a British legacy. Coloreds make up the largest proportion of Cape Town's population, with the Cape Malays forming a separate and very distinct group. For years, the city had few blacks, but since the end of apartheid, migration

159

from rural areas, notably Ciskei and Transkei, has increased. One by-product of this are such squatter settlements as Crossroads, on the city's outskirts; these serve to highlight the huge discrepancies between rich and poor.

City Tour

What remains of the old city center is characterized by narrow, straight streets. The most important and interesting sights are within easy walking distance of each other; and you can always orient yourself with the help of the main shopping street, Adderley Street, and the omnipresent Table Mountain. Start your tour is the **Foreshore** area, today crowded with high-rises. Originally, the waterline was somewhat further inland, but when the Duncan Dock was built (1937-1945), the excavated sand and soil was used as land-fill, thus providing an additional 494 acres

Above: Cape Town's City Hall is a frequent venue for concerts.

(200 hectares) of land ("foreshore"). Running through this area is Heeren-gracht, a broad, attractive boulevard with a strip of green park in the middle. Leading off this street to the left is Hertzog Boulevard, on the harbor side of which you'll find the **Nico Malan Theater Complex**; the opera house and theater here are famous for their excellent interior decor and acoustics. A walkway links the complex to the **Civic Centre**, home to the city administration; behind the center is the office of the Automobile Association.

At the end of Heerengracht, in front of a circular garden area with ponds and a fountain, the statues of **Jan van Rie-beeck** and his wife gaze at Table Mountain, roughly on the spot where their ship landed in 1652. Past this circle, Heeren-gracht becomes Adderley Street. Completed in 1970, the terminus of the **Main Train Station**, fronted by a bit of park, covers a lot of ground. **Captour** has a large publicity office in the **Tourist Information Centre** (**TIC**) on Adderley Street, providing comprehensive information, maps and so on. The complex also houses a branch of SATOUR and various car rental firms. From the street in front of the office, buses leave for the Waterfront; while the departure point for buses to and from the airport, as well as long-distance buses, is behind the office. On the other side of Strand Street in the large **Golden Acre** complex, which includes shops, restaurants and offices, SATOUR has its Cape Town office. Buses depart from the front of the building to the starting point of the Table Mountain cableway. Behind the complex is the **bus station** for city buses, located between Strand and Castle Streets.

Castle Street leads to the **Castle of Good Hope**, the city's oldest building, built between 1666 and 1679, which stands near the site of Riebeeck's original fort. It was built in the shape of a five-pointed star, with walls more than 30 feet

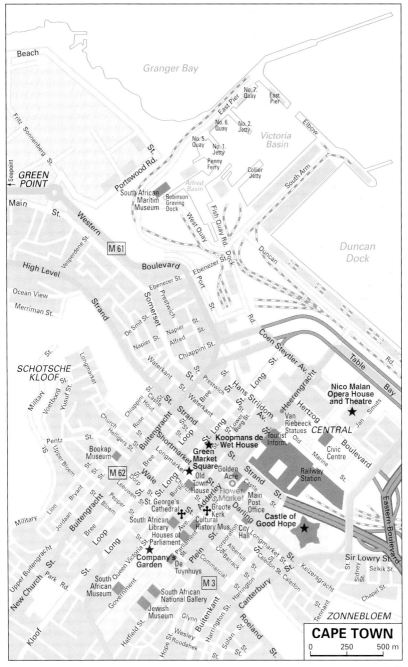

CAPE TOWN

0   250   500 m

(10 m) high, but it was never actually attacked, serving, rather, as a residence for the early governors. The state rooms have been restored and contain old furniture, paintings, porcelain and glass. The building is also home to a military and seafaring museum. East of and behind the castle is the Good Hope Centre, a large multi-purpose complex used for exhibitions, sporting events, trade fairs and congresses. The square in front of the castle, **Grand Parade**, which was once used for parades, is now a large parking lot. Market traders (fruit and flowers) have set up their stalls around its edge, and on Wednesdays and Saturdays there is a flea market. On Thursdays and Sundays, the Cape Town Symphony Orchestra performs in **Town Hall**, built along the south side of the square in 1905.

The main post office is on the corner of Castle and Parliament Streets. The Malay

Above: Music is in the air at the annual Coon Carnival. Right: Colorful row of houses in the Malay Quarter.

flower sellers who gather on weekdays opposite the post office in a passage leading to Adderley Street add a splash of color to the city. Continuing along Adderley Street towards Table Mountain, you come to the **Groote Kerk**. The first church was probably built here in 1678; the present bell-tower stems from the second church (1703); and today's church was completed around 1836. Note the carved wooden pulpit, a masterpiece executed by German sculptor Anton Anreith.The neighboring building (parts of which date back to 1679) was originally a lodge for the slaves hired by the Dutch East India Company to work in their gardens. It was renovated in 1809 and served as the seat of the Supreme Court for over 100 years. Today it houses the excellent **Cultural History Museum** which is well worth a visit. Opposite this, on the corner of Adderley and Wale Street, was the city's first hospital.

Adderly Street turns into Government Avenue, a splendid oak-lined promenade more than half a mile (1 km) long. It leads through the **Gardens**, a park which encompasses roughly one-third of the original vegetable garden planted by Jan van Riebeeck; strolling through this green oasis is a popular activity for tourists and Capetowners alike. To the right of the park entrance, next to **St. George's** (Anglican) **Cathedral**, is the **South African Library**, opened in 1812. In the Botanical Garden (on the right side of Government Avenue), there are more than 8,000 exotic trees and plants from all over the world. On the left side of the avenue stand the **Houses of Parliament**, of which the main entrance is, however, in Parliament Road. A little further along, **De Tuynhuys**, built in 1751 as a governor's residence, today serves as the residence of the President when Parliament is in session.

The **South African National Gallery** has a collection of works by contemporary South African painters as well as

English and Dutch painters (17th-19th centuries). Behind it stands South Africa's oldest synagogue (1862), now the **Jewish Museum**. The **South African Museum** at the end of the Gardens houses notable collections relating to natural history and archaeology; especially notable is a display on the life of the Bushmen, complete with works of Bushman art. The museum has an adjacent planetarium.

If you go past St. George's Cathedral and turn right from Wale Street into Burg Street, you come to one of the most charming and atmospheric places in the city's old section: **Green Market Square**. Paved with cobblestones and lined with trees, this former marketplace, where 17th- and 18th-century burghers strolled to see and be seen, still retains much of its Old World charm, despite the modern vendors who set up their stands here during the day. Built between 1755 and 1761, the **Old Town House** is a fine example of the architecture of the period. It served as Town Hall until 1905, and

today contains a small, but notable collection (Michaelis Collection) of 17th-century Flemish and Dutch painting.

St. George's Street (which runs parallel to Burg Street) is a pedestrian zone lined with stores, ideal for strolling. Near the intersection of Strand and Long Streets, the **Koopmans de Wet House**, built in 1701, is an excellent example of a Cape townhouse, reflecting then-contemporary lifestyles with its collection of European and South African furniture, porcelain, glass and silver. The **Malay Quarter** is on the other side of Buitengracht, the through road (M 62) to Kloof Nek, on the eastern slopes of Signal Hill; since the 19th century, this area has been a center of the Cape Malay population. The one-storey houses with their flat roofs, painted in bright colors, are arranged in a terrace system; between them are a number of small mosques with picturesque minarets. If you're in Cape Town at New Year's, don't miss the colorful Coon Carnival on January 1 and 2. The **Bo-Kaap Museum** on Wale Street,

housed in an 18th-century building, paints a fascinating picture of the life of a 19th-century Malay family.

After passing Green Point, a suburb with green areas and playing fields, Western Boulevard (M 6) reaches **Sea Point**. This built-up, densely-populated suburb stretches along the western slopes of Signal Hill. Attractive promenades invite you to stroll along the rocky coast, especially in late afternoon or early evening, when the powerful surf and the colors of the sunset cannot fail to impress.

The Harbor

Early explorers looking for a sea route to India visited Table Mountain, as did, after them, the trading ships of the colonial powers on their way to and from South and Southeast Asia. **Duncan Basin** has berths for passenger and freight ships, and the largest dry dock in

Above: In the Pumphouse Bar, Victoria & Albert Waterfront. Right: On Table Mountain.

the southern hemisphere, large modern refrigerated storage areas, and loading equipment. However, the volume handled here is only the fourth-largest in the country after Richards Bay, Saldanha Bay and Durban.

Since 1988, the older section of the harbor has been redeveloped to form an extensive shopping and recreational area, the **Victoria & Albert Waterfront** – comparable to Fisherman's Wharf in San Francisco or Sydney's Darling harbor. Though fishing boats still ply Victoria Basin, the area, these days specializes more in entertainment; you can go on harbor tours and pleasure cruises, prospect for semiprecious stones in the "Scratch Patch," shop, stroll, or sit in one of the many restaurants, bistros, pubs and coffee shops, watching the hustle and bustle until late into the night. Those interested in seafaring can visit the small **South African Maritime Museum** as well as three museum ships anchored in the harbor basin. The Waterfront has developed into a main tourist attraction. It's best to take a taxi or shuttle bus there (every 15 minutes from the information office at the train station, or every half hour from Seapoint to the central Victoria & Albert Hotel), since the modern freeway system, though impressive, cuts off Table Bay and the harbor from the city, and parking space is rare.

Table Mountain

An absolute must for visitors to Cape Town is a walk or hike on Table Mountain. There are breathtaking views of, to the south, the mountain ranges of the Cape Peninsula; of False Bay to the east; the Atlantic Ocean and the former prison island of **Robben Island** in the west; and, to the north, the city itself, which extends along the coast of Table Bay in all directions. Try to keep your itinerary for Cape Town flexible enough that you can ride up to Table Mountain as soon as the

weather permits; the weather conditions are extremely changeable here.

Table Mountain forms the northern end of the Cape Peninsula. It is formed of massive layers of sandstone and slate threaded with intrusions of grantie. The rocky plateau with its densely forested gorges reaches its highest elevation in the east: 3,551 feet (1,086 m) above sea level. It loses height to the south, descending to the lower plateau, where there are five reservoirs which provide Cape Town with water, and then dropping away steeply 650 feet (200 m) down to Orange Kloof, an area of dense forest not open to the public. The steep rock face to the north, roughly 2 miles (3 km) wide, towers over the city like a single, unbroken wall; actually, a narrow gorge, the Platteklip Gorge, divides it roughly in the middle from top to bottom.

This steep drop is flanked to the east by **Devil's Peak**, 3,273 feet (1,001 m), and in the west – separated by a wide valley – by **Lion's Head**, 2,188 feet (669 m). A narrow ridge runs north from Lion's Head to **Signal Hill**, from which an artillery battery used to be fired to greet ships or mark ceremonial occasions. You can drive up to a vantage point which yields fantastic views of the city, especially at night. At certain times, the face of Table Mountain is illuminated with spotlights after dark.

There are many walking routes, of varying degrees of difficulty, to the top of Table Mountain. The ascent takes about three hours; the easiest route is through Platteklip Gorge, but the hike is nevertheless potentially dangerous: lives are lost every year. The Mountain Club of South Africa can supply you with supplies, advice, maps, route descriptions and guides. As the weather can change very quickly, you should bring a warm jacket and waterproof clothing.

A quicker, safer means of ascent is the **Table Mountain Cableway** (opened in 1929). The lower station is easy to reach from the city center by car via Buitengracht/Kloof Nek Road; there is also a bus service from Adderley Street. From

the valley station, at an altitude of 1,197 feet (366 m) above sea level, the car ascends to an elevation of 3,489 feet (1,067 m) at the mountain station, running on a cable 4,068 feet (1,244 m) long. It holds 28 passengers and the journey takes only 7 minutes. However, be prepared to wait for your ride on weekends, public holidays and during vacations. A siren sounds at the summit if fog comes down; do make your way back to the mountain station as quickly as possible when this happens, as the cableway will stop running shortly afterwards.

THE CAPE PENINSULA

Visitors to Cape Town should also take the time to make the 30-mile (50 km) round trip along the peninsula's moun-

Above: Kirstenbosch National Botanical Gardens is one of the finest in the world. Right: Protea repens. Far right: The 18th-century gable sculptures in Groot Constantia.

tainous coastline. If you want to make the journey under your own steam, start off on the east side and return to Cape Town on the west side; this ensures that you'll make the best of light conditions in the morning and afternoon. Leave the city on Hertzog Boulevard, which runs into Eastern Boulevard (the M 4), or take Plein Street/Roeland Street to De Waal Drive (M 3). The M 3 and M 4 intersect just before the famous **Groote Schuur Hospital**, where Christian Barnaard performed the first heart transplant in 1967, to form Rhodes Drive. On the left-hand side you pass **Mostert's Mill**, a windmill dating from 1796, but still in operation, while on the right is Rhodes Memorial, a monument to Cecil Rhodes; Cape Town University; and the zoological gardens.

On the left side of the road is **Groote Schuur** ("big barn"); the grain silo built on this site in 1657 was incorporated into the magnificent country house which Cecil Rhodes had built in 1893 in the Cape Dutch style and later bequeathed to the nation. Since then it has served as the

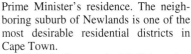

Prime Minister's residence. The neighboring suburb of Newlands is one of the most desirable residential districts in Cape Town.

A little further on, the M 63 branches off to the right, leading to the **Kirstenbosch National Botanical Gardens**. The gardens are uniquely situated on the densely wooded eastern slope of Table Mountain, where rainfall is high. In 1895, Cecil Rhodes purchased the area (in use as farmland since 1653), and bequeathed it to the nation on his death in 1902. The Botanical Gardens were subsequently laid out in 1913; they are considered to be among the most beautiful in the world. Some 148 acres (60 hectares) of its 1,304 acres (528 hectares) are cultivated. Around 22,000 types of plants have been collected, cultivated, and studied here. No matter when you go, something will be flowering, but spring is indubitably the best time to visit. The large herbarium, which is of considerable scientific interest, can only be visited by prior arrangement. There is an informa-

tion kiosk in the gardens, and a tea house serves snacks; an adjacent curio shop sells various indigenous plants and seeds, as well as books on South African flora. The walks are clearly signposted; there are a number of information boards around the grounds, and you can also pick up a map at the entrance. A bus runs to Kirstenbosch from the city bus station via Claremont.

On leaving Kirstenbosch, continue 3 miles (5 km) southwest on Rhodes Avenue to Constantia Nek, and then turn off southeast onto Constantia Road (M 41). After almost 2 miles (3 km), you come to **Groot Constantia**. Built in 1685 as the residence of Simon van der Stel, one of the most important Dutch governors, this building is one of the finest examples of Cape Dutch architecture. Today, it's a national monument, and contains a valuable collection of old furniture and paintings. The estate is superbly located in the midst of vineyards. Hendrik Cloëte, who bought the estate in 1778, improved wine cultivation here and had a spacious and

167

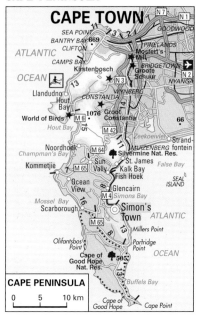

impressive-looking cellar built by the French architect L.-M. Thibault. German sculptor Anton Anreith fashioned the engraving on the gables. Cloëte's wines were esteemed at many European courts; but the estate's glory days came to an end in 1860, when the vine plague started to spread throughout the Cape Province. Today, however, the estate's wines are once again among the best in the country. There are two restaurants here – reservations are advisable for the Jonkerhuis restaurant – as well as conducted tours of the cellars and wine-tastings.

Somewhat farther north, near the M 3, is the former wine estate of **Alphen**, which also belonged to the Cloëte family; today, it's a national monument, and has been converted into a stylish luxury hotel. South of Groot Constantia, there are two wineries which were separated from the main Constantia property after

Right: You can collect your own bag of semi-precious stones at the "Scratch Patch."

Simon van Stel's death; these, too, also produce excellent wines. Called **Buitenverwachting** and **Klein Constantia**, they're both on the **Constantia Wine Route**, and you can visit their cellars by prior arrangement. At Buitenverwachting, you'll find an excellent restaurant, deservedly renowned.

To continue your journey, rejoin the M 3 and then turn off into Boye's Drive, a road which leads through the mountains high above the coast and offers magnificent views of False Bay. Just past Kalk Bay, this road joins up with the M 4 from Muizenberg. Another attractive alternative is to proceed from Buitenverwachting or Klein Constantia on the M 42 and the Oude Kaapse Weg (M 64). This route traverses the **Silvermine Nature Reserve**, which is abundant in indigenous flora. At the junction with Kommetjie Road (M 65), turn left, and you'll come to the coastal road at **Fisch Hoek**. This town, numbering some 12,000 inhabitants, is the only one in South Africa where no alcohol is served; a law was passed to this effect in 1818, and continues in force today. The beautiful sandy beach with its calm, clear waters at the southern edge of town is held to be one of the safest on the Cape Peninsula.

Just before Simon's Town, Dido Valley Road branches off from the M 4. Here, you can visit what is said to be the largest factory in the world processing semi-precious stones, **Topstones**, free of charge The adjoining store, **Mineral World**, sells a wide variety of articles made from and with semiprecious stones. For a small sum, you can acquire a "Scratch Patch Bag" to fill with stones you choose yourself from the heaps that comprise the "Scratch Patch" – great fun for kids and adults alike!

Simon's Town, named after Simon van der Stel and the southernmost point of the Cape Peninsula, is the terminus for the local electric train from Cape Town.

It was originally chosen by the Dutch East India Company in 1741 as a sheltered winter harbor, since Table Bay is often subject to harsh winter storms. The **Admiralty House**, built before 1760, has been a national monument since 1972. In 1814, it became the property of the British Admiralty: Simon's Town was, in fact, the main naval base for its South Atlantic fleet for 143 years. Not surprisingly, a strong English influence is still evident in the character of the town, with its narrow, winding streets and old-fashioned pubs. In 1957, the harbor and all its facilities became the headquarters and training center for the South African navy. Today, the navy is gone, and the harbor is home to a fair-sized fishing fleet and many oceangoing yachts. The **Simon's Town Museum** is housed in the former residency (built in 1777). The **Martello Tower** was built in 1796 as a gunpowder tower.

Take the road along the jagged coast, where the surf has hollowed out countless caves, until you come to the entrance of the **Cape of Good Hope Nature Reserve**. Occupying the southern tip of the Cape Peninsula, the reserve covers 19,142 acres (7,750 hectares), with 25 miles (40 km) of coastline. It was declared a conservation area in 1939 to protect the area's flora and fauna and prevent its beauty being destroyed by building. Eland, springbok, bontebok, black wildebeest, mountain zebras, baboons, ostriches, turtles, lizards, geckos and a wide variety of birds are at home here.

The **Cape of Good Hope**, which gave the peninsula its name, has been notorious for its storms since early seafaring days. Bartolomeu Dias, who was the first to sail around it in 1488, originally named it "Cape of Storms;" it was given its present, more optimistic name by the Portuguese king Henry the Navigator. The British circumnavigator of the globe, Francis Drake, called it "the fairest Cape" he had ever seen. The legend of the Flying Dutchman is said to have originated here; sightings of him are still reported today.

169

The road through the reserve ends at a parking lot around 409 feet (125 m) above sea level, with a kiosk and souvenir shop. Be careful of the often cheeky baboons which play in the area, and remember that visitors are not allowed to feed them! From here, you can take a bus or go on foot (an easy walk) to the most extreme tip of the peninsula, **Cape Point**, east of the Cape of Good Hope and 693 feet (212 m) above sea level. The lighthouse which was erected at the highest point in 1860 no longer functions; in 1914 a new one was built atop a cliff at a lower altitude, only 284 feet (87 m) above sea level. Its beam is one of the most powerful in the world. Cape Point's steep cliffs are home to numerous sea birds. If you're at all interested in the history of this region, you can hardly help being affected by the view from the summit; on the horizon to the

Above: Cape of Good Hope (left) and Cape Point (right) seen from a helicopter. Right: A good catch (Hout Bay).

south, you can see ships moving along what is one of the most important sea routes in the world. It's a curious feeling to remember that nothing lies between you and the South Pole but more water and ice. From here, an attractive walking trail leads to the Cape of Good Hope, along which the flora is notably interesting. There is also a road to a small parking lot, from which one can scale the Cape's famous cliffs.

From the entrance to the reserve, the M 65 continues west to the Atlantic coast. **Kommetjie**, a friendly little fishing resort, has, thanks to the favorable winds in summer, developed into one of the best surfing venues on the Atlantic coast.

The road then makes a long detour inland around the marshy hinterland of Chapman's Bay, and meets up with the M 6, which runs from the east and continues along the west coast to Cape Town.

Chapman's Peak Drive begins just after Noordhoek. Built in 1922, this road is considered a great engineering

achievement and acclaimed as one of the most spectacular coastal roads in the world. About 497 feet (152 m) above the crashing breakers of the Atlantic, it follows the line at the point where the brightly colored red, orange and yellow sandstone of Table Mountain rests upon the dark Cape granite, chunks of which stand exposed on the craggy slopes below the road. Along the way, you can pull over into lay-bys to enjoy the magnificent scenery; one virtually mandatory stopping place is at the road's highest point, before it turns inland away from the coast. From here, you have a splendid view across **Hout Bay** to the 981-foot (300 m) Sentinel, a cliff which drops away almost vertically to the sea, on the opposite shore. The area was once densely wooded – hence its name, "Wood Bay" – but these forests have long since been cut down, in part for shipbuilding. In 1869 the last two wild elephants here were shot. Today, the town is an important fishing port, especially for crawfish; and anyone who has-

n't seen enough bird life in the wild can look in at **World of Birds**, the country's largest bird park with more than 3,000 species. From early December to the end of April, Sunset Cruises runs boat trips to Cape Town on the launch *Circe*.

North of Hout Bay, the M 63 branches off on the right towards Constantia and Kirstenbosch. Near this turn-off is the estate **Kronendal**, a particularly fine example of Cape Dutch architecture, today a national monument housing a well-known restaurant. The M 6 leads back to the coast to the suburb of Llandudno with its quiet beach, which lies at the foot of Table Mountain's steep western drop, whose cliffs are known as the "Twelve Apostles." It continues of through Bakoven, Camps Bay (VIP beach) and Sea Point back to Cape Town.

ATLANTIC COAST

The main thoroughfare along the Atlantic, or West, Coast is the N 7; the smaller R 27 runs directly along the

coast, giving you a view of the cooling towers of the nuclear power plant at Koeberg, behind Melkbokstrand. After 75 miles (120 km) the road comes to the **West Coast National Park**. Covering some 49,400 acres (20,000 hectares), the park protects the ecosystem of the **Langebaan Lagoon** and its surroundinngs, including a 16-mile (26 km) strip of the Atlantic coast between Yverfontein and Langebaan. The wetlands are of international significance, playing host in summer to around 60,000 migratory wading birds. Numerous native sea birds, including the endangered jackass penguin, can breed and nest safely here on four islands off the coast. The cold, plankton-rich Benguela current near the coast attracts large numbers of fish, which the birds feed on. The lagoon is unique in South Africa, because it is not an estuary, but formed by an arm of the

Above: Many European sea birds winter in West Coast National Park. Right: Cape gannets, Lambert's Bay.

sea. Its water level is thus regulated by the tides alone, and not by an influx of fresh water. The salt marshes surrounding the lagoon are the largest in South Africa. The climate is dry, with an annual rainfall of 10.5 inches (270 mm), occurring mainly between May and August.

The park is divided into 3 zones. Zone A, at the entrance to the lagoon, is reserved for general recreation; you can hire a motorboat, waterski, fish, or dive here. In Zone B, only sailing and windsurfing (speed records have been set here) are allowed. Zone C, at the end of the lagoon, may not be entered at all. The Postberg section in the northwest is famous for its magnificent flowers (access only in August/September). Bird-watching is particularly rewarding in summer when the migratory birds have arrived from the north. In spring, whales stop off in the Plankiesbaai. Accommodation is available in the Langebaan Lodge on the northwest coast of the lagoon.

A little further north, past Langebaan, is **Club Mykonos**, South Africa's first private holiday club; its founder, inspired by a trip to Greece, had it built to resemble a Greek village. An ideal destination for anyone seeking activity and action, it even has a yachting harbor on **Saldanha Bay**, a large bay adjoining the lagoon in the south. The bay forms a natural harbor and was first discovered in 1601, but could not be used as a shipping post, because of the lack of drinking water. 1970 saw the construction of large loading terminals for the export of iron ore (open to the public); these terminals are linked to Sishen, where the ore is mined, by 534 miles (861 km) of railway track. Today, **Saldanha** is the largest harbor on the west coast of Africa; it's also home to a fishing fleet and an important center for crayfish. The drive north along the coast is charming, but the road is unpaved.

North of Cape Town, the N 7 first traverses the **Swartland** with the center

of Malmesbury, whose fertile black earth make it South Africa's most important wheat-growing area (Wheat Industry Museum in Moorreesburg). At **Citrusdal** the road reaches the Olifants River Valley. The river is used for irrigation and helped the area develop into one of the most important regions for citrus fruit. Not only is the small town a useful stop-off point for journeys to the north; it is also a good base for trips in the area.

The Olifants River Valley, which the N 7 follows from Citrusdal, is bordered to the east by the **Cedarberg Mountains**. A part of the Cape range, this chain is around 60 miles (100 km) long and reaches an altitude of 6,631 feet (2,028 m) at Sneeuberg, its highest peak. The **Cedarberg Wilderness Area** protects 175,370 acres (71,000 hectares). With its weathered sandstone formations, some eroded into bizzare shapes; waterfalls; caves with San rock paintings; fascinating views; and the sharp, clear light make this region a paradise for hikers, mountain climbers, nature lovers, artists and photographers. Apart from the Clanwilliam cedar (*Widringtonia cedarbergensis*) which gave the mountains their name, now an endangered species, other interesting flora (mountain fynbos) includes the white snow protea (*Protea cryophilia*), which blooms in March above the snow line and is not found anywhere else in the world. The network of hiking trails extends 157 miles (254 km).

Roughly halfway between Citrusdal and Clanwilliam, a road running east crosses the Olifants River and continues up to **Nieuwoudt Pass**, some 1,929 feet (590 m) above sea level, which commands fantastic views of the valley and mountains. The road then continues for 22 miles (35 km) through the reserve to **Algeria Forest Station**. It is here that permits for entering the wilderness area are issued; maps showing trails and huts and information brochures are also available. Finally, you can hire both a guide and a donkey (to carry baggage). As the number of hikers is limited, advance booking is a good idea; the best time to

173

visit the area is between September and April.

If you continue toward Ceres on the R 303 and turn left after 46 miles (74 km), you'll come the the nature reserve **Kagga Kamma** (9,139 acres / 3,700 hectares) in the southern part of the Cedarberg range. A few Bushman families have returned to the land of their ancestors, and visitors can get an impression of their traditional lifestyle. (Accommodation is in comfortable, fully-equipped thatched cottages.)

The small town of **Clanwilliam**, 32 miles (52 km) north of Citrusdal, is popular with waterskiing fans, who come to the 32-mile (18 km) dam on the Olifants River. Large areas of land are devoted to growing rooibos (*Aspalathus lineraris*), a shrub occurring throughout the province. Blacks have used its tender young leaves for centuries for medicinal purposes. Since about 1900, whites have been cultivating rooibos and using the leaves for tea: the beverage is caffeine-free and contains only minimal amounts of tannin, but is rich in vitamin C.

To the east, the R 364 leads over the **Pakhuis Pass** (2,959 feet/905 m above sea level) and through some lovely countryside to **Wuppertal**, some 43 miles (69 km) away. This picturesque little town at the eastern foot of the Cedarberg range was founded by the Rhenish Mission in 1830 and has changed little in the years since, making it popular with artists and photographers.

West of Clanwilliam, the R 364 runs to **Lambert's Bay** on the Atlantic coast. This fishing port (especially crawfish) is dominated by its fish-processing industry. A breakwater links **Bird Island** to the mainland. Resident here are large colonies of cormorants, Cape gannets, seagulls, terns and many other sea birds, including jackass penguins, which you can often see at quite close proximity. Some 47 miles (76 km) north of Clanwilliam on the N 7 is **Vanrhynsdorp**, a good base for excursions to Namaqualand.

WESTERN CAPE
Transportation

Three roads link Cape Town, the most important traffic hub, with the rest of the country. The N7 leads north (Namibia), the N1 runs from the seat of Parliament to Johannesburg/Bloemfontein/Pretoria, the N2, running nearly parallel to the coast, enables access from the south and east coasts to the interior of the country.

Bus: Intercity buses link Cape Town and all the country's major cities. Mainliner: via Springbok (6 hours) or Upington (10 1/2 hrs.) to Windhoek (16 hrs.); via George and Port Elizabeth (10 hrs.) to East London. Greyhound and Translux: along various routes (Bloemfontein, Kimberley, Beaufort West) to Johannesburg/Pretoria (about 18 hrs.) and Durban (via Bloemfontein, 19-20 hrs.). Along the mountain route to Port Elizabeth (10-12 hours), Translux stops at Paarl/Stellenbosch, Worcester, Oudtshoorn; along the coastal route, at Swellendam, Oudtshoorn, Knysna, Plettenberg Bay.

Train: The train trip to Johannesburg/Pretoria with the Trans-Karoo (daily, via Kimberley-De Aar) lasts 27 hrs.; to Durban with the Trans-Oranje (once a week, via Kimberley and Bloemfontein), 36 hrs. Electric high-speed trains run from Cape Town to Simonstown, Stellenbosch and a number of other towns in the area.

Air: Cape Town Airport, 13.5 mi/22 km from the city center (regular buses), is serviced by such international airlines as SAA, Swissair and KLM, as well as by Air Namibia (to Oranjemund/Lüderitz/Swakopmund, Windhoek, Harare/Livingstone/Lusaka). For domestic flights, as well as SAA, Sun Air offers service to Johannesburg and Sun City; Comair to Johannesburg; National Airlines to Springbok and Alexander Bay; South African Express (SAX) to Kimberley and Upington.

THE GARDEN ROUTE
Accommodations

ST FRANCIS BAY 6312: *MODERATE:* **Jyllinge Lodge**, 2, Mary Crescent, PO Box 65, tel: 0423/94-0270, fax: 94-0230.
JEFFREYS BAY 6330: *MODERATE:* **Savoy Protea Hotel**, PO Box 36, tel: 0423/93-1106, fax: 93-2445.
STORM'S RIVER 6308: *MODERATE:* **Tsitsikamma Lodge** (5 mi/8 km before Storm's River Bridge), PO Box 10, tel: 04 230/802, fax: 702. **Tsitsikamma Forest Inn**, Darnell St., tel: 042/541-1711, fax: 541-1669.
THE CRAGS 6602: *MODERATE:* (about 25 mi/40 km out of Storm's River on the N 2): **Forest Hall** (lovely historic country house), tel: 04 457/8869, fax: 8883.

PLETTENBERG BAY 6600: *LUXURY:* **The Plettenberg**, 40 Church St., PO Box 719, tel: 04 457/3-2030, fax: 3-2074. **Hunters Country House** (Silver), Pear Tree Farm, PO Box 454, tel: 04-457/7818, fax: 7878. *MODERATE:* **Beacon Island Resort** (Sun Hotel), Private Bag X1001, tel: 04 457/3-1120, fax: 3-3880. **Formosa Inn Country Hotel**, PO Box 121, tel: 04 457/3-2060, fax: 3-3343. *BUDGET:* **Bayview Hotel**, PO Box 1047, tel: 04 457/3-1961, fax: 3-2059.

KNYSNA 6570: *MODERATE:* **Knysna Protea Hotel**, PO Box 33, tel: 0445/2-2127, fax: 2-3568. **Yellowwood Lodge**, PO Box 2020, tel: 0445/82-5906, fax: 0445/2-4230. *BUDGET:* **Knysna Caboose**, PO Box 2044 tel: 0445/82-5850, fax: 82-5224.

SEDGEFIELD 6573: *MODERATE:* **Lake Pleasant Hotel**, Groenvlei, PO Box 2, tel: 04 455/3-1313, fax: 3-2040. **Lakeside Lodge**, PO Box 556, tel. and fax: 04 455/3-1844. *BUDGET:* **Island Lake Holiday Resort** (self-catering), PO Box 448, Wilderness 6560, tel. and fax: 0441/9 1194.

WILDERNESS 6560: *MODERATE:* **Karos Wilderness Hotel**, PO Box 6, tel: 0441/877-1110, fax: 877-0600. **Fairy Knowe Hotel**, PO Box 28, tel: 0441/877-1100, fax: 877-0364.

GEORGE 6530: *LUXURY:* **Fancourt Hotel & Country Club** (Golf hotel, national landmark, 2.5 mi/4 km N of the town center on the R 29), tel: 0441/70-8282, fax: 7605. *MODERATE:* **Hawthorndene Hotel**, Morning Glory Lane, PO Box 1, tel. and fax: 0441/74-4160 (ask for fax).

MOSSEL BAY 6500: *MODERATE:* **Old Post Office Tree Guest House**, PO Box 349, tel: 0444/91-3738, fax: 91-3104.

Tourist Information

Garden Route Tourist Information Centre, PO Box 1514, George 6530, tel: 0441/73-6355, fax: 74-6840. **Garden Route Accomodation Centre**. corner Union/Long St., PO Box 766, Knysna 6570. tel. and fax: 0445/2-1430. **Plettenberg Bay Business & Publicity Association**, PO Box 894, Plettenberg Bay 6600, tel: 04 457/3-4065, fax: 3-4066. **Knysna Publicity Association**, PO Box 87, Knysna 6570, tel: 0445/2-1610, fax: 2-1646. **George Tourist Information Centre**, PO Box 19, George 6530, tel: 0441/74-4000, fax: 73-5228. **Mossel Bay Marketing Association**, PO Box 25, Mossel Bay 6500, tel: 0444/91-2202.

OUDTSHOORN AND LITTLE KAROO
Accommodations

OUDTSHOORN 6620 *MODERATE:* **Kango Protea Hotel**, Baron van Reede St., PO Box 370, tel: 0443/22-6161, fax: 22-6772. **Holiday Inn Garden Court**, Baron van Reede St., PO Box 52, tel: 0443/22-2201, fax: 22-3003. *BUDGET:* **The Feather Inn**, 218 High St. PO Box 165, tel. and fax: 0443/29-1727. **Queens Hotel**, 218 High St., PO Box 19, tel: 0443/22-2101, fax: 22-2104.

PRINCE ALBERT 6930: *MODERATE:* **Swartberg Country House Hotel**, 77 Church St., tel: 04 436/332, fax: 383.

CALITZDORP 6660: *MODERATE:* **Die Dorpshuis**, Van Riebeeck St., tel. 04 437/3-3453. **Welgevonden Guest House**, PO Box 15, tel: 04437/33642, fax: 3-3603.

Museums and Sights

C.P. Nel Museum, Mon-Sat 8:30 am-1, 2-5 pm. **Ostrich farms:** guided tours (in several languages) daily every half-hour from 7:30 am-5 pm; tours last 1 1/2 to 2 hours. **Cango Crocodile Ranch and Cheetahland**, open daily 8 am-5 pm, hourly tours. **Cango Caves**, guided tours hourly in season (December to February and in April), 8 am - 5 pm; at other times every two hours between 9 am and 3 pm.

Tourist Information

Tourist Office Little Karoo, PO Box 1234, Oudtshoorn 6620, tel: 0443/22-6643, fax: 22-5007.

WINE COUNTRY
Accommodations

ROBERTSON 6705: *MODERATE:* **Avalon Grand Hotel**, 68 Barry St., PO Box 171, tel: 02 351/3272, fax: 6-1158.

WORCESTER 6850: *MODERATE:* **Cumberland Hotel**, PO Box 8, tel: 0231/7-2641, fax: 7-3613.

CERES 6835: *MODERATE:* **Belmont Hotel**, Porter St., tel. and fax: 0233/2-1150.

TULBAGH 6820: *MODERATE:* **De Oude Herberg**, 6 Church St. tel. and fax: 0236/30-0260.

PAARL 6038: *LUXURY:* **Grande Roche Hotel** (Silver), Plantasie St., PO Box 6038, tel: 02 211/63-2727, fax: 63-2220. *MODERATE:* **Goedemoed Country Inn**, Cecilia St. PO Box 331, tel: 02 211/61-1020, fax: 2-5430.

FRANSCHHOEK 7690: *LUXURY:* **Le Quartier Français**, Wilhelmina/Berg St., PO Box 237, tel: 02 212/2151, fax: 3105. *MODERATE:* **Swiss Farm Excelsior Hotel**, PO Box 54, tel: 02 212/2071, fax: 2177. **Le Ballon Rouge Guest House**, 12 Reservoir St., PO Box 344, tel: 02 212/2651, fax: 2651. *BUDGET:* **Huguenot Hotel**, Huguenot Rd., PO Box 27, tel: 02 212/2092.

STELLENBOSCH 7600: *LUXURY:* **Lanzerac Hotel** (Silber), Lanzerac Road, PO Box 4, Stellenbosch 7599, tel: 021/887-1132, fax: 887-2310. *MODERATE:* **d'Ouwe Werf Country Inn**, 30 Church St., tel: 887-4608, fax: 887-4626. **Dorpshuis**, 22 Dorp St., tel: 021/883-9881, fax: 883-9884. *BUDGET:* **Ryneveld Lodge**, 67 Ryneveld St., tel: 02 2317-4469, fax: 99-549.

Museums and Sights

WORCESTER: Kleinplasie Living Open Air Museum, daily 9:30 am-4:30 pm. **KWV Brandy Cellar:** guided tours Mon-Fri 9:30 & 11 am, 1:30 & 3:30 pm, Sat 9:30 & 11 am. **National Botanic Gardens**, daily 8 am-5 pm.

PAARL: Oude Pastorie, Mon-Fri 8 am-1, 2-5 pm, Sat 10 am-12, Sun 3-5 pm. **Afrikaans Language Museum**, Mon-Sat 9 am-5 pm. **KWV-Cellar**, guided tours (also in German; tours last 1 1/2 hours) Mon-Fri 9:30 & 11 am, 2:45 & 3:45 pm, Sat 10:30 am (Dec 1-Apr 30 also 11 am and 3:45 pm); tel: 02 211/2-3605.

FRANSCHHOEK: Huguenot Memorial Museum, Mon-Fri 9 am-5 pm, Sat 9 am-1, 2-5 pm, Sun 2-5 pm. **Boschendal**, Manor House, daily 11 am-4:30 pm; wine tastings and sales (also souvenirs) in Taphuis, Mon-Fri 8:30 am-4:30 pm, Sat 8:30 am-12:30 pm.

STELLENBOSCH: Kruithuis, Mon-Fri 9 am-1, 2-5 pm. **Dorp Museum**, Mon-Sat 9:30 am-5 pm, Sun 2-5 pm. **Libertas Parvas**, with the **Stellenryck Wijn Museum** and **Rembrandt van Rijn Art Gallery**, Mon-Fri 9 am-12:45 and 2-5 pm, Sat 10 am-1 and 2-5 pm, Sun 2:30-5:30 pm.

Tourist Information

Winelands Tourism Association, PO Box 19, Somerset werf 7130, tel: 024/51-4022, fax: 51-6207. **Robertson Publicity Association**, 54 Church St. Robertson 6705, tel: 02351/4437. **Worcester Publicity Association**, 75 Church Street, Worcester 6850, tel: 0231/7-1408, fax: 7-4678. **Tourist Information Ceres**, corner Voortrecker/Owen St., Ceres 6835, tel: 0233/6-1287. **Tulbagh Publicity Office**, 4 Church St. Tulbagh 6820, tel: 0236/30-1348. **Wellington Publicity Association**, 104 Main St., Wellington 7655, tel: 02 211/3-4604, fax: 3-4607. **Paarl Publicity Association**, 216 Main Rd., Paarl 7646, tel: 02 211/2-3829, **Wine Route**: tel. 02 211/2-3605. **Franschhoek Vineyards Wine Centre**, Main Rd., PO Box 280, Franschhoek 7690, tel: 02 212/3062, fax: 3440. **Stellenbosch Publicity Association**, 36 Market St., Stellenbosch 7600, tel: 021/883-3584, fax: 883-8017. **Stellenbosch Wine Route Office**, Doornbosch Centre, Strand Rd., tel: 021/886-4310. **Durbanville**: The Town Clerk, Main Road, Durbanville 7550, tel: 021/96-3020.

SOUTHWEST COAST AND FALSE BAY
Accommodations

SWELLENDAM 6740: *MODERATE:* **Swellengrebel Hotel**, 91 Voortrek St., PO Box 9, tel: 0291/4-1144, fax: 4-2453. *BUDGET:* **The Carlton Hotel**, 23 Voortrek St., tel: 0291/4-1120.

BREDASDORP 7280: *MODERATE:* **Arniston Hotel**, Beach Rd., Waenhuiskrans, PO Box 126, tel: 02 847/5-9000, fax: 5-9633.

HERMANUS 7200: *MODERATE:* **The Marine Hotel**, Marine Drive, PO Box 9, tel: 0283/2-1112, fax: 2-1533. **The Windsor Hotel**, PO Box 3, tel: 0283/2-3727. *BUDGET:* **Hermanus Youth Hostel**, 15 Church St., tel: 0283/2-1772 fax: 70-0004.

BETTY'S BAY 7141: *BUDGET:* **Hangklip Hotel**, PO Box 27, tel: 02 823/8700.

Museums and Sights

SWELLENDAM: Drostdy Museum, Swellengrebel St., Mon-Fri 9 - 5, Sat & Sun 10 am-4 pm.

HERMANUS: Old Harbour Museum, Mon-Fri 9 am-1, 2-4 pm, Sat 9 am-1 pm.

Rondevlei Bird Sanctuary, Perth Rd., Grassy Park, daily 8 am-5 pm.

Tourist Information

Swellendam Publicity Association, Voortrek St. PO Box 369, Swellendam 6740, tel: 0291/4-2770. **Overberg Tourism Association**, PO Box 258, Caledon 7230, tel: 0281/2-1511. **Hermanus Publicity Association**, PO Box 117, Hermanus 7200, tel. and fax: 0283/2-2629. **Hermanus Accomodation Centre**, 9 Myrtle Ave., tel. and fax: 0283/70-0004. **Captour**, Atlantic Rd., Muizenberg, tel: 021/788-1898, fax: 788-2269.

CAPE TOWN and CAPE PENINSULA
Telephone and fax area code: 021; postal code: 8000
Accommodations

LUXURY: **Mount Nelson Hotel** (Silver), 76 Orange St., Gardens, PO Box 2608, tel: 23-1000, fax: 24-7472. **Peninsula Hotel**, 313 Beach Road, Sea Point, tel: 439-8888, fax: 439-8886. **Cape Sun**, Strand St., PO Box 4532, tel: 23-8844, fax: 23-8875. **The Vineyard Hotel** (Silver), Colinton Road, Newlands 7725, tel: 64-2107, fax: 683-3365.

MODERATE: **Town House**, 60 Corporation St., PO Box 5053, tel: 45-7050, fax: 45-3891. **Victoria & Albert Hotel**, Waterfront, PO Box 16 157, tel: 419-6677, fax: 419-8955. **City Lodge**, Howard Place 7450, PO Box 124, tel: 685-7944, fax: 685-7997. **Holiday Inn Garden Court**, 10 Greenmarket Square, PO Box 3775, tel: 23-2040, fax: 23-3664. **Villa Lutzi**, 6 Rosmead Av., Oranjezicht, tel: 26-1468, fax: 26-1472.

BUDGET: **Breakwater Lodge**, Victoria & Albert Waterfront, PO Box 41 465, Seapoint 8060, tel: 406-1911, fax: 406-1070. **Zebra Crossing Travellers Lodge** (youth hostel), 82 New Church St., tel. and fax: 22-1265. **YMCA** (men and women under 30), 60 Queen Victoria St., PO Box 691, tel: 24-1247.

CONSTANTIA 8700: *LUXURY:* **The Cellars Hohenort Country House Hotel**, Hohenort Avenue, PO Box 270. *MODERATE:* **Southernwood**, 19 Avenue Bordeaux, tel: 021/794-3208, fax: 794-7551. **Alphen Hotel**, Alphen Drive, PO Box 35, Constantia 7848, tel: 794-5011, fax: 794-5710.

FISHHOEK 7975: *BUDGET:* **Avenue Hotel**, PO Box 22 161, tel: 021/82-6026, fax: 82-6080. **SIMON'S TOWN** 7995: *MODERATE:* **The Lord Nelson Inn**, tel: 021/86-1386, fax: 86-1009. **KOMMETJIE** 7975: *MODERATE:* **Kommetjie Inn**, PO Box 6, tel: 021/783-4230, fax: 783-1816. **HOUT BAY** 7800: *MODERATE:* **Hout Bay Manor**, Main Rd., PO Box 27 035, tel: 021/ 790-5960, fax: 790-4952

Restaurants

Most hotels have excellent restaurants. As in most major port cities, cuisines from around the world are offered in Cape Town; and the selection of fish and shellfish is marvelous. Here, furthermore, you'll find specialties of the Cape Province, which betray a distinctive Malay influence.

Biesmiellah Restaurant, Upper Wale St. (Malay quarter, closed Sun), tel: 23-0850 (Malay). **Aldo's**, Shop 153, Victoria Wharf (waterfront), tel: 21-7874. **Buccaneer**, 64 Orange St., tel: 24-4966 (steaks, seafood). **Hildebrand**, corner Strand St./ St. George's Mall, tel: 25-3385 (closed Sun). **Arlindo's**, Shop 155, Victoria Wharf, (waterfront) tel: 21-6888. **La Pasta**, 108 Beach Boulevard, Bloubergstrand, tel: 565-1591 (impressive view). **Peers**, Pierhead, Waterfront, tel: 21-7113 (closed Sun). **La Perla** (best lobster in Cape Town), Beach Rd., Sea Point, tel: 434-2471. **Kronendal** (closed Sun and Mon in winter), Main Rd., Hout Bay, tel: 790-1970. **Wharfside Grill**, Mariner's Wharf, Harbour Rd., Hout Bay, tel: 790-1100 (lobster, oysters, bouillabaisse). **Buitenverwachting** (closed Sun and Mon), Klein Constantia Road, Constantia, tel: 794-3522.

Museums and Sights

South African Maritime Museum, daily 10 am-5 pm. **Castle of Good Hope**, guided tours daily 10 and 11 am, 12, 2, & 3 pm; the museum closes at 4 pm. **Cultural History Museum**, Mon-Sat 9:30 am-4:30 pm. **South African Library**, Mon-Fri 9 am-6 pm, Sat 9 am-1 pm. **Houses of Parliament**, purchase tickets for the visitors' gallery when Parliament is in session in Room 12; at other times (July to January), guided tours Mon-Fri 11 am and 2 pm (register by phone: 403-2911). **South African National Gallery**, daily 10 am-5 pm. **Jewish Museum**, Tue and Thu 2-5 pm, Sun 10 am-12:30 pm. **South African Museum**, daily 10 am-5 pm. **Old Town House**, Mon-Fri 8:30 am-5 pm, Sat 9 am-12:30 pm. **Koopmans De Wet House**, Tue-Sat 9:30 am-4:30 pm. **Bookaap Museum**, Tue-Sat and holidays 9:30 am-4:30 pm. – **Table Mountain Cable Car:** May to November daily 8:30 am-6 pm, December to April 8 am-10 pm; tel: 24-5148. Table Mountain is illuminated after dark: from early September to early December every weekend until midnight; from then until Dec. 17, every night until midnight; from Dec. 17 to Jan. 10 every night; from Jan. 10 to the end of May, every night until midnight. **Kirstenbosch Botanical Gardens**, April-August 8 am-6 pm, Sept. to March 8 am-7 pm. **Mineral World Topstones**, Simon's Town and Waterfront, Mon-Fri 8:45 am-4:45 pm, Sat and Sun 9 am-5:30 pm. **Simon's Town Museum**, Tue-Fri 9 am-4 pm, Sat 10 am-1 pm. **World of Birds**, Valley Rd., Hout Bay, daily 9 am-6 pm.

Tourist Information

Tourist Information Centre (TIC), **Captour** (local information, Cape Peninsula) and **Western Cape Tourism Association** (regional information), Adderley Street, tel: 418-5214, fax: 418-5228, daily 9 am-5 pm. **SATOUR**, 10th floor, Golden Acre, Private Bag X9108, tel: 21-6274, fax: 419-4875. **Automobile Association**, AA House, 7 Hammerschlag Way (Foreshore), tel: 21-1550. **Tourist Assistance Unit** of the police, Tulbagh Square, tel. 418-2853.

ATLANTIC COAST
Accommodations

West Coast National Park, register with the National Parks Board.
SALDANHA BAY 7395: *MODERATE:* **Saldanha Bay Protea Hotel**, 51B Main Street, PO Box 70, tel: 02 281/4-1264, fax: 4-4093.
LANGEBAAN 7357: *MODERATE:* **The Farmhouse**, 5 Egret St., PO Box 160, tel: 02287/2-2062, fax: 2-1980. **Club Mykonos**, Private Bag X2, tel: 02 287/2-2101, fax: 2-2303.
CITRUSDAL 7340: *MODERATE:* **Cedarberg Hotel**, Voortrekker St., PO Box 37, tel: 022/921-2221, fax: 921-2704.
CLANWILLIAM 8135: *MODERATE:* **Clanwilliam Hotel**, PO Box 4, tel: 027/482-1101, fax: 482-2228.
NORTH PAARL 7623: *MODERATE:* **Kagga Kamma**, PO Box 7143, tel: 02211/63-8334, fax: 63-8383.
LAMBERT'S BAY 8130: *MODERATE:* **Marine Protea Hotel**, Voortrekker St., PO Box 249, tel: 027/432-1126, fax: 432-1036.
VANRHYNSDORP 8170: *BUDGET:* **Van Rhijn Inn**, Voortrekker St., tel: 02 727/9-1003.

Tourist Information

Tourist Information, **Langebaan Municipality**, The Town Clerk, PO Box 11, Langebaan 7357, tel: 02 287/2-2115, fax: 2-2825. **West Coast Publicity Association**, Oorlogsvlei, PO Box 139, Saldanha 7395, tel: 02 281/4-2088, fax: 4-4240. **Citrusdal Information Centre**, Private Bag X5, Citrusdal 7340, tel: 02 662/610. **Tourist Information**, PO Box 15, Lamberts Bay 8130, tel: 026 732/635, fax: 452. **Tourist Information**, The Town Clerk, Municipality, Church St., Vanrhynsdorp 8170, tel: 02 727/9-1030. For information on Namaqualand, see the Northern Cape chapter.

NORTHERN CAPE

NAMAQUALAND
RICHTERSVELD
AUGRABIES FALLS NAT. PARK
UPINGTON
KALAHARI GEMSBOK
NATIONAL PARK
EXCURSION TO KURUMAN
KIMBERLEY

NORTHERN CAPE

The Northern Cape province is at once the largest and the most sparsely populated of South Africa's new administrative districts. Though the province occupies some 29.7% of South Africa's total area, only 1.9% of its population lives here.

The cold Benguela current, which runs northwards along the coast, influences the climate considerably, causing both extreme dryness and frequent fog in the coastal region. Rainfall in Port Nolloth is 2.5 inches (63 mm) per year, while the temperature only reaches 62°-68° F (17°-20° C), although it is closer to the Equator. North of the Orange River, the seemingly endless plains of the upper Karoo, which adjoin the region to the east, gradually give way to the Kalahari, which is largely covered in reddish sand. The region's dryness is due less to the low annual rainfall of 8 inches (200 mm) than to the rain's quick absorption into the ground; there's plenty of water in the subsoil. In the province's eastern section the high plains are interrupted by several mountain ranges, between which lie

Preceding pages: A forest of kokerboom (quiver tree, or tree aloe) near Kenhardt. Left: Sheep auction at Upington.

enormous mineral resources, including iron and manganese ores, precious and semi-precious stones – sometimes just below the surface. The enormous manganese reserves are thought to be the largest in the world. The center for ore extraction is the territory between Kuruman and Postmasburg; in 1973, a railway line was built from here to the port of Saldanha on the Atlantic coast, from where the ore is shipped.

In the northeast, the land sustains extensive cattle farming, but settlements drop off progressively as you move northwest; you only find a few scattered karakul sheep farms. An exception to this is the extensive irrigated area near the Oranje, with Upington at its center.

Though the region has relatively good traffic connections and offers good accommodations, it has not developed into a major tourist region. However, those who do visit the province will encounter a unique area unlike any other South African province: a piece, one might say, of the genuine Africa.

NAMAQUALAND

Namaqualand is a rolling, barren, semidesert area stretching from the Atlantic coast across the Great Escarpment up to the high plateau, where it runs into

181

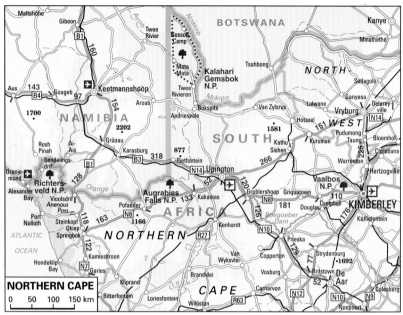

Bushmanland. Its southern edge, at **Vanrhynsdorp**, is still within the Western Cape province, but extends northwards into the increasingly arid region as far as the lower Orange River. Originally the area was inhabited by a handful of nomadic Bushmen and Hottentots, who were already away of the area's deposits of copper ore, and extracted them in small amounts. Whites did not settle in the area until the mid-19th century, when they began the systematic extraction of copper ore.

Namaqualand can turn into a great attraction in spring if there's been adequate rain and the hot, dry desert winds let up. Between mid-August and the end of September, hundreds of miles of this boulder-strewn, barren land are transformed into a rich, colorful carpet of flowers. The predominant flowers are Namaqua daisies (*Dimorhoteca sinuata*),

Right: Namaqualand's generally sparse vegetation is due to sandy, stony soil and an extremely dry climate.

members of the compositae plant family, which occur in white and every imaginable shade of yellow all the way through to deep orange. Multi-colored mesembryanthemums and other flowering plants are also common. These are seen to best advantage on sunny days between 1 and 4 pm.

It's not easy to predict beforehand exactly when and in what numbers the flowers will be in bloom. Most of the towns between Vanrhynsdorp and Springbok make suitable starting points for flower-viewing excursions. As a number of factors, however, influence the best flowering times and places from year to year, it's advisable to ask for advice; local residents will know where the best places to go are in a given season. The area east of the N 7 between Kamieskroon and Springbok seems to be particularly favored on a more or less regular basis. Because Namaqualand is particularly popular at these times, advance hotel booking is recommended. From June 1 to October 31, the Tourist

Information Center in Cape Town (Adderley Street) runs a "flower line" for anyone seeking more information.

Springbok, with 8,000 inhabitants, is the economic and administrative center of the region. Its history is closely linked to that of the copper mining industry, which originated here in 1862 but has since shifted to Okiep and Nababeep. Copper-generated wealth has led to the building of roads, attractive residential settlements and recreational areas in an otherwise inhospitable region. If you'd like to check out the Diamond Coast, travel up to Port Nolloth, where the first diamonds were found in 1925. To get there, drive to Steinkopf, 32 miles (52 km) north of Springbok, then continue westwards. After 11 miles (18 km), the **Anenous Pass** (3,106 feet / 950 m above sea level) offers a fine panorama of the coastal plain, provided it's not obscured by fog (a frequent occurence). **Port Nolloth**, once a shipping point for copper, is now a fishing port (with crawfish the main catch) and a small resort.

RICHTERSVELD

If you have a sense of adventure, the curiosity to seek out new experiences, and don't mind roughing it a bit, then you won't regret a visit to the 401,239 acres (162,445 hectares) of rugged, mountainous desert which was proclaimed the reserve of **Richtersveld National Park** in 1991. With this park, the National Parks Board is exploring new avenues. One cornerstone is a contract between the Parks Board and the inhabitants of the area, some 2,000 Namaqua farmers and herdsmen: the Namaqua can continue to keep their herds here, while the National Parks Board is allowed to protect the ecology of this unique countryside, safeguarding it from overgrazing and other damage. The Park is run by a Management Planning Committee, comprised of four members of the National Parks Board and five Namaqua from the Richtersveld Community. Two diamond mines on the banks of the Orange have also been allowed to continue operations.

Richtersveld was named after a German missionary who came to this region in 1830. The road along the so-called "Diamond Coast" was closed to the public for decades after the discovery of the first diamonds. Today it is open as far as **Alexander Bay**, center of the diamond mining industry, which you reach after 53 miles (85 km). The state-run company Alexcor mines the highest-quality diamonds for jewelry here. Oranjemund (Namibia), on the other side of the Orange, is not accessible. The river here forms South Africa's northern border, as well as the northern and eastern borders of the National Park.

A sandy gravel track leads to **Sendelingsdrif,** some 58 miles (93 km) away, where the park authorities have their offices in the Reuning mine. As the number of visitors and vehicles is limited, advance registration is a must; only four-wheel-drive vehicles are allowed. Since there are no accommodations or other facilities in the park, make sure to bring in enough food and above all enough water and gas with you (the last chance to shop is in Port Nolloth or Alexander Bay). If you're planning to cook, you'll also have to bring along firewood or a gas cooker; also remember a flashlight and – very importantly – a bag for garbage. Campsites do exist, but are as yet without facilities. Beware of poisonous scorpions! There is a speed limit of 25 mph (40 km/h), and driving is forbidden after dark. As there are, as yet, no accurate maps, only vague sketches of the area, it's not a bad idea to rent a four-wheel drive vehicle from the park authorities, with an experienced Namaqua ranger as a guide. Individuals traveling alone are not admitted to the reserve.

Though this may sound off-putting, your endeavors will be rewarded by a unique landscape: rugged, multicolored mountain ranges with peaks up to 3,925 feet (1,200 m) high. Erosion has sculpted

Above: The Orange River is the region's most important water supply. Right: The cascades of Augrabies Falls.

bizarre formations from the ancient volcanic, metamorphic and sedimentary rock. Photographers will have plenty to keep them occupied – especially in the early evening.

The main attraction is the exceptional and diverse vegetation, including succulents which only occur in this area; of these, the kokerboom or quiver tree (*Aloe dichotoma*) and the halfmens (*Pachypodium namaquanum*) are among the most noticeable. The mountain area in the west receives winter rain and coastal fog, making it somewhat wetter than the region along the Orange in the east, where it only rains occasionally – an annual average of 0.2-5 inches (5-125 mm) – generally in the summer during thunderstorms. While daytime temperatures can reach 104° F (40° C) in summer (there is no shade), nights can be pleasantly cool and even, in winter, very cold. Strong winds and sandstorms are a common occurrence. The best time to visit is mid-August to mid-October.

AUGRABIES FALLS NATIONAL PARK

From Springbok, the N 7 leads northeast towards Upington, some 240 miles (387 km) away, through the flat, dry, hot region of **Bushmanland**. At first, the region on either side of the road can still, in spring, boast the gorgeous wildflowers of Namaqualand; but as you go farther east, the land becomes increasingly barren and stony. After 185 miles (299 km), the R 359 branches off to the left at **Kakamas**, and leads a further 18 miles (29 km) to the entrance of Augrabies Falls National Park.

The unparalleled riverine landscape on either side of the Orange River, which splits here into several branches, has been a protected area since 1966. Roughly 500 million years ago, tectonic forces thrust an interior plateau above the earth's surface, and the Orange River began to wear

a deep ravine into the underlying granite and gneiss. It now crashes down in several cascades totaling 625 feet (191 m) in height – the main fall alone is some 183 feet (56 m) – into the 11-mile-long (18 km) canyon-like gorge. When the river is carrying a lot of water, especially in late summer, additional falls develop over the sides. The ravine is then filled with clouds of spray, and the place truly earns its name, which derives from a Bushman word meaning "place of great noise." However, since the Gariep Dam and P. K. le Roux Dam were built farther upriver, the volume of water has been more evenly regulated.

The park, which originally covered about 22,230 acres (9,000 hectares), was recently expanded to encompass 203,565 acres (82,415 hectares). Only part of it, however, is open to the public. Black rhinos have been resettled in the remaining area since 1985, and could become one of the park's special attractions. The annual rainfall here is 4.2 inches (107 mm) at most; summers are extremely hot, while

in winter the temperature can drop down to freezing point at night. There are three well-marked walking trails, all of which can be completed in an hour, and protected lookout points reveal the great diversity of this unique country. Allow 3 days for the **Klipspringer Hiking Trail**, which you can only walk between April 1 and September 30.

Countless lizards, geckos and agamas can be spotted darting about the rocks. The numerous rock dassie here have become accustomed to tourists; in addition, the park is home to springbok, kudus, and other small antelopes, including the graceful klipspringer, as well as baboons and suricate. Many types of aloe grow here, including increasing numbers of kokerboom, or tree aloe, along the banks of the tributaries, as do a number of green shrubs, such as stunted willows, olives, acacias, and the like, all of which

Above: In this sparsely-populated region, you seldom meet other people. Right: Moonrise over Upington.

form a vivid contrast to the dryness of the surrounding countryside. The best time to visit the park is between March and October. Open all year round, the rest camp has air-conditioned accommodation (with bathroom and kitchen), a restaurant, and a small store. There's a 20% reduction for anyone visiting the park between November 1 and the end of June (except during school vacations). There is a well-equipped campsite.

UPINGTON

From Kakamas, the well-traveled N 8 runs parallel to the Orange River, which is used intensively for irrigation along this stretch. The lush green fields form a fascinating contrast to the dry, rocky surroundings; the red dunes sometimes extend right up to the farmland. A large variety of semiprecious stones, including rose quartz, amethyst, tourmaline, and jasper, can be found here.

Upington lies 2,632 feet (805 m) above sea level on the northern bank of

the Orange River. Summers can be extremely hot here, but from April through October, the weather is virtually ideal: sunny during the day, cool in the early morning and evening, but with temperatures sometimes below freezing at night. About a quarter of the low annual precipitation falls in March.

The town has about 55,000 inhabitants (predominantly colored), and is the commercial center and traffic hub of the **Gordonia** district. A spacious town with broad streets, it offers everything you would expect for a comfortable stay and makes a good base from which to visit the two neighboring national parks. There is an extremely helpful **Tourist Information Office** in the foyer of the town library on Town Square, which can provides information on local sights as well as special events or excursions. The latter might include a visit to the Karakul Research Station; the South African Dried Fruit Cooperative, which produces and packs raisins (the second-largest in the world); or South Africa's north-ernmost winery, the large Oranjerivier Wynkelders.

Founded as a mission station named Olyvenhoutsdrift in 1871, the town developed quickly and was given its present name in 1884 after the then-British prime minister of the Cape Province. Since 1890, the abundant waters of the Orange River have been used to create an extremely fertile irrigated area, an oasis stretching some 174 miles (280 km) along the river banks in an almost desert-like region, which makes an impressive picture indeed when seen from an airplane. Wheat, corn, lucerne, cotton, grapes (for raisins, but more recently also for wine), fruit, peas and lentils are cultivated here. Karukul sheep are bred in the barren land around this; in Upington, their hides are industrially processed into pelts for coats and similar purposes.

On one of the Orange's islands, **Olyvenhoutsdrift**, which lies south of the town center and is linked to the mainland by a bridge, the city has built a holiday center with accommodation (cottages

and rondavels), caravan and camping sites, a restaurant, and sport and leisure facilities. Pride of the town is the **Palm Boulevard**, extending for more than half a mile (1 km). Upstream, Africa's second-longest railway bridge, measuring 3,505 feet (1,072 m), crosses the Orange River.

The former mission station and its church have been converted into a natural and cultural history museum (**Kalahari Oranje Museum**). An interesting collection of local minerals is housed in the library building.

KALAHARI GEMSBOK NATIONAL PARK

Allow at least three days for a visit to this national park, which is truly an unforgettable experience. Take the R 360 north out of Upington; the road is paved

Above: The sociable weavers' nests often cause problems. Right: South Africa's heraldic animal: the springbok.

for roughly half of the journey. The 222-mile (358 km) stretch to the park entrance offers very few opportunities to stock up on refreshments or water; take note, because, given the extreme heat, you'll need plenty of the latter.

Apart from a few scattered farms and the odd vehicle you pass on the road, you are virtually alone in a seemingly endless landscape characterized by white and rust-red dunes. Vegetation is largely semi-desert or occasionally park savanna with a palette of shades of green unfamiliar to non-African eyes. The light has an indescribable quality, and fantastic cloud formations soar, within it, over the broad circle of the horizon.

The huge thatched nests of the sociable weaver bird are seen on trees and even telegraph poles. From **Bokspits** (where there's a motel with swimming pool), the road follows the dry river bed of the Nossob for the last 37 miles (60 km) to the park entrance; down the middle of this river bed runs the Botswana border.

Twee Rivieren is both the entrance and one of the rest camps of **Kalahari Gemsbok National Park**. Created in 1931 and covering 5,952 square miles (9,600 square km), the park protects an incomparable ecosystem, a wilderness which has remained more or less intact. The reserve lies around 3,270 feet (1,000 m) above sea level, between the Namibia border in the west and the Botswana border in the east. On the Botswana side of the border, however, the park continues as the **Gemsbok National Park** (proclaimed a reserve in 1934). Not open to the public, it protects a further 16,120 square miles (26,000 sq. km), making the entire area larger than Kruger Park. There is no border between these two sections, so the game can roam around freely in an area larger than Belgium, making this one of Africa's largest game reserves.

The section within South Africa is flanked by two dry river valleys, the **Nossob** in the east and the **Auob** in the west,

both of which have their source east of Windhoek in Namibia and come together 4 miles (7 km) north of Twee Rivieren. They seldom carry water, but there is sufficient water below the surface to sustain the diverse and dense vegetation. A familiar sight is the unusual-looking camel-thorn tree (*Acacia erioloba*), reaching heights of 50 feet (15 m) and characterized by its sweeping, shade-giving branches. Water pumps driven by windmills keep the water-holes supplied with water. In the area between the river valleys, dunes up to 60 feet (18 m) high, dotted with shrub and tree vegetation, alternate with sand dunes wholly free of vegetation, open plains, and the occasional salt pan.

Both river beds are followed by roads, which, though unpaved and therefore dusty, are kept in good condition. The Auob road – which has more vegetation than the other road – leads, after 74 miles (120 km), to the **Mata Mata** rest camp on the Namibia border, which is closed at this point. The **Nossob Rest Camp** is reached after 102 miles (165 km) on the Nossob road; the road ends some 87 miles (140 km) further on at a picnic spot on the border to Namibia (also closed). Much further south there is one link between the two roads – 72 miles (117 km) north of Twee Rivieren on the Nossob road; 36 miles (58 km) on the Auob road. Drivers must keep to the roads and may only leave their cars at designated (picnic) spots. There speed limit is 31 mph (50 km/h).

Apart from the oryx or gemsbok antelope, which gave the park its name, you also encounter large herds of springbok, blue wildebeest and other types of antelope. You can also occasionally sight a Kalahari lion: larger than its counterparts in Kruger Park, it also has a darker mane and its coat is duller in color. Cheetahs, leopards, wild dogs, hyenas and small mammals such as the suricate are sometimes seen too. There are more than 200 species of birds in the park, but the sociable weaver is the most conspicuous on account of its large, intricate nests,

which can house up to 50 breeding pairs. Ostriches also live here. Although the large secretary bird, which only occurs in Africa, is usually seen on the ground, it can in fact fly, and builds its nests in tall trees. You can also occasionally spot eagles, vultures, hawks, bustards and many smaller birds.

The three rest camps offer pleasant accommodation; the one in Twee Rivieren even has a pool and restaurant. All three have stores as well as gas stations with gas and diesel fuel. The park is open all year round, but the best game-viewing period is from February to May when the vegetation is green. Daytime temperatures in this season may be high, but there are generally thunderstorms in the afternoons, which cool things off. As accommodation tends to be fully booked during school vacations, you should reserve in

Above: The red sand dunes of the Kalahari glow after a rainshower. Right: Wildebeest and springbok in Gemsbok National Park, Kalahari.

advance. Advance precautions against malaria are essential. If it is extremely hot, do take adequate water supplies and emergency rations with you on driving trips into the park, in case you break down and have to wait for help.

EXCURSION TO KURUMAN

Anyone traveling from Upington to Kimberley (249 miles / 401 km) or Johannnesburg – anyone, in short, driving east – can, although this part of the province is not particularly interesting, still find plenty of interesting places to visit along the way. The direct route to Kimberley is via the N 8 / N 10 which leaves Upington south of the Orange River in an easterly/southeasterly direction. Some 72 miles (116 km) before Groblershoop, the N 8 branches off to the east and crosses the Orange a little above the **Boegoeberg Dam** (campsite, fishing), a reservoir created to irrigate the valley. Here, the N 8 leads through an area rich in game; road signs and maps indicate to drivers the

animals which might be about. Kudus are especially common.

Some 84 miles (136 km) past Groblershoop you come to **Griquatown** (**Griekwastad**), founded around 1800 as "Klaarwater" by the Griqua people, a Hottentot tribe who migrated here from the Southwestern Cape province. The London Missionary Society set up a mission station in the town as early as 1802. Mary Moffat was born here, later to become David Livingstone's wife.

Vaalbos National Park, created in 1986, lies 37 miles (60 km) west of Kimberley, north of the N 8. Extending over 89 square miles (227 sq. km), the park is not yet open to the public: the vegetation is to be given the chance to regenerate; and black rhinos, buffalo and other game have been resettled here.

If you drive east out of Upington on the N 14, you come, after 130 miles (210 km), to two recent settlements. **Sishen** was not founded until 1953, when people arrived to start mining the region's huge reserves of iron ore; **Kathu** was established during the construction of the rail link to Saldanha in 1973. In 1980, the two settlements were merged. The area north of here has been a center for manganese mining since 1958; its manganese reserves are the largest in the world.

Kuruman, some 31 miles (50 km) further east, is a pretty little town at the foot of a low range of hills; today, it's the center of an important cattle-breeding area, and asbestos is also mined in the region. The town owes its existence in this extremely dry area to a natural spring, which has broken through the bedrock layer of dolerite here to emerge, in the middle of the park, as a picturesque pool known as "the Eye." It yields an amazing 20 million liters of water a day, thereby supplying water for the town and feeding both the Kuruman River and two four-mile (6 km) irrigation channels. Kuruman became famous because of its mission station, founded in 1821, where the missionary Robert Moffat worked until 1870. It was from here that David Livingstone (who married Moffat's

daughter in 1845) set off on his pioneering explorations into the African interior, from here that Robert Moffat explored Matabeleland (now Zimbabwe). Moffat translated the Bible into Tswana – which had previously had no written form – and printed it on a simple press. The church, built between 1831-38, holds 1,000 people and has incredible acoustics; it has been a national landmark since 1938.

On the R 31 toward Kimberley (148 miles/238 km away), just after Danielskuil, you'll come to the Finsch Diamond Mine, which belongs to the De Beers concern. The mine started its (open-pit) operations in 1965, and is the largest in the country today. In 1869 the first diamonds were found in the river gravel of the Vaal near **Barkly West**. The town, which today still has something of its original "diamond rush" atmosphere, became the headquarters of the British col-

ony Griqualand West in 1870. People still try their luck during the dry months (June through September), but tend, these days, to find more semiprecious stones (tiger eyes) than diamonds. In the **Mining Commissioner's Museum**, you can learn more about the diamond-rush years.

KIMBERLEY

The capital of the Northern Cape province lies some 3,917 feet (1,198 feet) above sea level on the highveld. After the first diamonds were found here in 1871, other miners arrived on the scene. Their efforts resulted in the largest crater ever made by man, the "Big Hole." The local miners' camp, New Rush, quickly grew into a town which was named for the then-British colonial minister in 1873. By 1889, the Big Hole was already 1,308 feet (400 m) deep. As it was impossible to continue the work with the open-pit method, the work was mechanized, shafts were constructed, and in 1892 the first winding tower was set up.

Above: The "Big Hole" left by diamond miners in Kimberley. Right: Inside the Kimberley Mine Museum.

Kimberley was the first town in the southern hemisphere with electric street lighting and an electric tram. Shortly afterwards, South Africa's first stock exchange opened for business. Henriette Stockdale, an Anglican nun, founded the first nurses' school, and in 1891, thanks to her, South Africa recognized nursing as a profession – the first country in the world to do so. During the Boer War, the town was under siege by the Boers for 154 days. In 1912, South Africa's first flying school was created here. The Kimberley School of Mines, founded by De Beers, predated the renowned University of Witwatersrand in Johannesburg.

A second center which grew up around Bultfontein was merged with Kimberley in 1912, and Ernest Oppenheimer was elected its first mayor. The story of its foundings and its vast wealth have brought Kimberley worldwide renown. It is headquarters of the diamond cartel which controls 80% of the world's diamond production; and it was also this area which paved the way for the mining industry around Johannesburg and Witwatersrand, which laid the foundations for the development of South Africa's industry and wealth.

Unlike other South African cities, Kimberley did not develop as the result of clear, organized city planning. The city center around **Market Square** is surrounded by small, narrow, winding streets where you can still occasionally see houses from the early period. The **Information Office** is housed in **City Hall** which was completed in 1899. From here, you can ride a historical **tram** (dating from 1913) to the **Big Hole**, which is now part of the **Kimberley Mine Museum,** as is the winding tower (completed in 1892). The hole, which had reached a depth of 3,597 feet (1,100 m) when the mine closed in 1914, is partly filled with water today. It is 1,547 feet (473 m) in diameter, with a circumference of 5,232 feet (1,600 m). Looking down into this gigantic hole from the viewing platform, it is difficult to imagine how such enormous amounts of "blue ground" – 25 mil-

lion tons by 1914 – were moved by hand, hauled up by means of a veritable spider's web of ropes and pulleys. In the museum, you can see photos of this, as well as newspaper clippings from around the world reporting on diamond fever and life in Kimberley. There is also a collection of diamonds of varying shapes, colors and sizes, including the largest uncut diamond ever found (616 carats). Cecil Rhodes' private railway carriage, or reconstructed sections of street with houses, a church, stores, a pub, Barnato's "Boxing Academy," workshops, and more, peopled by nearly life-sized mannequins, recreate something of the atmosphere of the days of diamond fever.

The **Alexander McGregor Memorial Museum** at the center of town (Chapel Street), not only houses some prehistoric finds, but also has an interesting collection of rocks and minerals. In the **African**

Above: Memorial to the diamond miners in the Oppenheimer Memorial Gardens, Kimberley.

Library (9 Du Toitspan Road), there's an excellent collection of Africana as well as the original Bible which missionary Robert Moffat translated into Tswana and the press he used to print it on.

Central feature of the **Oppenheimer Memorial Gardens** is a fountain-cum-memorial for Kimberley's diamond miners; it features five life-sized figures, each holding up a diamond. The nearby **Harry Oppenheimer Building,** in which all South Africa's diamonds are graded and valued, is not open to the public. Also in the vicinity, the **William Humphreys Art Gallery** displays, in addition to a collection of paintings by Dutch, English and French artists, works by South African painters.

The new **McGregor Museum**, a marvelous Victorian-era building, is between Egerton and Atlas Street near the border of one-time Beaconsfield (the original border stone still exists). Rhodes intended this house as a sanatorium; it later became a hotel. Today it is a museum with collections of cultural and religious history.

The **Duggan-Cronin Gallery** is well worth a visit. It displays a unique collection of more than 8,000 photos taken between 1919 and 1939 by an Irishman named Alfred Martin Duggan-Cronin, who emigrated to the country in 1897. He worked in the mine himself and took photographs of the blacks who poured into the area from all over the country looking for work. Historically and ethnologically, as well as artistically, the photographs are true treasures; capturing their subjects in traditional tribal dress and regalia, they preserve many details of traditions that have since, irrevocably, been lost.

From Kimberley, you can get to Johannesburg on the N 12 through the Northwestern Province (289 miles / 467 km), or by taking the N 8 to Bloemfontein and then the N 1 through the Free State, a distance of 328 miles (592 km).

NORTHERN CAPE
Transportation

Bus: Among the local bus routes from Upington (Mainliner, four times a week), the ones to Cape Town (10 hours) also stop at Vanrhynsdorp and Citrusdal; Springbok lies on the Cape Town/Windhoek route. The trip from Upington to Johannesburg (via Kuruman) takes 8 1/2 hrs., to Windhoek 10 hrs. Greyhound links Upington and Kimberley (4 hrs.) with Bloemfontein (6 1/2 hrs.) and Durban (15 1/2 hrs.), Kimberley with Pretoria/Johannesburg (7 1/2-9 1/2 hrs.). Kimberley also lies on many of Translux's long-distance routes: to Cape Town via Beaufort West (12 1/2 hrs.); Johannesburg (5 hrs.), to Knysna (11 hrs., via Oudtshoorn, Mossel Bay, George).

Train: Upington and Kimberley are on the Johannesburg/Windhoek train route; Kimberley is also on the main Cape Town/Johannesburg line, which the Blue Train also uses.

Air: South African Express has taken over from SAA the regular flights to and from Upington and Kimberley. National Airlines runs regular flights between Namaqualand (Springbok, Alexander Bay) and Cape Town Mon-Fri; and two flights a week between Sishen and Johannesburg (Lanseria). The airports at Upington (4 mi/7 km) and Kimberley (7 mi/12 km from the city center) can only be reached by taxi or rental car.

Richtersveld Challenge, PO Box 142, Springbok 8240, tel: 0251/2-1905, fax: 8-1460, offers five-day tours into Richtersveld (with Land Rovers and an optional 28-mi/45-km hike; qualified, certified guides; everything except bedding is provided).

Accommodations

SPRINGBOK 8240: *BUDGET:* **Kokerboom Motel** (at the edge of town), PO Box 340, tel: 0251/2-2685, fax: 2-2257. **Springbok Hotel**, Van Riebeeck St. PO Box 46, tel: 0251/2-1161, fax: 2-2257. **Springbok Lodge** (quite renowned; permanent collection of rocks and minerals), PO Box 26, tel: 0251/2-1321, fax: 2-2718. **Masonic Hotel**, Van Riebeeck St., PO Box 9, tel: 0251/2-1505.

PORT NOLLOTH 8280: *BUDGET:* **Scotia Inn**, PO Box 9, tel: 0255/8353.

AUGRABIES 8874: **Augrabies Falls Hotel**, PO Box 34, tel: 0020, ask for 18.

UPINGTON 8800: *MODERATE:* **Upington Protea Hotel**, 24 Schroeder St. PO Box 13, tel. and fax: 054/2-5414. **Oasis Protea Lodge**, 26 Schroeder St.PO Box 1981, tel. and fax: 054/31-1125. **Oranje**, Scott St., tel: 054/2-4177, fax: 2-3612. **Die Eiland Resort**, Private Bag X 60003, tel: 054/25211 (chalets and campsites).

KURUMAN 8460: *MODERATE:* **Eldorado Motel**, Main Street, PO Box 313, tel: 05 373/2-

2191, fax: 2-2191. *BUDGET:* **Grand Hotel**, 15 Beare St., PO Box 2, tel: 01 471/2-1148.

BARKLY WEST 8377: *BUDGET:* **Queens Hotel**, PO Box 17, tel: 05 352/, ask for 85.

KIMBERLEY 8300: *MODERATE:* **Holiday Inn Garden Court**, 120 Du Toitspan Road, PO Box 635, tel: 0531/3-1751, fax: 2-1814. **Savoy Hotel**, De Beers Rd., tel: 0531/2-6211, fax: 2-7021. **Hotel Kimberlite**, 162 George Street, Kimberley 8301, tel: 0531/81-1967.

BUDGET: **Kemo Hotel**, Aster Rd., PO Box 465, tel: 0531/4-1341. **Kimberley Youth Hostel**, Bloemfontein Rd., tel: 0531/2-8577.

Accommodation for Augrabies Falls National Park and Kalahari Gemsbok Park (**Twee Rivieren, Nossob Camp** and **Mata Mata**): National Parks Board, Pretoria.

Museums and Sights

UPINGTON: **Kalahari Oranje Museum**, weekdays 8 am-1:30 and 2-5 pm.

KIMBERLEY: **Kimberley Mine Museum**, daily 8 am-6 pm. **Alexander McGregor Memorial Museum**, Mon-Fri 9 am-5 pm, Sat 9 am-1 pm, Sun 2-5 pm. **African Library**, Mon-Fri 8 am-12:45, 2-4:30 pm. **William Humphrey Art Gallery**, Mon-Sat 10 am-1, 2-5 pm, Sun 2-5 pm. **McGregor Museum**, Mon-Sat 9 am-5 pm, Sun 2-5 pm. **Duggan-Cronin Gallery**, Mon-Fri 9 am-5 pm, Sat 9 am-1, 2-5 pm, Sun 2-5 pm. You can visit the **Bultfontein Mine** (De Beers) Mon-Fri, 9-11 am (to register for tours, call 0531/2-9651). The historic **Kimberley Tram** runs daily 9 am-4 pm.

BARKLY WEST: Museum, Mon-Fri 8 am - 4:30 pm.

Tourist Information

Telephone information (June 1-Oct. 31) about the flowers in Namaqualand: 021/418-3705.

Tourist Information, The Town Clerk, PO Box 17, Springbok 8340, tel: 0251/2-2071. **The Public Relations Officer Alexkor**, Private Bag X5, Alexander Bay 8290, tel: 256/360. **Tourist Information**, The Town Clerk, Main Rd. Port Nolloth 8280, tel: 0255/8230. **The Warden, Richtersveld National Park**, PO Box 406 Alexander Bay 8290, tel. and fax: 0256/506 (office: Reuning Mine, Sendelingsdrif).

Tourist Information Office, Town Square (Public Library), Upington 8800, tel: 054/2-6911. **Kimberley Tourist Information**, corner Old Main/Transvaal Rd., Private Bag X5030, Kimberley 8300, tel: 0531/806-2645.

SATOUR, Suite 620, Flaxley House, Du Toitspan Rd., Private Bag X5017, Kimberley 8300, tel: 0531/3-1434, fax: 81-2937.

Automobile Association, AA House, 13 New Main St., Kimberley 8300, tel: 0531/2-5207.

FREE STATE

BLOEMFONTEIN

GOLDEN GATE

HIGHLANDS NATIONAL PARK

DAMS

FREE STATE

At the heart of South Africa, between the Vaal River in the north and the Orange River in the south, lies the province of Free State. It takes up 10.6% of the country's total land area, but is home to only 6.9% of the population of whom 56% speak Sesotho and 14% Afrikaans. This was the first area beyond the Orange River to be settled by whites in the course of the Great Trek; it was an independent Boer state from 1854-1910, and after that became the province of Orange Free State, since 1995 named Free State. The capital was and still is Bloemfontein, but there are plans to change its name.

The province covers the central high-veld: a broad region of flat or gently rolling grassland, with hardly any trees, scattered with a few table mountains. It lies 4,578 feet (1,400 m) above sea level and is flanked in the east by spurs of the Maluti mountains, Lesotho and the Drakensberg, which reach an altitude of 8,100 feet (2,477 m) above sea level in the Rooiberg range.

Preceding pages: The countryside near Clarens. Left: The National Women's Memorial in Bloemfontein commemorates the women and children who died in concentration camps during the Boer War.

For more than 100 years, agriculture formed the backbone of the economy. Around 31% of South Africa's arable land is in this province. While the country's most important corn- and wheat-growing area lies in the eastern section, the west is devoted to animal farming, above all merino sheep. Then in 1946 gold fields were discovered around Welkom, Odendaalsrus, and Virginia, which rank alongside Witwatersrand as some of the world's richest. Mining has therefore become an important economic factor. As yet, tourism does not play an important role, even though the province is conveniently located and offers a large number of attractions.

BLOEMFONTEIN

The province's capital, 263 miles (425 km) from Johannesburg and 626 miles (1,010 km) from Cape Town, is also the judicial capital of South Africa. The first white settler arrived here in 1840; in 1846, British soldiers established a garrison and administrative headquarters. The city's name, "spring of flowers," is thought to refer to a spring near the first settler's farm, which had long been used by passing hunters and traders. Today the city, which has around 235,000 inhabitants, is an important traffic hub, a

199

university city, and a popular center for conferences and congresses.

Hoffmann Square is the center of the downtown area and a favorite meeting point. City buses depart from here, and it is here that the most important government offices are located. Go east along Maitland Street and you come to the main railway station; to the west, it brings you to the wide, splendid President Brand Street, site of several historically important buildings. **First Raadsaal**, built in 1849, is one such. The small, thatched building has served as a school, a conference center, Parliament, City Hall, church and museum, in that order. A little further north stands the **Old Presidency**, completed in 1885, which was once the President's residence and is today a museum. Two blocks further on the other side of the street stands the **Supreme Court**, a neo-Classical building dating from 1909. In front of the **Old Govern-**

Above: A rest stop on the Great Trek; 19th-century woodcut.

ment Buildings, which used to serve as a third Raadsaal, there is a statue of the esteemed President Brand, elected in 1864, whose campaign slogan was: "Everything will be fine if everyone does his duty." Brand did his duty for the next 25 years. Today, the building accommodates a museum and research center for Afrikaans literature. The adjoining **Appeal Court** is well worth a visit for its woodcarvings and panelling of black stinkwood. North of here, set in a verdant garden area, stands **City Hall**, completed in 1936. Further down Charles Street is the fourth Raadsaal, a brick building fitted out with a dome and columns, built in 1893, which houses the Provincial Assembly. Also on Charles Street is the **National Museum**, housing an interesting anthropological collection, including a large number of fossils, as well as collections of archaeology and ethnology.

Towering over the city is the plateau-like form of **Naval Hill**. Extending over its slopes and heights is the **Franklin Game Reserve**, where you can see –

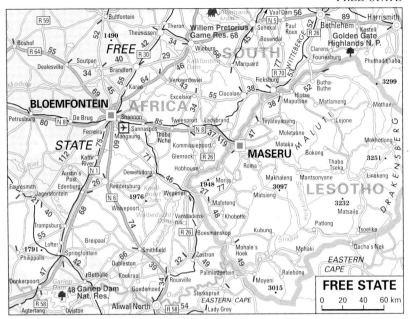

within city limits – springbok, blesbok, eland and wildebeest. West of President Brand Street, St. Andrew Street leads to the city's most attractive park, **Kings Park**, which has a rose garden and, in its western section, a zoo. The Botanical Garden is outside the city to the north. The **National Women's Memorial** on Memorial Road, at the southern edge of the city, was erected in memory of the more than 26,000 women and children who died in British concentration camps during the Boer War.

GOLDEN GATE HIGHLANDS NATIONAL PARK

Drive east along the N 8 from Bloemfontein and after 40 miles (64 km) you'll come to **Thabu Nchu**, the "Black Mountain." Some 6,991 feet (2,138 m) above sea level, it towers above the little town (with a Sun Hotel and casino) which shares its name. After another 40 miles or so (65 km) you reach Ladybrand. From here you can either make a 12-mile (19

km) detour to **Maseru**, Lesotho's capital, or drive northeast along the R 26, which runs parallel to the Lesotho border. **Ficksburg**, the center of this fertile area, is famous for its asparagus and cherries; there is a Cherry Festival in November. **Fouriesburg** became important on account of the nearby border crossing at **Caledoonspoort**. The latter, in turn, became tremendously important during construction work on the Lesotho Highlands Water Project. After passing through some impressive scenery, the road brings you to **Clarens**, which you can also reach from Bloemfontein by taking the N 1 to Winburg and then the N 5 east to Bethlehem.

A few miles east of Clarens, at the foot of the Maluti mountains, you come to **Golden Gate Highlands National Park**. The sandstone, which is colored yellow, red and orange due to the presence of iron oxide, has been eroded into bizarre forms; in the sun, and most of all at sunset, the rock appears to be bathed in golden light. This is especially true of the

Golden Gate, a kind of portico of two rocky cliffs more than 325 feet (100 m) high, which stand on either side of the road to form an "entrance." Founded in 1963, South Africa's first landscape park measures 28,726 acres (11,630 hectares) in area. With its altitude of 6,187-9,277 feet (1,892-2,837 m) above sea level, the park's climate is characterized by pleasantly cool summer days, cold and sometimes snow in the winter. As in all mountain areas, the weather can change very quickly.

What makes this park so special is its grandiose scenery; you don't need to be fascinated by geology to appreciate it. The highest sandstone rocks are covered by layers of resistant quartzite or remains of the area's once-thick basalt layer which is still about 1,962 feet (600 m) thick on the highest peak, Ribbokop.

Above: Brandwag Camp lies at the foot of the impressive cliffs of Golden Gate Highlands National Park. Right: The Free State is the granary of South Africa.

The typical vegetation of the highveld, especially grassland, is not exactly lush. This explains why there are fewer birds and animals here than in other areas of the country. Of the 140 species of bird here, the black eagle, bearded vulture and bald ibis are among the most rare. Apart from zebras, there are also antelope such as eland, blesbok, black wildebeest, and common and mountain reedbuck.

At the foot of an impressive sandstone face stands **Brandwag Camp**, one of the most comfortable choices of accommodation in all the parks. Apart from the main building, a former hotel, there are motel-like chalets, a restaurant, self-service restaurant, tennis courts and bowling greens, swimming pool, and horses available. If you are looking for something less exclusive, try the **Glen Reenen Camp**, less than a mile (1 km) away; as well as permanent accommodation, this camp has caravan and campsites and a gas station.

If your idea of a vacation is to unwind in crystal-clear mountain air and lovely

scenery, this beautiful, quiet national park with its comfortable accommodation is ideal, either for hiking or simply relaxing.

If you cross the park and continue east towards Harrismith, a road 13 miles (21 km) after Glen Reenen Camp leads off south to **Phuthaditjhaba**, the former capital of the homeland Qwaqwa, today a noted artisan center. Mohair wall hangings, wickerwork, and glass articles are made and sold here. From the neighboring town of Witsieshoek, a former mission station founded in 1874, the road continues south through a fascinating mountainous region. After 12 miles (20 km), you come to a toll-booth on the border of the Qwaqwa nature reserve. The road ends 6 miles (10.5 km) further on at the foot of the Sentinel, at an altitude of 1,661 feet (2,680 m). From here, you can walk in about 2 hours to the summit of **Mont-aux-Sources**, 10,732 feet (3,282 m) above sea level. It is one of the most scenically rewarding walks in South Africa. Accommodation is available in the Witsieshoek Mountain Resort about 3 miles (4 km) from the toll-booth.

DAMS

There are a number of manmade reservoirs, here known as "dams," in the Free State for the provision of water and irrigation purposes, but the **Gariep Dam**, with a capacity of 7,745 million cubic yards (5,958 million cu. m), is the largest in South Africa and the fourth-largest on the whole continent. It was constructed in 1971 on the border of the Northern Cape province as part of the Orange River Project, and extends over 135 square miles (374 sq. km). To get there from Bloemfontein, take the N 6 south to **Smithfield** and continue southwest on the R 701 to Bethulie, or take the N 1 to Springfontein and then go southeast to **Bethulie**, an old mission station set up in 1829. One of its buildings, the oldest dwelling constructed by Europeans in the Free State, is today a small museum. On one shore of the dam is **Midwaters**, a holiday village

(with campsite) with excellent facilities, ideal for fans of water sports and anglers. The **Gariep Dam Nature Reserve** on the northern banks of the reservoir is the largest nature reserve in the province and home to springbok, black wildebeest, other antelopes and ostriches.

Continuing further south on the N 6 from Bloemfontein, you reach **Aliwal North** after 128 miles (206 km). The town lies 4,480 feet (1,280 m) above sea level on the south bank of the Orange River, but is within the Eastern Cape province. Two hot mineral springs yield 2 million liters of water a day from a depth of 4,186 feet (1,280 m). This water has long been used in the treatment of rheumatic illnesses. The town has developed into a popular spa resort, with several pools and a biokinetic center.

Near the N 1 north of Bloemfontein, there's another dam, the **Allemanskraal**, just after Winburg. It was created when

Above: Vaal Dam reservoir is a venue for a wealth of recreational pursuits.

the Sand River was dammed up in 1960 to supply the nearby gold-mining regions with water. Here, too, a holiday center (called Aldam) has developed, complete with accommodation, a caravan park, sports and fishing opportunities.

A 29,640-acre (12,000 hectare) area including the dam was proclaimed the **Willem Pretorius Game Reserve**, where many nearly-extinct highveld species, mainly antilopes, have been successfully resettled. Apart from a herd of about 300 black wildebeest, there are white rhinos, giraffes and buffalo.

Vaal Dam, close to the Free State's northern border, is a 117-square-mile (300 sq. km) dam with bilharzia-free water which supplies water to Witwatersrand. It also allows water sports and fishing, and is often referred to as the "mini-French Riviera." A range of accommodation and activities are available.

Just a few miles north of Vaal Dam, you come to Vereeniging and the industrial area of Gauteng Province.

FREE STATE
Transportation
Bus: Translux runs regular buses from Bloemfontein (buses depart from 17 Cricket Street) to Cape Town (about 12 hours), Durban (8 hrs.), Johannesburg (5 hrs.), Port Elizabeth (about 8 1/2 hrs.); Greyhound (depart from Ultra City, pit stop on the N1 – Western Bypass) runs to Johannesburg, Kimberley (2 hrs.) and Upington (4 1/2 hrs.), Cape Town, Port Elizabeth.

Train: Amatola long-distance trains stop at the station here: Johannesburg (7 hrs.) / East London (around 13 1/2 hrs.); Algoa: Johannesburg (6 1/2 hrs.) / Port Elizabeth (12 hrs.); and Trans Oranje: Cape Town (21 hrs.) / Durban (16 hrs.).

Air: The airport is on the N8, 6 mi/10 km E of Bloemfontein (rental car, taxi). It's serviced by both SAA and Airlink (to Johannesburg, Durban, East London, Port Elizabeth).

BLOEMFONTEIN
Telephone and fax area code: 051, postal code: 9300

Accommodations
MODERATE: **Bloemfontein Hotel**, Sanlam Plaza, East Buirger St., tel: 30-1911, fax: 47-7102. **Naval Hill** (Holiday Inn Garden Court), 1 Union Ave., PO Box 1851, tel. 30-1111, fax: 30-4141. **City Lodge**, Voortrekker Str., PO Box 3552, tel: 47-9888, fax: 47-5669. **De Oude Kraal** (country lodge, 22 mi/35 km S of the city near the N 1), PO Box 8331, tel: 05215-636, fax: 05215-635. *BUDGET:* **Bloemfontein Inn**, 17 Edison St., PO Box 7589, tel: 22-6284, fax: 22-6223. **Die Herberg**, 12 Bame St., PO Box 12 165, Brandhof 9324 (near the city), tel: 30-7500, fax: 30-4494.
MODERATE: **Maselspoort** (holiday village on a reservoir, 14 mi/23 km NE of Bloemfontein), Private Bag X20 519, tel: 051/41-7848, fax: 41-7865.

Museums and Sights
First Raadsaal, Tue-Fri 10 am-3 pm, Sat/Sun 2-5 pm. **National Afrikaans Literary Museum**, Mon-Fri 7:30 am-12:15, 1-4 pm, Sat 9 am-12. **National Museum**, Mon-Sat 8 am-5 pm, Sun 8 am-6 pm. **Sand du Plessis Theatre**, advance registration for visits, tel: 47-7771. The **orchid house** at the foot of Naval Hill is open daily 10 am-4 pm.

Excursions
It's 88.5 mi/143 km to Lesotho on the N 8, N of the main train station, past the **airport** and **Thaba Nchu** (Sun Hotel with a gambling casino in the Maria Moroka Nature Reserve), and Ladybrand to **Maseru**, capital of Lesotho, a center for artisan crafts and a notable tourist destination.

Tourist Information
Bloemfontein Publicity Association, Hoffman Square, PO Box 639, tel: 405-8911, fax: 47-3859.

SATOUR, Sanlam Parkade, Shop No. 9, Charles Street, PO Box 3515, tel: 47-1362, fax: 47-0862. **Automobile Association (AA)**, 13 Sanlam Plaza, Maitland Street, tel: 47-6191. **Lesotho Tourist Board**, PO Box 1378, Maseru 100, tel: 00266/31-2896, fax: 31-0108.

GOLDEN GATE NATIONAL PARK
Accommodations
THABA NCHU 9780: *LUXURY:* **Thaba Nchu Sun Hotel**, PO Box 114, tel: 05 265/2161, fax: 2521.
LADYBRAND 9745: *MODERATE:* **Travellers Inn**, 23 A Kolbe St., PO Box 458, tel: 05 191/4-0191, fax: 4-0193.
MASERU 100 (Lesotho): *MODERATE:* *Lesotho Sun*, Private Bag A68, tel: 09 266/31-3111, fax: 31-0104. **Maseru Sun**, Private Bag A 84, tel: 09 266/31-2434, fax: 31-0158.
FICKSBURG 9730: *MODERATE: Nebo Farm* (guest farm), PO Box 178, tel. and fax: 05 192/3947.
FOURIESBURG 9725: *MODERATE:* **Fouriesburg Hotel**, 17 Reitz St., PO Box 114, tel: 058 222 ask for 30, fax: ask for 284. **Witsieshoek Mountain Resort**, PO Box 17 311, Witsieshoek 9870, tel: 058/789-1900, fax: 1901.
For reservations in **Brandwag** or **Glen Reenen Camps** in Golden Gate National Park, contact the National Parks Board, Pretoria.

Tourist Information
Tourist Information, Town Clerk, PO Box 116, Ficksburg 9730, tel: 0563/2122. **Highland Tourism Association**, PO Box 927, Ficksburg 9730, tel: 05192/5447, fax: 5449.

DAMS
Accommodations
GARIEP DAM 9922: *MODERATE:* **Verwoerd Dam Motel**, 2 Aasvoël Ave. PO Box 20, tel: 05-2171, ask for 60, fax: ask for 268. **Aventura Midwaters**, Private Bag X10, tel: 05-2171, ask for 45, fax: ask for 135. For holiday lodging on the highveld (near **SMITHFIELD** 9966: *MODERATE:* game and merino sheep farm **Hamolapo Game Ranch**, PO Box 71, tel: 05562/2104, fax: 05 562/32.
VENTERSBURG 9450: *MODERATE:* **Aventura Aldam** (holiday village, Willem Pretorius Game Reserve), Private Bag X6, tel: 05 777/4229, fax: 4078. *BUDGET:* **Fanny Preiss House** (youth hostel), Louis Trichardt Square, Marquard 9610 (29 mi/47 km SE of Winburg, which lies on the N 1, 15.5 mi/25 km S of the dam), tel: 05272, ask for 195.

Border crossing to Lesotho
Opening times of the most important border crossings: Maseru Bridge 6 am-10 pm; Ficksburg Bridge and Caledonspoort are open round the clock.

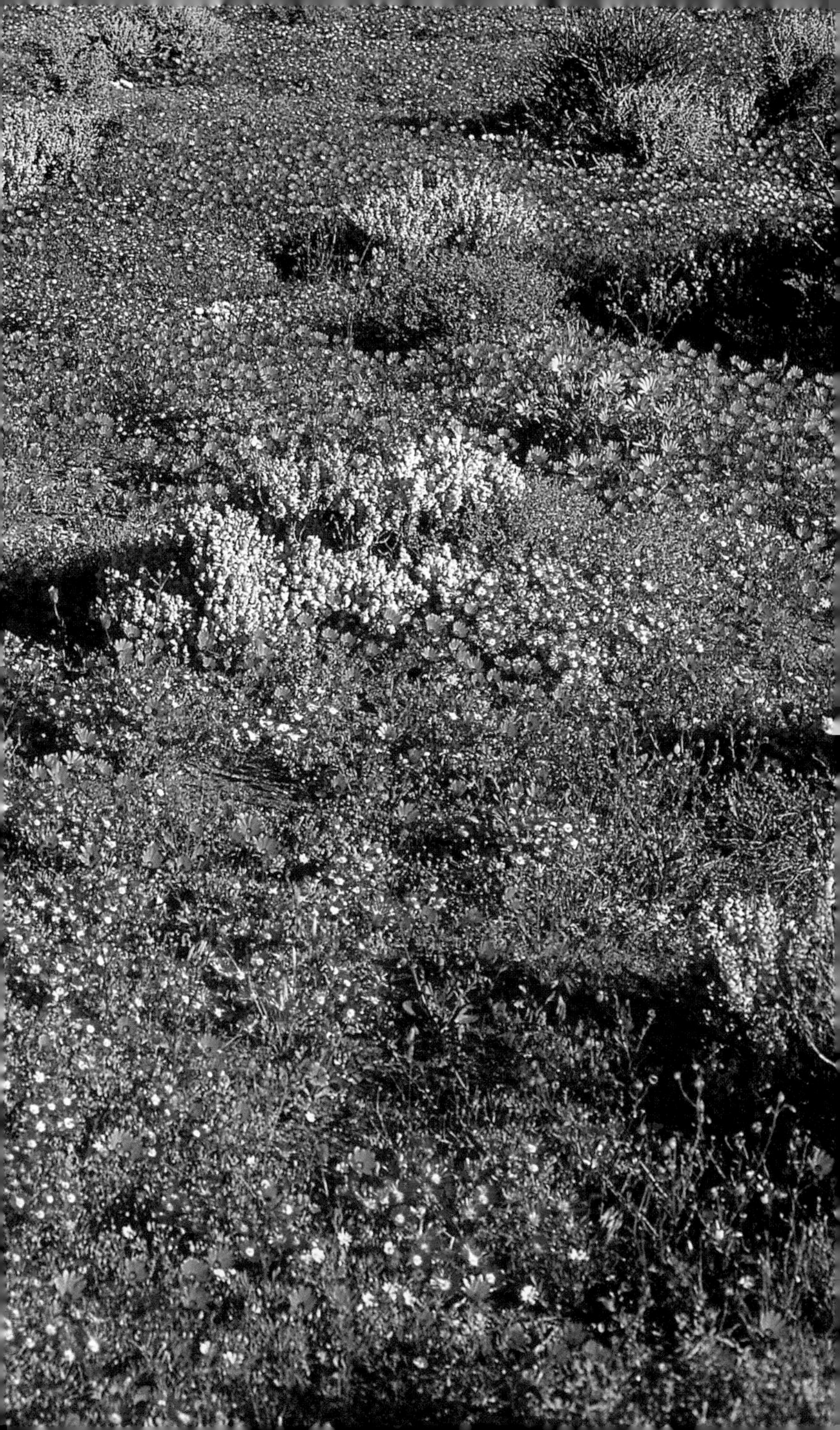

NATURE AND WILDLIFE CONSERVANCY

Despite their seeming vastness, South Africa's many nature preserves and wildlife refuges comprise only 6-8% of the country's total land area. And yet, although it's becoming necessary to expand the facilities, South Africa is one of the world's leaders in terms of nature conservancy. The need to protect rare and endangered species of plants and animals was recognized early on, but today often runs up against financial limitations. One option is collaboration of the state and private investors, such as the Conservation Corporation, which takes over the task of protecting nature and links this with economic enterprise.

Preceding pages: Namaqualand. Paraglider in Camps Bay. Above: Antilope hunting (chocolate ad, c. 1900). Above right: The white rhinoceros was threatened with extinction. Right: Private wildlife parks – committed to conservancy.

As the country was increasingly settled, and particularly after the onset of large-scale big-game hunting around 1840, South Africa's wealth of wildlife was drastically reduced. The first public protest was raised when it became known that in Zululand, in the former British colony of Natal, the white rhino was threatened with extinction; to protect it, the country created the nature reserves Hluhluwe, Umfolozi and St. Lucia.

The animal plague "nagana" devastated hordes of domestic animals, but by and large spared the country's wildlife; people thus blamed wild animals for the disease, not yet realizing that it was transmitted by the tsetse fly. As a result, another spate of wildlife extermination began in 1917: 25,000 wildebeest alone were killed in the first onslaught. As the plague continued to spread, white settlers demanded the dissolution of all the game preserves – fortunately in vain. When, the plague flared up again in 1928, settlers saw to it that the herds of wild animals again appreciably decreased.

In Transvaal, in 1898, President Paul Kruger turned a region of farmland into the Sabie Game Reserve; in 1926, considerably expanded through the National Parks Act, this became the Kruger National Park. Today, the National Parks Board administers an additional sixteen National Parks throughout the country; ten of these have convenient and low-budget accommodations. These reflect a portion of the tremendous variety of South Africa's landscapes, from the lonely, desert-like Kalahari Gemsbok Park in the north to the coastal preserve of Tsitsikamma National Park on the Indian Ocean, from the West Coast National Park on the Atlantic coast, home to a large number of sea birds, to Kruger National Park on the eastern border, which, as the country's largest national park and the one with the widest variety of animals, is a prime destination for foreign visitors. The newest park is Richtersveld National Park in the northwestern part of the country, featuring a completely new concept, opened in 1991.

In addition to these, there are also provincial parks, especially in KwaZulu/Natal. The Natal Parks Board in Pietermaritzburg administers 20 parks and reserves, including Umfolozi, Hluhluwe and St. Lucia; others, among them Ndumu, Tembe and Kosi Bay, are run by the KwaZulu Department of Nature Conservation. The situation is similar in the other provinces. Even outside of the actual reserves, there are strict regulations about nature conservancy. It's forbidden, for example, to pick or dig up plants within 100 yards on either side of a road. Beyond the efforts to save individual species from extinction, one major goal is to preserve examples of South Africa's natural ecosystem for future generations. The country belongs to a number of international environmental protection organizations. Since 1968, the most important nature organization has been the Southern African Nature Foundation, a branch of the World Wide Fund for Nature (WWF); since 1995, it's been called the WWF South Africa.

211

ANIMALS AND PLANTS
Animals

South Africa's wealth and variety of wildlife is one of the country's prime tourist attractions. Many of the large mammals who once ranged over the whole southern part of the continent and were then threatened with extinction in the course of the last century now dwell safely in wildlife reserves, where visitors can observe them living tranquilly in their natural habitat.

Of the big cats, the one you'll see most frequently is the largest, the lion, which lives in packs and observes a strict hierarchical system. Life is quite different for the leopard, a smaller animal who's a definite individualist; he usually spends his days in the shade of leafy trees, where his coat with its roseate spots makes him hard to sight. When stalking his prey, the

Above: Two generations of giraffes. Right: Buffalo belong to the "Big Five," the most popular targets of big-game hunters.

long-legged cheetah can reach speeds of up to 60 mph over short distances. The cheetah's coat has simple spots; the animal's most distinctive markings are the black stripes running from the inner corner of the eye to the mouth. Smaller (measuring some 60 cm at the shoulder), but sporting similar markings, is the nocturnal serval. Hyenas and jackals, which generally feed on carrion, are still fairly common, but the wild dog is threatened with extinction.

The largest of all animals, elephants live in small herds and eat grass, lesves, roots and tree bark. The bulls reach weights of up to 13,200 pounds, and their dietary needs are correspondingly enormous (330-440 pounds of food a day, and up to 220 l – about 50 gallons – of water). They are carefully tended in the game preserves; as poaching is no longer a problem here, preserve officials are forced to kill several animals each year in order to preserve the natural ecological balance.

Elephants are exceeded in size only by giraffes, who also live in small herds and reach heights of up to 16 feet, enabling them to find food among the treetops (leaves and fruit) without fear of competition. These animals are exceptionally curious, but very peaceful. You'll often see them in the company of zebra herds, generally Burchell's zebras, which you can recognize from the fact that between the black stripes, as individuated as a human fingerprint, you can see yellow or gray "shadow stripes." Nearly extinct a few decades ago, the somewhat smaller mountain zebras have more black stripes, but no shadow stripes; the best place to spot them is in Mountain Zebra National Park.

It was for rhinoceros (both black and white rhinos), threatened with extinction, that South Africa's first wildlife preserves, Hluhluwe and Umfolozi, were created at the end of the last century. Since then, thanks to exemplary care, their numbers

have so increased that some of the animals have been resettled in other areas of the country.

Among the "Big Five," the traditionally-sought trophies of visiting big-game hunters, are, as well as lions, leopards, rhinos, and elephants, buffalo. These animals live throughout the country in large herds; most other animals maintain a respectful distance.

But the animals you'll encounter most often, all over the country, are the 29 species of antilope who live here; at first, certainly, it's far from easy to tell them apart. Apart from gemsbok or oryx (not to be confused with the mountain goats seen in Europe), springbok, bontebok and blesbok, you can sight most of the species in Krüger Park. The endangered bontebok resides under special protection in the Bontebok National Park near Swellendam; you'll also find them in the nature preserve on the Cape of Good Hope. The gray oryx, with distinctive black-and-white facial markings and sharp horns up to three feet long, lives predominantly in the Kalahari, which is also home to blue wildebeest and large numbers of springbok. The latter, a particularly lovely and graceful antilope, is one of the country's national emblems, as well as a symbol of South African sports. Equally graceful, if somewhat larger, are the numerous blackfoot impala, animals which can jump incredibly high and far (up to 30 feet). Only the males of this species have horns. This is also true of the mid-sized kudu, generally gray in color, whose spiralling horns, up to six feet long, are perhaps the loveliest of any antilope's. Smallest of the antilope is the blue duiker, measuring 13-15 inches at the shoulder; the largest is the eland (60-75 inches). Occasionally, you can see antilope, particularly impalas, grazing at pasture; game farms are starting to cultivate these animals with increasing frequency.

The warthog, about 27 inches (70 cm) high, has bumps of skin (the eponymous "warts") on his head, a mane, and tusks up to 15 or 16 inches (40 cm) long. Wart-

213

hogs tend to amuse observers by holding their tails erect when they run.

The only primates native to South Africa are breeds of monkeys belonging to the family of long-tailed monkeys, such as the vervet or white-throated monkeys, as well as baboons (bear baboons, chacmas); feeding the latter is severely punishable by law. If baboons are about, as, for instnce, on the Cape of Good Hope, it's wise to close your car windows, as they may make a quick grab for cameras or pocketbooks.

Of the smaller mammals, common in many areas of the country are squirrels, bush babies with enormous eyes, rock dassies (which are related to elephant), and suricate.

Crocodiles, which can reach lengths of up to 20 feet (6 m), live in the warm rivers of Kruger National Park and the wildlife preserves of KwaZulu/Natal. Only 35 of the country's indigenous

Above: The eyecatching colorful plumage of the plumed turako (knysna lourie).

snakes are poisonous; these include puff adders, cobras, green and black mambas, and tree snakes. You can learn interesting facts about snakes, and how to deal with them, at daily demonstrations in the snake parks of Durban and Port Elizabeth, or at the Halfway House, where snake poison is extracted for later use in medical serum. Under strict protection are South Africa's twelve species of indigenous land turtle and five freshwater turtles, as well as the five species of sea turtle you can encounter along the coast. Of the latter, only two species actually breed here, including the leatherback turtle, which reaches weights of up to 880 pounds and frequents the northern coast of KwaZulu/Natal. And no traveler can fail to notice the wide variety of lizards, geckos, iguanas, and other reptiles sunning themselves on the rocks.

Bird-watchers can have a field day; South Africa boasts some 900 species. One of these is the largest flightless bird, the ostrich, which is even bred in the Little Karoo, and the largest flying bird, the Karoo koerhaan, which lives predominantly in the Kalahari and the Great Karoo. Near flowering bushes and plants, especially proteas, you can see smaller species, especially the long-tailed sunbird. You can also spot eagles, vultures, cranes; the funny long-legged secretary bird, only found in Africa; many kinds of weaver bird, known for their complex nest structures; colorful kingfishers and bee-eaters; wydahs with astonishingly long and ornate tails; hornbills and tokos with their huge beaks. On inland lakes or along the coast live countless water and sea birds, including osprey, flamingos, heron, pelicans, marabus, cormorants, or black darters.

Among the many insect species native to South Africa, visitors are most impressed by the colorful varieties of butterfly; there are more than 800 different kinds. You can't miss the termite hills, especially in grasslands and bushlands. The less pleasant representatives of the insect world include the tsetse fly (nagana fly), a carrier of sleeping sickness, now almost extinct. The anopheles mosquito, however, which carries malaria, has certainly been decimated in the warm and humid marsh areas, but has developed resistance to a number of medications, and has therefore come to represent a renewed danger. In forested areas, there are also ticks, equally feared as disease carriers. The country's arthropod insect residents include scorpions; the ones with the thick tails are especially poisionous. Also dangerous are bilharzia worms, which prevent swimming in most South African waters.

Fish about in the country's rivers and numerous reservoirs. Along the coast, the ocean currents foster a remarkable variety of sea life. You can sometimes spot whales and dolphins beyond the breakers (in Hermanus, for example, or Plettenberg Bay). And bathing beaches are surrounded with nets to keep away the sharks.

ANIMAL NAMES
English-Afrikaans

Baboon	Bobbjaan
Black Rhino(ceros)	Swartrenoster
Blue Wildebeest	Blouwildebees
Buffalo	Buffel
Caracal	Rooikat
Cheetah	Jagluiperd
Eland	Elenantilope
Elephant	Olfant
Gemsbok	Oryx, Spiessbock
Giraffe	Kamelperd
Hippo(potamus)	Seekoei
Impala	Rooibok
Jackal	Jakkals
Leopard	Luiperd
Lion	Leeu
Rock Dassie	Klipdas
Sable Antelope	Swartwitpens
Squirrel	Eekhoring
Suricate	Stokstertemearkat
Vervet Monkey	Blouaap
Warthog	Vlakvark
Waterbuck	Waterbok
White Rhino	Witrenoster

Plants

In no other region of the world has such a wide variety of plant species and types developed in such a small area as in South Africa. The country boasts some 22,000 kinds of plants, more than the entire United States, a land mass 17 times larger. South Africa is also the only country which contains one of the earth's six floral kingdoms entirely within its borders; the Cape floral kingdom is the world's smallest, but has the largest number of species. On the Cape peninsula alone, more than 2,600 kinds of flowering plants grow within an area of a mere 195 sq. miles (500 sq. km) – more than on the entire British Isles, which exceed it in area by 500 times.

In past centuries, human settlers have wreaked profound changes on the re-

Above: Strelitzia. Right: Immortelles are common in the fynbos vegetation of the southern Cape Peninsula. Far right: A half-mens tree in Richtersveld.

gion's original vegetation. Still, however, the various climactic conditions of the various regions, particularly the fact that rainfall decreases noticably as you move from east to west, have created the following, distinct vegetation zones.

The relatively well-irrigated highveld, together with the eastern part of the Great Escarpment, is a region of grass plains. On the slopes of ravines and in river valleys you can still make out the remains of what was originally a fairly dense forest. Bordering this to the north and northwest, the lower-lying, dry, warm regions of Northern Province and Eastern Transvaal, the park-like savannahs of the lowlands, are sprinkled with various kinds of acacia, notably the characteristic umbrella thorn and the extremely useful sweet thistle (*acacia karoo*), one of the most widespread plants in South Africa, with small, spherical, yellow flowers; other trees include wild figs as well as mopane bushes and trees with their butterfly-shaped leaves. Between these grow the striking baobab trees, eye-catching because of their thick trunks, where they store water; fever trees with yellow-green bars; and elephant trees, also called sausage trees for their huge, sausage-like, and wholly unappetizing fruit.

Adjacent to this on the west, the thorn savanna of the Kalahari is dominated largely by camel-thorn acacia bushes and a sparse covering of grass. To the south is the semidesert of the Great Karoo; this region's flora is mainly comprised of tufts of grass and knee-high bushes. Alternating with these are a variety of succulents, including many species of aloe, characterized by their "crests," which, like the various euphorbias or spurges, can reach heights of more than 6 feet (2 m). Stone plants ("flowering stones"), adapted to extreme dryness, also grow here, but it's almost impossible to find one unless it happens to be blooming at the time. Such succulents as mesembryanthemum, euphorbia (spurge) and aloe, in-

cluding the kokerboom (quiver tree, or tree aloe), are also the main flora of Namaqualand; in spring, however, this area can be transformed into a sea of blossoming wildflowers, dominated by the daisies, a kind of aster, which seem to spring up veritably overnight. Only in the far northwest do you encounter the unusual tree halfmens, a member of the family Apocyaceae.

In South Africa, natural, virgin forests take up less than 1 % of the landscape: in some valleys of the highveld, for example, or in the Great Escarpment with its high rainfall. By the coast on the Garden Route, near Knysna, you can see an area of original, native high forest with numbers of ironwood, stinkwood, and yellowwood trees. Some trees have reached heights of up to 145 feet (45 m) and are as much as 800 years old; they are prized for their wood, used to make furniture. Remains of the original native forest have also survived in the valleys and ravines of the Cape provinces. South Africa's trees have been classified in a

"National List of Trees;" and trees in nature reserves, parks, rest camps and other such spots actually bear numbers to make identification easier for visitors.

Because of the increasing need for wood for building, paper manufacture, and the like, reforestation has been going on since 1876 on a broad scale with quick-growing, usually foreign trees (pine, eucalyptus, or species of acacia), especially in Transvaal and Kwa-Zulu/Natal; more than 70% of these forests are in private hands.

And one can't neglect to mention the trees which line the roads; although these aren't always native, they give many places their characteristic, signature flair. Take the old oaks in Stellenbosch, the pear trees in Beaufort West, and, above all, the jacarandas, which are found all over the place, but which in October veil the streets of Pretoria in a cloud of pale lilac blossoms.

As you move northeast from East London through the coastal region, the bushy undergrowth is increasingly interspersed with various types of palm, Natal strelitzia, and mangrove. Because of the warm, humid air from the Indian Ocean, the region sports lush, subtropical flowering vegetation all year round. From July to October/November, parks and gardens flower with magnificent scarlet coral trees, laburnum, hibiscus, flamboyant, azaleas, rhododendrons, camelias, bougainvillea, and many other flowers, both indigenous and imported.

The evergreen vegetation which predominates in the Cape floral kingdom, along the coast, and also in the mountains is related to the macchia found around the Mediterranean; in South Africa, it's called fynbos (fine bush). Its main representatives are the 600-odd species of heather or erica; the protea family, with 82 species in South Africa, and 117 types of the grass-like restio family.

To these, one must add the flowers from the aster family (daisies, Gerbera), lilies (agapanthus, fire lilies), geraniaceae (geraniums, pelargoniums), and other plants indigenous to the country. Many of these have become common in Europe and North America, as well. There are more than 100 kinds of orchid in the Cape floral kingdom alone, and this is only one-quarter the number found throughout the whole country. Most famous of the former is the red disa (*disa uniflora*), also known as "Pride of Table Mountain." The bushes of the protea family reach heights of 10 feet (3 m) or even higher, but there are also small, creeping varieties. These come in a virtually inconceivable range of sizes and colors; the blossom of the King Protea (*protea cynaroides*), South Africa's national flower, reaches diameters of 10 inches (25 cm) and more.

The most important of the fynbos trees, of which there are only a few (silver tree, 16-22 feet / 5-7 m, but can reach

heights of 50 feet and more (16 m); wild almond, up to 26 feet / 8 m high), also belong to the family of the evergreen proteas. Members of this family – which is also found in Australia and South America – also grow in the Drakensberg. Irises and lilies bloom magnificently in spring, particularly after a bush fire, an event not uncommon in the dry summers. These fires actually play an important role in the growth of the fynbos, in that they create, within the usually dense undergrowth, room, light and air for bulbs and seeds to sprout and grow.

What can create a problem are plants that have been brought in or even imported for agricultural purposes, which can start to expand and crowd out indigenous vegetation, thereby threatening the natural ecological balance. As most of them haven't got natural enemies in this environment, and thanks to the high resistance of their seeds or their rapid growth, they can wholly displace or suffocate the local flora. Among these foreign interlopers are opuntia, or prickly pear; these plants have even been declared damaging weeds, and planting them is prohibited. Water hyacinths from Central and South America have expanded to threaten the ecosystems of entire bodies of water. Brought in for agricultural reasons, large-scale plantings of eucalyptus, a tree native to Australia, draw disproportionate amounts of water from the environment.

There's no one definite answer to the question of when the best time of year is to view the flora of South Africa; something or other is sure to be blooming whatever time of year you come. However, spring (September to November), with its abundant profusion of flowers, is always an unforgettable experience. As well as observing the wealth of flora in its natural environment, anyone with a particular interest in plants should make sure to visit some of the botanic gardens, particularly Kirstenbosch Gardens in Cape

Right: Diamond mining in South Africa, after a woodcut of 1872.

Town, as well as Betty's Bay, Bloemfontein, Caledon, Durban, Nelspruit, Pietermaritzburg, Roodepoort, Stellenbosch, Worcester, and a number of others.

DIAMONDS, GOLD, AND OTHER TREASURES

Diamonds are born at extreme temperatures and extreme pressures from kimberlite, a volcanic stone which was forced along narrow veins from the center of the earth to the earth's crust between 140 and 80 million years ago. The blue-green "blue ground" kimberlite weathers to a brownish-yellow "yellow ground." The proportion of diamond in kimberlite is extremely low: an average of about 1 carat to every 5 tons; while a large portion of kimberlite veins contain no diamond whatsoever. Diamonds found in rivers or on the coast have been eroded and washed out of kimberlite veins which happen to contain diamonds.

In the small village of Hopetown, 74 miles (120 km) southwest of present-day Kimberley, diamonds were first found in 1866. One of these, an 83.5-carat rock which later became known as the "Star of South Africa," last changed hands in 1974 at an auction in Geneva for the impressive sum of $552,000. When similar stones were found in the riverbeds of the Vaal, it kicked off a true "diamond rush." Treasure-hunters from around the world poured into this remote region; their camp Klipdrift was a forerunner, if somewhat north, of today's Barkly West.

But South Africa's true economic ascendancy didn't begin until 1869, when a diamond was found in the wall of a farmhouse not far from present-day Kimberley. The territory was within the Oranje Free State, but was also claimed by the Griqua, a Hottentot tribe, as well as by the Boer Republic of Transvaal. Such claims were silenced in 1871, when the British simply annexed the region as the crown colony of Griqualand West; it was later appended to the Cape Colony.

In 1871, diamond-hunters struck it rich near present-day Kimberley on the farm

219

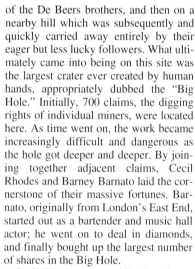

of the De Beers brothers, and then on a nearby hill which was subsequently and quickly carried away entirely by their eager but less lucky followers. What ultimately came into being on this site was the largest crater ever created by human hands, appropriately dubbed the "Big Hole." Initially, 700 claims, the digging rights of individual miners, were located here. As time went on, the work became increasingly difficult and dangerous as the hole got deeper and deeper. By joining together adjacent claims, Cecil Rhodes and Barney Barnato laid the cornerstone of their massive fortunes. Barnato, originally from London's East End, started out as a bartender and music hall actor; he went on to deal in diamonds, and finally bought up the largest number of shares in the Big Hole.

Cecil Rhodes, meanwhile, bought up the most claims from the De Beers

Above: In Cullinan Diamond Mine today.
Above right: A cut diamond. Right: A gold bar in its rough form.

brothers. Rhodes had come to South Africa in 1870 for health reasons; but by 1871, he was already involved in the diamond rush. In 1880, he founded the De Beers Mining Company; in 1888, he took over Barnato's mine holdings, at a price of 5,338,650 pounds; and from 1890-96, he was Prime Minister of the Cape Colony. De Beers, initially led by Rhodes, was taken over by Ernest Oppenheimer in 1929, and later (1957-84) by Oppenheimer's son, Harry. Over the years, the firm gradually took over most of the other diamond mines in the area, most recently (1964) the Finsch Diamond Mines northwest of Kimberley, one of the largest in Africa. Today, diamonds are also mined around Pretoria and in Namaqualand. South Africa ranks third worldwide as a producer of diamonds for jewelry, topped only by Botswana and Russia.

Only a few years after the first diamonds were found, the first gold veins were discovered in Witwatersrand, not far from Johannesburg. This discovery kicked off the country's gold-mining industry, a field which has seen tremendous growth in the century since its inception. For the most part, only microscopic amounts of the precious metal are present; one ton of ore yields an average of 15 grams of gold. To get this, stone is brought up to the surface, processed to a fine powder, and treated with chemicals. The resulting gold is melted and cast into bars; these ingots also contain about 8% silver and 3% other metals.

Germiston, southeast of Johannesburg, is home to the largest gold refinery in the world; here, the gold is brought to a level of purity of around 99%. To produce one ounce of gold, it takes, in addition to expensive equipment, an average of 3.3 tons of ore, 39 working hours, 5441 liters of water, 572 kilowatts of energy, and 12 cubic meters of compressed air, as well as explosives, chemicals, and other items. A large mine processes about 8 million tons of ore a year; over the last few years, South Africa's annual gold production has averaged out to about 600-700 tons. Most of the veins in the central Witwatersrand region have been exhausted, and the mining industry has gradually moved eastward (Evander), especially into the gold fields of the Orange Free State.

Among the country's other treasures are the huge reserves of iron and manganese ore in the Northern Cape Province. The warehouses of the Bushveld complex, north of Pretoria, contain 82% of the western world's platinum reserves, 74% of its chrome, the world's largest amount of vanadium, and the third-largest of fluorite. Andalusite, an aluminum silicate valued in industry because it's fire-resistant, is also found here; South Africa has the largest resources of this mineral in the world, and produces 47% of its volume worldwide. In the volcanic veins of Phalaborwa are copper ore, phosphate and vermiculite, an insulating material; of the latter, South Africa has half of the western world's total reserves. The antimony mine near Gravelotte (west

of Phalaborwa) alone produces some 10% of the world's antimony ore.

There are also rich coal deposits from a more recent era of the earth's history in South Africa, above all in Eastern Transvaal, Northern Natal, and the Free State. A large portion of the valuable coal lies near the earth's surface, and can therefore be mined at a relatively low cost. South Africa stands in fourth place in terms of worldwide coal production; more than a quarter of its yield is exported (notably from the coal port of Richards Bay, among others), most of it to Japan. Of the coal used within the country, more than 20% is used in the production of synthetic gasoline. For the past several years, there's been drilling for natural gas off the coast of Mossel Bay; this, too, is processed into fuel.

South Africa's other riches include semiprecious stones, such as tiger's eye, jasper, chalcedony, amethysts, and others; and rare and quite valuable minerals such as zirkon and the titanium compounds ilmenite and rutile.

221

SOUTH AFRICAN WINE

The climate of the winelands in the southwest corner of Africa is not unlike that of the Mediterranean countries. Winters are mild, with adequate rainfall; and there's a lot of sun. The Cape region's varied landscape, with its steep mountains and green, fertile valleys, different soils and numerous climactic zones in miniature, provide the ideal conditions for wine cultivation. Accordingly, this is practiced throughout the region around Cape Town, extending northward parallel to the Atlantic coast into the fertile valley of the Olifants River, and eastward to the Little Karoo. Grapes are also grown in the irrigated area along the Orange River near Upington; but most of these grapes are destined to become raisins. South Africa's grape harvest begins in January and lasts until April.

Above: South Africa produces many excellent wines for connoisseurs (wine cellar of Neethlingshof, near Stellenbosch)

Seven years after Jan van Riebeeck arrived at the Cape, the first wine was bottled on Table Mountain at Wynberg and Constantia. When the area around Stellenbosch was settled a few years later, it opened up thereto-undreamt-of possibilities to vintners. Subsequent settlers, mainly Germans and Huguenots from France who brought with them knowledge and experience in the field of wine, produced excellent wines which were enjoyed at royal tables throughout Europe. The local wine industry saw a renewed ascendancy after World War II, when new grape varietials were brought in, accompanied by new and improved methods of production.

White grapes are cultivated in 85% of the country's vineyards. One-third of these are *chenin blanc*, also called *steen*, a South African variety of the *chenin blanc* grape grown in the Loire Valley. Also increasingly popular, besides the *Sauvignon blanc*, is the Cape Riesling; this is an offshoot of the Southern French *Crouchon blanc*, and is wholly unrelated to the classic, or Rhine, Riesling, which is relatively new to this region. *Chardonnay*, the classic grape from Burgundy and the Champagne region, still represents only a small portion of the country's grapes, but has been responsible for a whole series of great wines on the market. Concentrated in the Breede River valley and in the Little Karoo is the *Muscat d'Alexandrie*, known as *Hanepoot* in South Africa, mainly used in the production of dessert wines.

Many of the country's best red wines are products of the *Cabernet Sauvignon* grape from Bordeaux, which has been grown here for around 70 years; these wines, however, take a long time to mature. Quicker are the *Shiraz* and *Merlot*, which also yield excellent wines, but are often – like merlot in Burgundy – blended with Cabernet. The second most common red wine grape is the *Cinsault*, originally from the Rhone; in 1927, this was crossed with the *Pinot noir* from Burgundy to create South Africa's first indigenous grape varietal, the *Pinotage*.

Only around 50% of the grape harvest is used for wine. Also extremely important are the production of brandy and liqueurs. Among the latter is Jerepigo (sweet grape juice strengthened with alcohol), Muscadel, and Hanepoot, as well as port and sherry. Centers for this industry are Robertson and the Little Karoo. Sparkling wine is also produced from rosé and red wines.

Since 1973, the South African Council for Wine and Spirits has carried out official quality control. After tests, it confers the seal "Wine of Origin," which confirms the label's claims regarding place of origin, year, and grape varietal. Only 4% of South Africa's wines are Wines of Origin; most of them, even some of the very top wines, are blended. If the various grape varietals are listed on the label, they have to be listed in the order of their percentage in the blend. If they comprise less than 20% of the total, the exact percentage has to be given. Since 1992 – with a two-year period of grace to allow the law to take effect – alcohol content also has to be indicated on the label. Because the sun is stronger, this content is usually higher than that of European wines. Domestically, the wine can vary from the percentage given by up to 1%, but for wines destined for EU countries, there's only room for free play up to 0.5%.

At the annual South African National Wine Show (SANS), awards are given for particular quality; the double gold, gold, silver and bronze medals may then be printed on a wine's label. These replace the designation "Superior" which was conferred upon special wines until 1990. The description Premier Grand Cru, on the other hand, says nothing about a wine's quality, but rather denotes an extra-dry white wine.

Even without an seal of approval, a wine may be truly excellent; many vintners don't even apply for the official designations.

In listing the sugar content, wine lists include, as well as dry (up to 4 g/l) and semi-dry (4-12 g/l), wines designated as off-dry, of which the sugar content is somewhere between the two. Semi sweet wines contain between 4 and 30 g/l. In wines of the Late Harvest (20-30 g/l), the maturity of the grape at its harvesting helps determine between Special Late Harvest and Noble Late Harvest, which also includes the mold *botrytis cinerea*. In Noble Late Harvest wines, the sugar content is more than 50 g/l.

Cooperatives process some 80% of the grape harvest. The umbrella organization and market leader with some 70% of the country's export is the KWV (*Ko-operatieve Wijnbouwers Vereeniging*), based in Paarl. Founded in 1918, it's the private property of the vintners, and today boasts the largest wine-cellar in the world. About 94% of the country's 4,650 vintners are members.

LITERATURE IN SOUTH AFRICA

South Africa's literature includes works in Afrikaans, the dominant language among the whites, which is also spoken by many coloreds; in English, a literary language for many black and colored residents, as well as for most Indians; and in the Bantu languages, which have been increasingly coming into their own as a literary force to be reckoned with: about a fifth of the books published in South Africa appear in African languages.

Literature in Afrikaans

The first literary works in Afrikaans, which didn't become a written language until 1875, appeared around the turn of this century. Initially, most of these works were poems. The most important,

Above: The great South African writer Nadine Gordimer shows her pleasure in her Nobel Prize for Literature (1991).

and most popular, writers of this period were C. L. Leipoldt (1880-1947) and C. J. Langenhoven (1873-1932), poet of the national anthem of white South Africans, *"Die Stem van Suid-Afrika."* N. P. van Wyk Louw (1906-1970), a member of the "Dertig" group of poets, wrote masterpieces in virtually ever major poetic form: odes, sonnets, ballads. His historical dramas (*Dias*, 1952; *Germanicus*, 1956; others) are among the best works of their kind. The same can be said of the dramas of Uys Krige (1910-87) the romantic member of this group of writers; his works include *Alle paaie gaan na Rome* (1949). Krige also enriched the literature of his language with countless translations and editions of works of European, Arabian, and Latin American literature. The social and political situation of the colored population found its first literary expression in the works of S. V. Peterson, born in 1914; he was followed by Adam Small (born in 1936), with his poems of liberation and his play *Kanna hi ko hystoe* (Kanna comes home, 1965), about the residents of District Six in Cape Town, a residential slum which was destroyed in 1966.

Most important poet of the younger generation, the so-called Sestiger, is Breyten Breytenbach, born in 1936. His works are strongly influenced by Zen Buddhism; because he is married to a Vietnamese woman, he had to leave the country, and he has lived in France for many years. He collected his impressions of a three-month trip to South Africa in 1973, when he received a permit to enter the country to attend a writers' congress, in his *Seisoen in Paradys* (1977). In 1986, Breytenbach, who had received a number of international awards, received a literature prize in South Africa for two volumes of his poetry.

One notable Afrikaans novel is *In a Strange Land*, by Karl Schoeman. Other members of the Sestiger group who have written a number of highly regarded novels include Etienne Leroux and André Brink. Brink, who has received several international literary awards, has translated a number of his own works into English. Particularly well-received was his novel *Houd - den - Beck*, or *A Chain of Voices* (1982), which illustrated South Africa's current problems through its depiction of an actual historical event of 1825. A number of Brink's other novels are available in English, such as *The Wall of the Plague* or *An Act of Terror*; *A Dry White Season* (1979) was even filmed in 1989. Dalene Mathee's first novel, *Kringe in 'n bos* (1984), which the author herself translated in to English, focuses on a mystical relationship between man and nature.

Literature in English

The first South African novel in English was *The Story of an African Farm* (1883), a story of people and their lives set in the Great Karoo; it brought its author, Olive Schreiner (1855-1920),

tremendous recognition. Also extremely popular was Jock of the Bushveld (1907), a story about dogs by J. P. Fitzpatrick (1862-1931). Sir Laurens van der Post (born in 1906), has written short stories and novels, notably the marvelous *Story Like the Wind* (1972), which tells of a young boy's coming of age against the setting of the conflict between tribal culture and white settlers, and its sequel, *A Far-Off Place*. Van der Post is, however, perhaps best known for his travel books. *Venture into the Interior* (1952) was a best-seller; 1955 saw the publication of *The Dark Eye in Africa*; 1958, *The Lost World of the Kalahari*. Sarah Gertrude Millin (1899-1968) was the first author to make social questions and racial problems the stuff of literature (*The Dark River*, 1919; *God's Stepchildren*, 1924).

But South Africa's internationally best-known authors have also taken the country's political and social situation as their theme: Alan Paton and Nadine Gordimer. Alan Paton (1903-1988) wrote the novel *Cry, the Beloved Country* (1948), which has been translated into many languages, dramatized, and filmed. Said to be the most-read South African novel ever written, it's an impressive narration of the story of a black man who comes from a small rural settlement to the white-dominated metropolis of Johannesburg. Another of Paton's novels, *Too Late the Phalarope* (1953), deals with the problems of apartheid; Paton was also politically active in efforts to end the system. *Ah, But Your Land is Beautiful*, the first part of a trilogy, published in 1981, is set in South Africa in the 1950s. Paton's short stories have been collected under the title *Tales from a Troubled Nation* (1961).

Nadine Gordimer, born in 1923, was the first South African author to win the Nobel Prize for Literature. Her first novel, *The Laying Days* (1953), was followed by *The Burger's Daughter* (1979) and many others. *July's People* (1981) postulated a situation in which the roles and interdependencies of the races were reversed. Critics see Gordimer's greatest strength, however, as lying in the short story genre (with collections such as *Six Feet of the Country*, 1956; Penguin has published a *Collected Stories*, as well as several other works).

Next to the short stories of other authors such as Olive Schreiner and Alan Paton, the volume Mafeking Road (published in 1947) by Herman Charles Bosman (1905-51) has a special place. Another author who's received international recognition is J. M. Coetzee, whose novels include *Dusklands* (1974), *The Life and Times of Michael K.* (1983), and *Foe* (1986).

The country's most important contemporary English-speaking dramatist is indubitably Athol Fugard, born in 1932, who is also active as a stage director and actor. His works, which have also been extremely successful internationally, deal primarily with racial tensions (*No Good Fryday*, 1958; *The Blood Knot*, 1962; *Master Harold and the Boys*, 1984; *My Children, my Africa*, 1989). Fugard has been active in the support of black theaters in the townships.

Known for his satirical writings, as well as for his acting and cabaret work, is Pieter-Dirk Uys.

Founded by whites in 1951, and initially run by whites, the literary magazine *African Drum* was the first forum for black authors, concentrating mainly on short stories. A leading author to emerge from this endeavor was Es'kia Mphahlele, whose works dealt with daily life in the townships. He ran the magazine from 1955-57 before leaving the country, like many other authors and artists; he returned from abroad in 1983. A

Right: Archaic magic of big-game hunters – the dawnings of South African art lie in the rock paintings and engravings of the Bushmen.

prime example of the literature of South African writers in exile is his autobiography *Down Second Avenue*, published in 1959. Prominent among the ever-increasing number of English-language works by black South Africans is the poetry collection *Sound of a Cow Hide* (1971), by Oswald Mtshali, and the verse epic *Africa, My Beginning* (1979), by Ingoapele Madingoanes.

Literature in Bantu Languages

Originally, the black tribes had no written language, but rather a rich oral tradition of literary texts handed down from generation to generation. The translations from English texts attempted by missionaries, such as J. W. Colenso in Zulu and R. Moffat in Tswana, were the first written documents in these languages. The novel *The Pilgrim's Progress* (published 1674-84), by British author John Bunyan, was the first work of world literature to be translated, first to Xhosa in 1866, and then into virtually all of the major African languages in the course of the ensuing 100 years. After the translation of numerous other international works, the first great work of black African literature appeared in 1925 with the publication of the novel *Chaka*, by Thomas Mofolo (1875-1948), in the Sotho language. The work was translated into English in 1932 and into German in 1953 and 1988; it marks the beginning of an independent and rich literature of black Africa. Many of these works have been translated into English.

THE CULTURAL EXPERIENCE

Until apartheid was abolished, culture in South Africa was primarily something for the white population. Opera houses, concert halls, and ballet were open to them. The first theater was founded in Cape Town in 1801, and the first academy of music in 1826; Carl Maria

von Weber's *Der Freischütz* was the first opera to be performed in South Africa when it was staged there in 1831. Government subsidies for cultural institutions began to make room for a new kind of cultural thinking in the "New South Africa." The festival at Grahamstown, for example, the largest gathering of art and artists in Africa, is no longer merely a venue for "white art"; rather, it's open to the art of all of South Africa's many ethnic groups, as well as that of neighboring countries.

Art

The greatest treasury of works of representational art, and at the same time that art's earliest manifestation, are the rock paintings and engravings which visitors can see on cliff sides or in caves in many regions throughout the country. The paintings are mainly executed on sandstone, predominantly in the mountain regions (Drakensberg, Cape range). The engravings are found mainly on low smooth blocks of rock, generally dolerite or a similar fine-pored stone (also on high plateaus in the Northern Cape Province and the Great Karoo). According to eyewitness accounts of the 18th and 19th centuries, the more recent rock paintings were the work of Bushmen; however, it's also widely held to be established that most of the earlier works are by Bushmen, as well. Most of the engravings are depictions of animals, which are generally quite easy to identify: most common are eland, elephants, and, north of the Orange River, giraffes. The paintings often portray people, as well; modern researchers associate these to the work of medicine men. The colors, mainly red and brown, but also black and white, were produced with metal and vegetable pigments as well as a mixture of burnt chalk and blood; some of them have proved astonishingly durable. Many of the images are on an extremely high artistic level.

Outside the country, people don't tend to know much about the visual arts of

227

traditional ways of life, little is evident in the big cities. You can, however, find them in rural areas where some of these traditions have managed to survive: take the colorful wall paintings on the Ndebele houses. Often, weavings and rugs, ceramics, and wickerwork are produced for the tourist market. Beadwork also figures largely, especially among the Nguni groups, whether as a part of traditional dress, jewelry, a status symbol, or an elements of rites and ceremonies. Among the Swazi and Zulu, beadwork was used to convey messages, particularly love letters. The beads were originally made of natural materials such as seashells, ostrich-egg shells, or seeds, but European traders introduced glass and, later, plastics, which enabled the beadworkers to follow a range of new artistic avenues.

Architecture

South Africa has made a significant contribution to world architectural styles with Cape Dutch architecture, which you can see to best advantage in Stellenbosch, Tulbagh and Graaff-Reinet. At first, the homes of the early settlers were simple rectangles, with thatched roofs and thick, whitewashed walls. In the course of time, the characteristic central gable was introduced, as well as the side gable; both clearly demonstrated the influence of the European Baroque, with its curves and relief and sculptural ornamentation. European artists such as French architect Louis-Michel Thibault (1750-1815) and the German sculptor Anton Anreith (1755-1822) were notable contributors. Many of the country's 19th-century buildings, by contrast, reflect increasing British influence, with neo-Classical and neo-Gothic elements.

white South Africans, which betray the strong influence of Great Britain and the Netherlands. The outlines of this largely uncharted territory are set forth in the country's art museums, especially those in Pretoria and Cape Town.

After World War II, most of the works by independent black artists were executed in the townships; known as "Township Art," many of these works and their artists have come into the international spotlight and found a ready market. Artists recognized abroad include painters Mslaba Dumile and Leonard Matsoso; Asaria Mbatha, who creates impressive linoleum cuts; and sculptors Sydney Kulmalo and Lucas Sithole.

Of black folk art and artisan work, which is closely tied to customs and

Above: Beadwork and ceramics demonstrate high artistic quality. Right: Whitewashed, thatched houses with ornate curving gables are characteristic of Cape Dutch architecture (Meerlust winery near Stellenbosch).

The Victorian style evident at the turn of the century has been dominated since the beginning of the 20th century by British architect Sir Herbert Baker (1862-

1946), whose designs include the Union Buildings in Pretoria and the Rhodes Memorial in Cape Town. The modern buildings which have come to dominate the skylines of the big cities since the 1950s stem mainly from the drafting tables of foreign architects, such as the Germans Helmut Jahn (Diagonal Street 11 in Johannesburg) and H. Hentrich (the Harry Oppenheimer Building in Kimberley), or the American firm Skidmore, Owings, and Merrill (the Carlton Centre in Johannesburg).

Music, Dance, and Theater

Until quite recently, music in South Africa was divided into two worlds. Since their arrival, the whites sought to keep up the traditions of European music; while the music of the black population was born of a long ethnic tradition in which both music and dance figure prominently. This close cultural connection to music has given rise to the idea that blacks have a natural innate musicality, vocal abilities, and sense of rhythm.

For some time, it's been in the field of choral music that these two worlds have encountered one another; these days, you can see a gradual growth of interest in each of these groups for the music of the other. After the end of apartheid, pop and rock groups from the black townships, such as Harari and Mango Groove, attracted the attention of the international music scene by virtue of their unique sound, still free of the influence of mainstream international pop. Miriam Makeba (born in 1932), who returned to South Africa in 1991 after 31 years in exile (in America, among other countries), was catapulted to world fame as early as 1967 with her hit *Pata-Pata*, recorded with Harry Belafonte. She sings African folk music in addition to pop and Afro-American music with elements of blues and jazz. Other internationally known artists are the jazz pianist Abdullah Ibrahim and the jazz trumpeter Hugh Masekela, who, working with author

229

Mbongeni Ngema, wrote the music to the hit musical *Sarafina*, which dealt with the students' uprising in Soweto. In 1987, the musical began a sensational, 22-month run on Broadway; it was performed in Vienna and Hamburg in 1989; and a film version was made in 1992 with Miriam Makeba. Ngema, now generally regarded as the best-known black dramatist in South Africa, subsequently wrote and composed another musical, *Township Fever*, which premiered in 1990 and was also a considerable success. This work, based on the true story of a railway workers' strike in 1987, marked the first stage treatment of black-against-black violence.

One reason for the musical's success was the extensive use of dance, which is strongly entrenched in the culture of the

Above: Under apartheid, the Market Theatre in Johannesburg became a forum for black protest theater. Right and far right: Bowls and trout fishing are two beloved South African sports.

black peoples. One black dance company that's attracted considerable attention was founded 16 years ago in Soweto by Carly Dibankoane. In addition to white ballet companies, centered at the Cape Town Opera House, new groups have sprung up aspiring to more contemporary forms of expression, such as the Free Flight Dance Company in Johannesburg.

Mbongeni Ngema's name is also closely linked with the history of the Market Theatre in Johannesburg, which from its inception didn't observe racial segregation. This was the most important platform for black protest theater. Theaters with roots in white cultural traditions received government subsidies on a provincial level: the Nico Malan Theatre in Cape Town, as well as the State Theatre in Pretoria, have opera and playhouses; and Bloemfontein's Sand du Plessis Theatre and the Natal Playhouse in Durban both also present opera, drama, and ballet. Cape Town's most important private theater is the Baxter Theatre.

SPORTS

Partly because of its favorable climate, South Africa is a veritable paradise for athletes and sportsmen; here, you can find nearly every sport imaginable. After having been excluded for years from international sporting events (including, after 1960, the Olympic Games), the country has, since the lifting of apartheid laws in 1992, once again been allowed to send athletes to international competitions.

Football, or soccer, has recently displaced rugby as the national sport par excellence; since 1992, South Africa has again been a member of the International Football Association. Rugby and cricket come out of the British tradition, as do tennis and golf; in these sports, South African athletes now figure once again in international rankings.

The 56-mile (90 km) Comrades Marathon between Durban and Pietermaritzburg takes place every year at the end of May. More than 10,000 people partici-

pate, and millions more line the roads as spectators.

The most important horse-racing events are the Rothman July Handicap held in Durban on the first Saturday in July and the South African Derby (April) in Turffontein, near Johannesburg. Also near Johannesburg is the Kyalami motorway for Formula One and motorcycle racing; this track could play a significant role in international races in future.

The best conditions for the extremely popular sports of surfing and windsurfing (or surfsailing) are along the shores of the Cape Peninsula, in St. Francis Bay, and around Port Elizabeth and Durban. Diving and snorkeling fans frequent Tsitsikamma National Park as well as the northern coast of Natal.

Jukskei, which dates back to the pioneer days of the Boers, is not unlike ringtoss; it's played with wooden pickets resembling the neckpieces of an ox-yoke.

You can pick up interesting and/or current information on a variety of sports and sporting events from SATOUR.

231

SOUTH AFRICA – TOMORROW

In 1994, the "New South Africa" started out on a long and difficult road. A mood of exuberance accompanied the first free elections and, subsequently, the swearing in of the country's first black president, Nelson Mandela. In his first public appearance after 27 years in prison, in 1990, Mandela had also requested the population to "let bygones be bygones," thereby laying the cornerstone for a mood of reconciliation that was to bridge all differences of skin color, language, ideology, classes, religions, and values. Such reconciliation is a precondition for the solution of the problems which now face the country.

Above: Blacks and whites have to work together to solve South Africa's problems. Nelson Mandela and Frederik W. de Klerk received the Nobel Peace Prize in 1993. Right: Education for everyone is an important factor in smoothing out disparities and paving the way to a better future.

The new government is faced with the black population's high expectations on the one hand, and the tremendous tasks before it on the other. Migration from rural areas into the cities has created huge slum areas which have to be dealt with; and the ANC has to try to fulfil its campaign promise of building a million new houses within five years. House-building has thus become a hot topic. And building up the economy, which could help combat high unemployment, especially among young blacks, requires investment, particularly foreign investment.

A brake to progress is the inadequate level of education; establishing an effective system of education and training is, therefore, of paramount importance. And tremendous efforts will have to be made in order even partially to improve living conditions for the black population, with such measures as bringing electricity to large areas of the former homelands, building water and sewage lines, and improving health care. Bringing living conditions in these regions up to the stand-

ards enjoyed by whites remains a dream for the distant future. Increasing the effectiveness of agricultural measures and securing water rights, not only for the population but for agriculture, forestry, and industry are other major tasks.

Tourism, hitherto something for the white population and a very small number of international visitors, is one of the great hopes for the country's economic future; every ten new tourists create a new job. Word has gotten out that South Africa is a dream destination for travelers; the few people who used to sing its praises have, since the end of apartheid, been joined by veritable choruses. Necessary, therefore, are new investments to build tourist facilities, as well as improvements in education and vocational training to help raise the standards of customer service.

The bad example set by many tourist-oriented countries should serve to warn South Africa from making the same mistakes: the land's great tourist resources, its incomparable landscapes and wild animals, would not be able to support the ills of mass tourism. Large on many agendas are "gentle tourism" and "ecotourism;" in places, these have already been put into practice. In some areas, such as Richtersveld, national parks are working together with the inhabitants of protected areas, or, as along the edge of Kruger Park, operate their game reserves in conjunction with private companies. Private tourist facilities invest part of their profits into local community facilities, such as schools, and make jobs available to local residents. South Africa should not sacrifice its identity as an African country on the altar of the Western model of profit-seeking.

South Africa's black population, like Zimbabwe's black population before them, have recognized that the country's problems can only be solved through collaboration with the whites. A new mood of openness and desire for reconciliation could enable the South Africans to inspire other countries to abandon policies of violence and oppression.

233

PREPARING FOR YOUR TRIP

PLANNING YOUR TRIP

In spite of the country's size, its many facets, and the virtually infinite number of possible combinations, it's not difficult – especially given the wealth of informational materials available to the would-be traveler – to plan a trip to South Africa: the only difficulty, in fact, is to make a decision, given such a broad palette of options. The main tourist magnets are Cape Town; the Cape Peninsula and the winelands; the Garden Route and the Little Karoo; the seaside resorts along the Indian Ocean, especially Durban; and, most of all, Kruger Park. Anyone with a bit more time, or who's been to South Africa before, or simply wants to depart from the standard tourist paths and truly get to know the country, should explore the mountains of the Cape Provinces, such as the Cedarberg range with its fascinating flora; the varied wildlife reserves of Natal; the tranquil Golden Gate National Park; or desert-like areas such as Kalahari Gemsbok Park or Richtersveld.

When you're planning your trip, your local representative of the South African Tourism Board (SATOUR) can provide you with information (no reservations), a "Travel Guide and Map," and other travel-related material. In Great Britain: 6 Old Grove, London SW19 4DZ, tel. (0181) 944 6646, fax: 944 6705. In the United States: 747 Third Avenue, 20th floor, New York, NY 10017, tel. (212) 838 8841, fax: 826 6928.

If you want to save yourself the time and trouble of figuring out where and how you want to go and worrying about other preparations, you can book a package tour through most travel agencies. Helpful in choosing such a tour are the annual brochures put out by South African Airways, as well as the catalogue of qualified individual operators, which also appears every year, called "Best of Af-rica" (available at most travel agencies). If you prefer to get to know a country and its people at your own pace and under your own steam, you'll still find that these catalogues are a helpful crutch in your planning.

From a financial standpoint, it's generally preferable to book all travel reservations in your country of origin; travel agencies often have deals with South African organizers that enable them to offer much lower rates.

When to Go / Climate

As South Africa lies south of the Equator, the seasons are the inverse of those in the northern hemisphere: Christmas comes at the height of summer, while winter lasts from May to August. However, the climate is generally mild, so there's not really a "bad" time to visit the country. High tourist season falls together with the long school holidays in December and January; Easter is also a busy time. At these times, hotels are often booked out, and national parks and beaches which are usually tranquil and empty can be both more crowded and more expensive than at other times of year. You can swim along the Atlantic coast in summer, and at the Indian Ocean resorts all year round. Gardeners will always find some flowers to admire, but spring in August/September, especially in Namaqualand, is an unforgettable experience, and if you don't want to miss the flowering jacarandas in Pretoria, you should plan to be there around the end of October or early November. If you want to visit the game reserves, wintertime is generally held to be the best time. In April and May, you can witness the wine harvest in Cape Province, while March and April are the best times to visit Cape Town itself.

Clothing / What to Pack

Because of the mild climate, you'll generally need to bring summer clothes no matter when you go; men in shorts are the rule rather than the exception. At higher altitudes or on the Cape, you'll need a light jacket or sweater in the evenings. In winter, too (June, July, August), somewhat warner clothing is advised, particularly as the heating is poor or even non-existent in some buildings. For the game reserves, you should bring light clothes that breathe; if you do any hiking or join a Wilderness Trail walk, you should avoid bright colors CKCK so as not to scare the animals. Both for these and for hikes in the mountains, you will, of course, need sturdy shoes. Some of the better restaurants may require formal attire (jacket and tie for men).

If you're bringing a camera or video camera, you should bring all your equipment, including batteries and film, as these items are more expensive in South Africa than in many other countries. Don't forget to bring good binoculars, one pair for each person. One pair for a group of people is not enough; you'll regret it no end when you're on a game reserve trying to glimpse a lion with your naked eye! You'll also need to bring anything and everything to protect you from the intensive sun: hats, sunglasses, sun cream (with a high UV protection factor). Insect repellent isn't a bad idea, especially in the lowveld; and a flashlight also comes in handy. Airline weight restrictions (often as little as 44 pounds/20 kg if you're flying tourist class) will keep you from bringing too much. And of course, when you get to South Africa it's no problem to buy any items you may have forgotten to pack. Hotels sometimes offer cleaning and laundry service, often cheap and efficient; and there's the usual complement of coin-operated laundromats and dry cleaners in all the big cities.

Entering the country (visas)

To enter South Africa, you need to have a valid passport which is good for at least six more months. There's no visa re-quirement for citizens of Great Britain or the Republic of Ireland; citizens of other countries are issued visas free of charge by the local South African diplomatic representative, a process which can take a couple of weeks. If you want to visit Swaziland or Lesotho, visas are issued at the border. If you want to stay in the country for more than three months, you should ask about residency requirements at the nearest diplomatic representative before you go. No special inoculations are required, but prophylactic malaria shots are recommended for certain parts of the country (see "Health," page TK). Proof of your inoculation history is only required if you're travelling in from a country within the yellow fever region.

Diplomatic Representatives of the Republic of South Africa

AUSTRALIA: Rhodes Place, Yarralumla, Canberra ACT 2600, tel. (062) 732424, fax: 732669.

CANADA: 15 Sussex Drive, Ottowa KIM 1M8, tel. (613) 744 0330, fax: 744 8287.

GREAT BRITAIN: South Africa House, Trafalgar Square, London WC2N 5DP, tel. (0171) 930 4488, fax: 839 1419.

U.S.A.: 3051 Massachusetts Ave NW, Washington, DC, 20008, tel. (202) 232 4400, fax: 265 1607.

Currency

The country's unit of currency is the Rand (R), divided into 100 cents (c). Bank notes circulate in denominations of 200, 100, 50, 20, 10 and 5 Rand; there are 5-, 2-, and 1-Rand, as well as coins for 1, 2, 5, 10, 20 and 50 cents. You can only bring R500 into the country. The currency exchange offices at the international airports are open for the arrival of every international flight. Credit cards are quite common throughout South Africa; international credit cards – Visa, Eurocard/Mastercard, American Express and Diners Club – are widely accepted.

An exception are gas stations: here, you can only pay cash. For cash payments, it's a good idea to bring plenty of travelers checks, such as American Express Travelers' Checks, which you can cash at the American Express office in any big city free of charge. Small banks, especially in the country, tack on hefty commissions to cash traveler's checks. You can't use Eurochecks in South Africa.

Customs

Objects for person use can be brought into the country duty free. Adults can also bring in a liter of alcohol, two liters of wine, 400 cigarettes, 50 cigars, 250 g of tobacco, 250 ml eau de toilette, and 50 ml of perfume, as well as presents worth up to R200.

GETTING THERE

Many international airlines (including **South African Airways-SAA**) fly daily or several times a week from major international airports to Johannesburg and Cape Town; some lines also fly to Durban. Since the end of apartheid, there's been a lot of competition among the major airlines on South Africa routes, so it's worth it to have your travel agent scout out which airline is currently offering the best prices. British Airways flights are generally reasonable.

Ship travel no longer plays much of a significant role, but there are a few shipping lines (such as the **St. Helena Shipping Co.**; contact Curnow Shipping Ltd., Halston, England, tel. (013265) 63434, or R. M. St. Helena Line, Cape Town, South Africa, tel. (021) 25165) which take passengers on their freight ships. Since 1990, the South African line **Safmarine** takes up to 12 passengers on four container ships specially outfitted for the purpose. The trip from London to Cape Town, Port Elizabeth or Durban takes 16 days. (**Safmarine**, PO Box 2171, Cape

Town 8000, tel. (021) 4086151, fax: 4086513; in London, tel. (0171) 283 30883). South Africa has also again become a stop-off for many cruise ships.

TRAVEL IN SOUTH AFRICA

By Air

For domestic travel in South Africa, planes are virtually essential, especially if you have limited time. The distances are simply tremendous. **SAA** flies – sometimes several times a day – between Johannesburg, Cape Town, Durban, Bloemfontein, George, Port Elizabeth, East London and Richards Bay; the new airline **SA Express** (SAX) has taken over the flights to Kimberley and Upington. Destinations of the private airlines **– Airlink**, **Comair**, **Inter Air**, **National Airlines**, **Sun Air**, **Theron Airways** and **Transkei Airways** – are listed in the individual chapters. Domestic flights should also be booked before you go, and well in advance. There are also charter flights available, as well as airplane rentals (for more informationen, contact SATOUR).

By Train

In South Africa, trains are not a particularly important mode of transportation. Apart from local traffic around the big cities, there are only a few long-distance trains, such as those from Johannesburg to Kimberley-Cape Town, Durban, Port Elizabeth, Pietersburg / Messina, Nelspruit / Komatipoort. One of the most famous luxury trains in the world, the legendary Blue Train, which went into operation in 1972, Einer der berühmtesten Luxuszüge der Welt, der legendäre, takes 25 1/2 hours to travel the some 990 miles (1600 km) between Pretoria and Cape Town. Although this trip costs considerably more than a regular flight, which takes about 2 hours, the train is almost always completely booked out, so you'll have to reserve well in advance if you're interested (around 11 months before your trip). The most scenic stretch of the route, east of Cape Town, is crossed by day in both directions, but because of the light, the way out of Cape Town is held to be more attractive than the way into it.

During the summer months, the Blue Train also makes excursion tours combined with sight-seeing (Worcester, Tulbagh, Saldhana) and overnights (3-4 days; details from SATOUR).

In 1989, the Blue Train got some competition in the form of the nostalgic steam train **Rovos Rail**, which is supposed to be even more luxurious and atmospheric than the legendary Orient Express. It takes 3 days to get between Pretoria and Cape Town; it also follows a route between Pretoria, Kruger Park, and Komatipoort/Maputo, as well as to Daressalaam.

Fans of steam locomotives will also be enthused by the "Choo Tjoe," which goes from George to Knysna in around 3 hours; by the "Apple Express," which once transported apples from the Langkloof Valley to Port Elizabeth; and by the "Banana Express› out of Port Shepstone.

By Bus

The most important mode of inter-city travel are buses, which run between the country's main cities daily, or at least several times a week. They're faster than the train, and are generally air-conditioned and have reclining seats. More information about travel times is listed in the Guideposts at the end of each chapter.

Translux, Greyhound, Citiliner Express and Intercape Mainliner have the largest networks; these lines also have offices in all the major cities of South Africa. You can also make reservations (up to 3 months in advance) at any travel agency, as well as through Computicket when you're in South Africa. Good value for money is offered by the **Southern Africa Coach Travel Pass,** a bus pass is-sued by Translux. For information, contact Travel Pass Office in Southern Africa c/o Tourlink (Pty) Ltd, PO Box 169, Cresta 2194, Merchandise Centre, 90 Nugget Street Johannesburg, tel. 011/404-2617, fax: 011/402-7299 (also see "Prices," p. 245).

South African tour organizers offer a range of bus tours, most of them out of Johannesburg, Durban or Cape Town; tours are offered both on large coaches (by, for instance, Springbok Atlas) and minibus (such as Welcome Tours). Prices aren't cheap, but they do include overnights, meals, and visits to museums and other points of interest.

By Car

The excellent, generally navigable roads that cross the whole country make it a pleasure to travel on your own by car. You can reserve rental cars at quite reasonable prices before you embark on your trip, either through a travel agency or through one of the major international firms: Avis, Budget and (eapecially reasonable) Imperial have offices at every airport and in most big cities. There are also a number of local firms which often offer even lower prices, and may be more cost-efficient for short distances. To rent a car, you need a valid driver's license from your country of origin, with an English translation when applicable, or – better yet – an international driver's license. You also have to be at least 23 years old, and some companies set a top limit of 70. Rental costs always include insurance. There are some particularly low-priced package offers which combine a rental car with your flight and/or motel (SAA, for instance, has a few such deals). Most companies offer four-wheel drive vehicles, and you can sometimes even rent a driver.

If you rent a car from one of the major companies, you can return it at any branch of that company within South Africa at no additional charge, but there are limits on driving in neighboring countries. If you belong to an automobile association, you can, by showing your membership card, get service from the **Automobile Association of South Africa** (AA); it's the first listing (AA) in every telephone book. The central office is in Johannesburg (Braamfontein), 66 De Korte Street, tel. 011/4071000, fax: 3392058. Services include a breakdown service, a tow service, and a variety of free maps and brochures.

In South Africa, everyone drives on the left-hand side of the road; if you're not used to this, you'll be surprised how quickly you adapt. You only have to keep in mind that traffic signs are on the left side of the road. The speed limit on expressways is 74 mph (120 km/h); on country roads, 62 mph (100 km/h); and 35 mph (60 km/h) in towns. Higher speeds are allowed on some country roads, where indicated. Seat belts are required by law.

Before driving long distances through sparsely-populated regions, check your gas tank; gas stations can be few and far between, and you're not allowed to carry a reserve tank. As gas stations don't take credit cards, always make sure you have enough cash on hand, as well. In hot weather, it's also wise to bring along enough to drink.

It should also be mentioned that the rate of automobile accidents in South Africa is relatively high, so visitors are advised to drive carefully and yield the right of way if there's a question. One potential danger are the countless minibus taxis operated by black drivers, which comprise a large part of local public transportation, and which generally go very fast. You should also drive slowly in rural, sparsely inhabited areas, as children and animals can run out onto the street without looking. You should also take seriously road signs indicating game in the area (see also Practical Tips, Roads).

By Motorcycle

Motorcycles can also be rented. Drivers must have had their motorcycle license for at least two years, and be at least 21 years old for motorcycles up to 250, at least 23 for machines over 250 cc. Rental agencies include: **Le Cap Motorcycle Hire**, 45 Bloem St. Cape Town 8001, tel. 021/23-0823, fax: 23-5566; in Johannesburg: **Dirk de Play**, tel. 011/839 16 60, fax: 011/839 16 61. If you'd like to explore South Africa on your own motorcycle, an expensive but fast option is **Lufthansa's** "Fly & Ride Program," which allows you to fly into the country on the same plane as your motorcycle. A slower but cheaper option is to ship it (see "Getting There," p. 236).

PRACTICAL TIPS

Accommodations

South Africa has a wide range of excellent accommodations facilities to offer the visitor. In 1993, the once-obligatory system of testing and rating all of the country's hotels was replaced with a new system of classification by SATOUR, which the various establishments – regardless of what type they are – have to apply for themselves. If an application is accepted, the establishment receives a burgundy-colored sticker which indicates the number of stars assigned (one star for a comfortable standard hotel; five stars for the highest class of luxury hotel) and the type of accommodation (hotel, guest house, etc.). In addition – and independently of the number of stars – another set of classifications is awarded for particular quality of facilities or service (to date, there are ten establishments in the silver class). You can, therefore, be certain that a given accommodation will live up to its advertising, as it were, and offer service at the level you expect. But you can also stay at one of the many hotels which have not yet been classified, or which used to have only one star. These are generally clean and fitted out with all the necessities and conveniences, and both reception and service tend to be extremely friendly. The classifications given in this boook are made on the basis of price: **Luxury hotels** (*LUXURY*): R 300 and up, **simple hotels** (*BUDGET*) less than R100. The hotels in the middle price class, designated as *MODERATE*, are between these prices, regardless of whether they're two- or four-star establishments. Classification in the Silver Class, which is independent of the number of stars or the price, is also listed in parentheses (Silver).

A large number of hotels and guest houses or country hotels have joined large hotel chains or other, similar groups. If you book several nights in different hotels of the same chain, either directly or through a travel agent or airline, you may be able to get considerably lower rates. A few possibilities include:

Southern Sun Group, which in addition to the Sun Hotels also owns the chains Holiday Inn and Holiday Inn Garden Court (which provides fewer services and facilities); for information, write or call: 7th Floor Twin Towers Sandton City Sandhurst 2196, PO Box 5087 Johannesburg 2000, tel. 011/0780-0155, fax: 780-0259, central reservation service: tel. 011/780-0001. (These are generally larger hotels in the mid-range and luxury price categories, often in the big cities.)

Protea Hotels, information and reservations: in Great Britain: Reservations Africa, 2 Ely Street, Stratford-upon-Avon, Warwickshire, CV37 6LW, tel. (01789) 414200, fax: 414420. (Usually individual, smaller hotels, including establishments in the country or in small towns, most of them in the moderate price category.)

Portfolio of Country Places and **Portfolio's Town & Country Retreats**; information, brochures (also available from SATOUR) and reservations at Portfolio of Places, Shop 5E Mutual Square, Oxford Road, Rosebank Johannesburg 2196, tel. 011/880-3414, fax: 788-4802. (These are establishments in particularly beautiful settings which provide individual lodgings with a personal touch, some only with bed and breakfast, some with complete board, in every price category.)

City Lodge and Town Lodge, PO Box 782 630, Sandton 2146, tel. 011/884-5327, fax: 883-3640. (Establishments away from downtown areas with good transportation connections, with all the modern comforts but with a deliberate effort to avoid unnecessary luxury, offering only overnight and breakfast, but with restaurants nearby; middle and lower price classes, with reduced weekend rates.)

Central reservation service for **Aventura Resorts**: Aventura Ltd., PO Box 720, Groenkloof, Pretoria 0027, tel. 002 712/346-2277, fax: 346-2293. (Holiday towns with chalets, rondavels, tents, campsites and caravan facilities, most of them in the Free State, PWV region, Norther Province, and Eastern Transvaal).

Club Caraville Resorts (annual membership fee) provide cut-rate accommodation or special tariffs for all club establishments (hotels, lodges, chalets and self-catering apartments, caravan- and campsites). Central reservation office: PO Box 139, Sarnia 3615, tel. 031/701-4156, fax: 701-4159.

The increasing number of **"Bed & Breakfasts"** are not only generally cheaper than hotels, but also give you a chance to get to know some of the hospitable South Africans on a slightly more personal level. Central reservations: 20 8th Ave., Melville, PO Box 91 309, Auckland Park 2006, Johannesburg, tel. 011/482-2206, fax: 726-6915. Local tourist offices can also provide you with relevant information about establishments in a given area; another useful source is the brochure Portfolio's Bed and Breakfast Guide (Portfolio of Places). A specialty of South Africa are the accommodations within most of the national parks and nature reserves, the so-called **rest camps**. These can range from simple rondavels to accommodations with all the modern conveniences – in Kruger Park, for example, you can find both ends of the spectrum. They're all very clean and tidy and fitted out with modern comforts; most of them have toilets and showers, refrigerators, and kitchen equipment. Reservations can be made at the following offices:

For National Parks: the National Parks Board, 643 Leyds Street, Muckleneuk, PO Box 787, Pretoria 0001, tel. 012/343-1991, fax: 343-0905.

For wildlife reserves in KwaZulu/Natal: Natal Parks Board Reservations, PO Box 1750, Pietermaritzburg 3200, tel. 0331/47-1981, fax: 47-1980. (Information: tel. 47-1961, fax: 47-1037); Ndumu, Tembe, Kosi Bay at: KwaZulu Department of Nature Conservation, 367 Loop St., Private Bag X 9024 Pietermaritzburg 3200, tel. 0331/94-6696, fax: 42-1948.

It's at the private nature reserves that you'll find the greatest pricing differences; they can range from R 2,500 a day (including meals and "Game Drives") for a suite in Ngala, Eastern Transvaal, to R 350 in the Greater Kuduland Lodge (Tshipise, Northern Province).

Banks

There are banks in most towns (generally open Mon-Fri 9 am-3:30 pm, sometimes also Sat 9-11 am; in smaller towns, they'll usually close for an hour at lunch time).

You can also change money or cash traveler's checks at travel agencies, such as American Express or Rennies Travel; these facilities are usually open longer hours than are most banks (see "Currency," p. 235)

Books and Maps

Most South African bookstores carry a range of informative books about South Africa, particularly ones with marvelous photos of the country's landscape, plants and animals.

Apart from bookstores, you can get a variety of different maps from SATOUR, car rantal agencies, or the Automobile Association of South Africa (AA). If you're going to be traveling around South Africa for an extended period of time, it may be worth your while to pick up *the New Southern African Book of the Road*, published by AA; this contains, as well as road maps, small city maps of some 165 cities, information about cars and breakdown assistance (with a listing of important expressions in Afrikaans and six Bantu languages), and illustrative information about weather conditions and notable plants, animals, and even buildings you can see along the road.

Camping and Caravaning

The climate and the excellent roads provide ideal conditions for both camping and caravaning – traveling, that is, with a mobile home or camper. You can rent fully-equipped vehicles from **Campers Corner**, PO Box 48 191, Roosevelt Park 2129, tel. 011/789-2327, fax: 787-6900; **CI Leisure Rentals**, PO Box 137, Pinetown 3600, tel. 031/701-2203, fax: 701-2200, Knysna Camper Hire, PO Box 1286, Knysna 6570, tel. 0445/22-444, fax: 82-588.

There are more than 700 caravan parks in South Africa, most with adjacent campsites. Camping off site is not permitted anywhere in the country. These sites are affordable, and generally completely equipped, with modern sanitary facilities and, often, places to cook, do laundry, iron, and wash dishes. Often, these sites also offer fixed accomodation (rondavels, chalets, and the like), a swimming pool, restaurants, and shops. SATOUR has a listing of 76 such facilities.

Computiticket

The central ticket system for the whole country sells tickets for every imaginable event (movies, sports, concerts, theater, etc.), and even makes reservations for long-distance bus travel.

This service enables you, upon arrival, to find out what kinds of events and concerts are going on ll over the country during your trip, and to order tickets for the events that interest you. There are Computiticket offices in most big-city supermarkets; you can also look up local addresses in the phone book.

Doctors

In South Africa, you hve to pay medical costs yourself; it's a good idea to get overseas medical insurance (available at travel agencies) before you go, if you're not already covered for medical expenses abroad through your insurance or a major credit card. Doctors are listed in the telephone book under "Mediese Praktisyns" oder "Medical Practitioners," dentists under "Tandartse" or "Dentist." You can also receive out-patient treatment in a hospital; there's one located in nearly every city.

Eating and Drinking

South African cuisine is not significantly different from that of other Anglo-Saxon countries. The meat – usually served in huge portions – is generally excellent; the barbecue, or *Braaivleis*, when it's grilled over an open fire, together with *Boerewors* (sausage), is a special South African activity, and you see grills all over the place expressly for this purpose. Game is sometimes on the menu: ostrich, impala, kudu,and even, sometimes, crocodile. Fish and seafood lovers are in for a treat in South Africa, most of all, of course, along the coast. The most common types of food fish include *kingklip, stockfisch, steenbras, yellowtail, sole*, and many others. If you see *"Line Fish"* on a menu, don't confuse it with a species; it's simply the fresh catch of the day (off the line). Crayfish are also known as *Cape Rock Lobster*; you can also get p*rawns, shrimps, and mussels. Oysters* are most common around Knysna, Langebaan, Saldanha Bay and Port Elizabeth. Perlemoen (also called abalone, or *Haliotis*), of which the large, mussel-like shells, covered in mother-of-pearl, are also sold as souvenirs, are most common along the coast between Saldanha Bay and Transkei.

Nearly all meals are served with potatos and vegetables. The land also produces nearly every fruit you can think of, including bananas and pineapples. Also excellent are the dried fruits, most of which come from the area around Ceres.

Each of the various groups of immigrants has enriched the country's cuisine with its own specialties, notably the Indian curries, especially in Durban. In the Cape Province, the Malay influence is evident in *sosaties* (skewers of meat made of marinated lamb or pork) *or bobotie* (a casserole made of ground meat with curry and raisins); *in bredi*, a casserole made of mutton and vegetables, the addition of the chopped stems and flowers of *waterblommetjies*, a water plant indigenous to the Cape region, is particularly prized.

Biltong, dried meat, is most popular when made from game, such as kudu, elephant, or ostrich.

Hotel breakfasts tend to be in the English tradition: large and good. Some hotels also offer a somewhat simpler continental breakfast, at a lower price. Also in the Egnlish tradition, the tea tends to be better than the coffee. Some hotels have preserved the custom of *Early Morning Tea*, which you can have brought to your room (with tea or coffee) at the hour you specify. One very popular beverage is rooibos-tea, which is free of tannin and rich in vitamin C.

Take-away food, whether you're looking for snacks or full meals, hot or cold, is widely available in self-service restaurants, cafés, etc.

Alcoholic beverages are available from the so-called "bottle stores," which are open until 6 pm. Supermarkets have also recently begun to sell wine and beer. South African wines have earned their good reputation, and they're usually quite reasonably priced, even in restaurants. Sherry, port, brandy or liqueurs are often taken as aperitifs, the so-called "sundowners" on the veranda. You can get wide range of excellent sugar-free fruit juices; make sure to stock up on these before long road trips.

Electricity

In general, the voltage in South Africa is 220 V; in Pretoria, it's 250 V. The plugs for electric razors may be two-pronged, but most other electrical appliances have three-pronged plugs, especially in older houses. These are hard to find overseas; the best idea is to buy an adaptor when you get to the country, unless you can borrow one from your hotel.

Fishing

With its miles of coastline and legion lagoons, estuaries, and inland lankes, South Africa is a fisherman's paradise. This also holds true for fans of deep-sea fishing or surf fishing; late summer and autumn are the best times for the latter. One special attraction is fishing in the wake of the sardine schools off Natal's southern coast. For fresh-water fishing, you'll need a license (which you can pick up for a small fee from the local authorities). Trout are the only fish with a protected season (June, July, and August). SATOUR issues an information sheet with suggestions for good spots and addresses of tour organizers, boat rental agencies, and fishing clubs.

Health

There are good medical facilities throughout the entire country, so that you're never far from good medical assistance no matter where you are. There are hospitals even in smaller cities. There is, however, no National Health Servcie or anything comparable, so that you should consider purchasing overseas medical insurance coverage before you go (see "Doctors," page 241).

As hygenic regulations are extremely strict, you can drink the tap water anywhere in the country with no problem; and you don't have to worry about ice cubes in your drinks, ice cream, fresh fruit, or salads.

To protect yourself against the strong sun, even when the sky is overcast, you'll need sun cream, a hat, and a good pair of sunglasses.

There are sharks off the Natal coast, but most bathing beaches are protected by nets. The water is quite clean almost everywhere. A tip for involuntary encounters with sea urchins: if you put a dressing with normal household vinegar on the affected spot, you'll escape the worst of the consequences, which can otherwise last for a long time and be quite uncomfortable. In the north and east of the country, most of the inland lakes are contaminated with bilharzia (a kind of parasite), which can cause bilharziasis, a dangerous parasitic disease. If you don't know for a fact that a given area is free of bilharzia, you shouldn't swim in the river or lake, or even dip your hands or feet in the water.

As protection against insects (including ticks, which are often carriers of dangerous diseases) in the lowveld and in the hot, humid coastal region of KwaZulu/Natal – especially in the evening – one of the best options is long-sleeved clothing, long pants, and socks; and you should avoid using perfume or aftershave. Insect repellents (which you can buy at any drug store) can be useful, especially against the Anopheles mosquito, which carry malaria. This disease, which seemed on the verge of being wiped out, has started to spread again; if you plan to visit Kruger Park, Swaziland, or Kwa-Zulu/Northern Natal (Zululand), you should take prophylactic malaria medication. Consult a good doctor or an institute for tropical medicine in your own country before you go.

You can get the medicines at a pharmacy without a prescription; you need to start taking them about a week before you travel into the endangered region. If, after you return, you start to get sick, manifesting grippe-like symptoms, for instance, inform your doctor right away that you've been in an area with malaria.

Although there are only a few truly dangerous kinds of scorpion, it's best to avoid going barefoot in rest camps or at campsites, to avoid them. Similarly, there isn't much danger of your being bitten by a poisonous snake; but if it does happen, try to remember what the reptile looked like, so that when you get help – as quickly as possible – the doctors will be able to determine the right serum.

Helicopter Tours

A helicopter tour over Cape Town and Table Mountain, or along the Cape Peninsula to the Cape of Good Hope, is an unforgettable experience. For information and reservations, contact Court Helicopters, Volkmar "Dick" Hilland, tel. 25 29 66/ 21 59 00, fax: 25 19 41/21 59 20.

Hiking

Hiking is still a relatively new pastime in South Africa, but it's rapidly become extremely popular. Steadily built up since 1973 , the network of hiking rails is administered by the state organization of the National Hiking Way Board, an institution which aspires to protect the environment and teach people more environmentally-conscious behavior in their dealings with nature. The hiking trails cover a whole range of elengths and degrees of difficulty, with and without guides, with and without overnights;

they're indicated by a yellow-and-white footprint painted on a rock or a tree trunk. Only a limited number of hikers is allowed on a trail at any given time, so you have to register in advance, and there's usually a small fee. When you register, you're given a brochure with a map of the route and useful information about the trail and its peculiarities, as well as interesting material about the environment, flora, fauna, and cultural history of the area. Information: National Hiking Way Board, Private Bag X93, Pretoria 0001, tel. 012/310-3839, fax: 320-0949. (SATOUR can also supply you with the brochure "Follow the Footprints.")

Additional hiking trails are administered by nature conservation authorities, city governments, or run across private property. More information on these can be obtained from the Hiking Federation of South Africa, PO Box 1420, Randburg 2125, tel. 011/886-6507. For more information about *Wilderness Trails*, guided hikes led by experienced rangers, contact the National Parks Board in Pretoria, the Natal Parks Board, or the KwaZulu Dept. of Nature Conservation in Pietermaritzburg.

Some travel agencies also organize small group hikes, providing guides and sometimes also arranging for equipment, luggage transportation, accommodations, and meals. Two such organizers are: Drifters, PO Box 48 434, Roosevelt Park 2129, tel. 011/888-1160, fax: 8-8102; Wilderness Safaris, PO Box 651 171, Benmore 2010, tel. 011/884-1458, fax: 883-6255.

An informative, interesting and helpful aid to planning and preparing for hikes in the country is Jaynee Levy's book *Complete Guide to Walks & Trails in Southern Africa*, published by Struik in Cape Town; there are also a number of books and brochures with suggestions for and descriptions of local walks, available in most book shops. When hiking in South

Africa, remember, for purposes of orientation, that the sun is in the north, rather than the south, at noon. On cloudy days, a compass is useful; flashlights can also come in handy in an emergency, and tables of the tides will help if you're planning to do any beach hiking: river mouths may be impassable at high tide.

Information

Most towns and tourist centers have tourist information offices (Publicity Associations), where you can get up-to-date information free of charge, as well as brochures and maps – the latter sometimes at a price. Perhaps the largest of these is the **Visitors' Information Bureau** in Cape Town (Adderly St., tel. (021) 418 52 14; fax: 418 52 27), which joins car rental agencies and a number of tourist services under the Captour umbrella. You can get advice, pick up current information – the state of the spring flowers in Namaqualand, for example – and book excursions and accomodation throughout South Africa.

The most important sources of information abroad for potential visitors to South Africa are local **SATOUR** offices (see "Planning," p. 234).

Minerals

South Africa is a true paradise not only for amateur minerologists and rock hounds, but for anyone with even the slightest interest in the beauty of rocks and minerals. You're not allowed to bring gold, diamonds, emeralds, or fossils with archaeological significance out of the country. But you can collect any semiprecious stones you like, except for tiger-eyes.

Newspapers

The South African newspapers with the largest circulation are published in Johannesburg, and both appear in English: *the Sowetan* (circulation: about 220,000) and *The Star* (208,000). Some of the national Sunday papers have higher circulations: *the Sunday Times* (522,000) and the Afrikaans publication *Rapport* (359,000).

Opening Hours

Since 1989, there haven't been any uniform legal hours of business. Most stores are open Mon-Fri from 8:30 am to 5 pm, Sat 8:30 am-1 pm; pharmacies, small shops and some supermarkets are open longer. Many shops are closed Monday mornings.

Pharmacies (Chemists)

Pharmacies (in the telephone book under "Apteek" or "Chemists") generally sell a variety of goods, rather than simple medications; in large cities, there are usually a couple open past regular business hours.

Photography

With its long hours of sunshine, the dry climate, generally ideal lighting conditions, and dramatic cloud formations, South Africa is the perfect travel destination for anyone even slightly interested in taking pictures. In the national parks, wild animals often come up so close to you that you can photograph them with a regular camera; for shyer animals which keep their distance, or smaller creatures such as birds or butterflies, or for close-ups of, for example, flowers, a telephoto lens is indispensable. You should use a more light-sensitive film (ASA 200 or 400) so that you can keep your shutter speeds down.

Take plenty of film along with you; of course, you can buy it everywhere in South Africa, but it's considerably more expensive. In big cities, you can generally have film developed and printed very quickly and cheaply.

Photographing buildings and facilities used for the country's defense or security is prohibited; and this prohibition extends to police buildings and even prisons.

Post and Telecommunications

Most post offices are open Mon-Fri 8 am-4:30 pm, Sat 8 am-noon. It costs R 1.90 to send an air mail letter overseas; post cards cost R 0.75. Air mail letters to overseas destinations usually take from 4 to 7 days; packages, which have to be sent from the customs counter of the post office CK, take around 6 weeks. The red-painted mailboxes, usually in the form of a column, are not all that plentiful. As there's relatively little mail delivery in South Africa, addresses are often in the form of a PO box or Private Bag. The four-digit postal code is written after a town or city's name, or given its own line at the bottom of the address.

The long-distance phone line network functions quite well throughout most of the country, generally with direct dialling. You need a whole pocketful of coins to place an overseas call, and hotels generally demand much higher rates for telephone calls; your best bet for calls home is to go to the post office, where you can pay at the counter. Furthermore, telephone cards are also available (R10), sold at all airports and in shopping centers.

Dialling codes for the United States and Canada: 0901; to Great Britain: 0944; to Australia, 0961; to New Zealand: 0964. If you're placing a call to South Africa from overseas, the country code is 27, preceded by whatever the international prefix is from your country; you then leave off the 0 from the prefix of whatever local number you're calling. Faxes have the same area code as telephones. If only one number is listed for telephone and fax, it often means you have to ask on the phone to be connected to a fax machine.

Prices

For the most part, prices in South Africa aren't greatly different from those in other Anglo-Saxon countries. To stay the night in a luxury hotel (concentrated in the big cities) costs around R500 and up; outside of major cities, this sum will be considerably lower. During the high season, however, prices usually soar, particularly for hotel accommodations.

The price fluctuations between the various private wildlife reserves (for bed and board, game-sighting tours, and the like) are often extreme. Mala Mala, for example, costs more than R1500 a day; while a day at Tanda Tula Game Lodge goes for about half that price.

SAA, car rental agencies, and other travel organizers often offer discount hotel passes for the larger hotel chains. You can often get lower prices on weekends (City Lodges) zu erzielen, but generally only off season, from May to August. In rural areas, it's often cheaper, and also more convenient, to book dinner, bed and breakfast at one establishment.

If you're cooking your own meals, you can travel relatively cheaply. There's a wide and varied palate of prepared meals and snacks on offer, and they're generally reasonably priced. Restaurant costs may be cheaper than some travelers are used to; even at the most expensive gourmet temples, you may escape for about R60-80 per person. And the wine, too, is quite reasonable, particularly in light of its high quality.

Where the prices are notably high is in domestic travel. The flight from Johannesburg to Cape Town costs R570 if you fly at the normal tourist rate; at the Africa Explorer rate, it's R440. If you reserve three months in advance, you can get even lower prices; for the same flight under these conditions, Comair charges R262. Here, as well, therefore, it's a good idea to check out all the various possibilities in advance. The bus trip from Pretoria to Cape Town costs R299 with Greyhound; with Translux, it's about 20% less. Senior citizens get a 20% discount on Greyhound routes, and 40% off train travel. An attractive bus ticket option for overseas travelers is Translux's Southern Africa Coach Travel Pass (see page 237); this allows you to travel on 7, 10, or 15 days within a month, or 21 or 30 days within two months, as far and as often as you like on Translux buses, as long as you reserve at least 24 hours in advance. In 1995, these tickets cost between R995 and R2995.

The catalogues mentioned above in the section on preparing for your trip (SAA tours, Best of Africa, and others) include offers for rental carzs in all categories; using these isn't a bad idea, as the prices are generally a great deal lower than the rates you'll get if you book normally once you arrive in the country. In Kruger Park, admission for day visitors cost R 10 in 1995; overnights in the park were an additional R 10; and cars were R 20. A cottage for 1-2 people (with kitchen and bathroom) costs between – in, for example, Olifants Camp – R 220 and – in Shingwedzi – R 160.

Listed prices are increased by the addition of VAT (Value Added Tax), which amounts to 14%. If you make any purchases of more than R 250, you can get the money back if you submit an application at the airport when you're leaving the country.

Prices, of course, change quickly, so these listings can only be taken as rough indications to help you with orientation in planning a South Africa trip.

Radio and Television

Most hotel rooms are equipped with radios, and increasingly also with televisions. Most radios receive one station in English and one in Afrikaans. Television was not introduced until 1976; the South African Broadcasting Corporation, which is about to be reorganized and restructured, currently broadcasts on two channels, in English, Afrikaans, and other languages. In some hotels, you can get the American news channel CNN, and there's also usually *pay tv*.

Restaurants

South Africa has eateries to suit every taste, from fast food chains through the cuisines of the world to exclusive gourmet temples. On entering a restaurant, it's customary to wait to be seated; and at very good or well-known restaurants, it's a good idea to reserve a table in advance. Not all eateries are licensed to serve alcohol; the level of license is posted next to the entrance: Y = License for wine and beer only with meals; YY = License for wine and beer; YYY = License for wine, beer, and hard liquor.

Any drinks you order in a restaurant have to be paid for when they're served, rather than with the meal. If a restaurant doesn't have a license, you can bring in your own alcoholic beverages with you.

Generally, a "café," in South Africa, isn't a place where you linger over a cup of coffee and a croissant (except, perhaps, at the Cafe Suisse in the Workshop mall in Durban); most cafés here sell groceries and produce, take-away meals, cigarettes, sweets, and newspapers and magazines.

Pubs are open Mon-Sat from 10 am to midnight; on Sunday, alcohol can only be served with meals – even in hotels. Pubs and bars are still basically off-limits to women, although men are, of course, served as well in the *Lady's Bars*. But this, too, is gradually changing.

Roads

Of South Africa's approximately 124,000 miles (200 000 km) of roads, only around 52,700 miles (85,000 km) are paved. Most of them, however, are in excellent condition. They are numbered according to a uniform system (expressways in white or yellow on a blue ground, other roads on a green ground): national highwasy with N, provincial highways with R, and highways in metropolitan areas with M. Signposting and directional indications are generally excellent, and as there are also excellent road maps (also from car rental firms), it's quite easy to find your way around. Along some stretches of expressway, or toll roads (marked with a black T on a yellow ground), you have to pay a small toll; but you can always detour onto a smaller, toll-free, if somewhat longer route.

There are a number of different markings on the roadways themselves. Marked in yellow are such indications as the edge of the road (an unbroken line); bus lanes (dotted line, with the indication "BUS"); directional arrows for turn lanes; no-parking zones (yellow line). Letters within an oval denote reserved parking places (L for loading zone, B for bus, T for taxi, FB for fire brigade, A for ambulance).

A road sign bearing an S with a slash through it desingates a no-stopping zone. Of road signs in Afrikaans, it may be useful to know that "Ompad" indicates a detour. Traffic lights, often known as "robots" in South Africa, are set behind, rather than in front of, intersections. Road signs with information usefu to tourists bear white symbols on a brown background.

Security

Visitors to wildlife reserves will be perfectly safe as long as they follow the safety regulations. The country's inland waters may contain not only bilharzia, but also hippos and crocodiles, while there could be sharks swimming off unprotected coasts. Be careful, in short, if you're planning to go for a swim.

In addition to generally driving carefully and responsibly, you should take seriously the roadside street signs indicating the presence of wild animals; a collision with an animal such as a hippo – and hippos often cross roads at night in their search for food " can be decidedly unpleasant for all concerned.

One consequence of the country's economic straits and the population ex-

plosions in urban areas brought about by the continuing migration from rural areas to the cities is dire poverty in areas; and this leads, in some large South Africa cities – as in most large cities the world over – to a notable crime rate. This shouldn't spoil your pleasure at traveling through this country, but it should move you to take a few simple precautions to avoid potential problems. After dark or on weekends, for instance, there are certain areas you should avoid walking around in alone; at night, too, it's best to take taxis, which you can have called in a hotel or restaurant. Don't bring any valuable jewelry with you, and leave other valuables, your passport, and your return flight ticket in the hotel safe when you go out. And valuable, flashy camera equipment is often best left at home if you're in a questionable area. Using credit cards and traveler's checks will keep you from having to carry around large sums of cash.

Shopping

Shopping in South Africa can mean browsing in one of the country's countless flea markets, cruising through a well-stocked supermarket, or entering one of the luxurious shops in an exclusive Cape Town or Johannesburg mall (Sandton, Rosebank). Prices tend to be fairly reasonable, except for import goods, such as cameras, which may be considerably more expensive than in, for example, America. You can buy gold jewelry, diamonds, and other precious stones duty-free from an officially certified jeweler if you shuw your passport and return flight ticket (information: *Jewellery Council of South Africa*, Kine Centre, Commissioner Street, Johannesburg, tel. 011/331-5631); one popular place to buy gold is Gold Reef City in Johannesburg. You can find semiprecious stones and jewelry in curio shops, as well as at The Scratch Patch at Mineral World in Simonstown and Cape Town (Waterfront).

Another popular souvenir is leather, particularly ostrich and buffalo leather; other local wares include pelts or clothing made of mohair, angora, or merino wool, as well as ostrich feathers or ostrich egg shells. You can also buy antilope hides and horns. Note, however, that according to the Washington Treaty of 1975, you're not allowed to bring a number of endangered plant and animal species, or products made of them, into your country, or can only do so with certain certificates and a special import permit. Check with your local consulate to see which regulations apply to your country.

Completely prohibited is any kind of trade with the big cats, rhinoceros, various turtles (including all sea turtles), many kinds of crocodiles and snakes, elephants, two of the three species of zebra that live in South Africa, bontebok and sable antilope, as well as palm and tree ferns and a variety of orchids. Any infringements of these laws are punishable by high fines.

You can find artisan works by the Bantu peoples, such as their colorful beadwork, woodcarvings, woven rugs (which often come from Lesotho), basketwork, and other objects, in curio shops, even in smaller cities, as well as in the shops at the rest camps in a number of the national parks; the latter also have an excellent selection of groceries.

At the end of your trip, you can pick up bouquets of dried flowers or hand-packed fresh proteas at stores in the international airports, as well as local wine, sherry, port, or brandy at the duty-free shops.

Taxis
You can't simply hail a taxi on the street. In general, you have to order one by phone; there are only a few taxi stands. Rates vary from city to city; but there's generally an initial fee, and then per-mile charges measured on the meter.

Minibus taxis are generally operated by black drivers, and can be hailed on the street; they're usually extremely overcrowded, and, as they also tend to go far too fast and lack proper safety precautions, are not really recommended for tourists.

Time
South African time is 2 hours later than Greenwich Mean Time; 7 hours later than Eastern Standard Time; 10 hours later than Pacific Time; 8 hours earlier than East Australian Time, and ten hours earlier than New Zealand Mean Time. Therefore, when it's noon in South Africa, it's 10 am in London, 5 am in New York, 2 am in Los Angeles, 8 pm in Sydney, and 10 pm in Auckland. During daylight savings time in Europe and the United States, this difference is one hour less, as South Africa doesn't observe a daylight savings time. Opening hours of offices, museums, etc., are generally given with a.m. and p.m., rather than on a 24-hour clock.

Tipping
Porters will expect at least 1 Rand per piece of luggage; for the suppliers of other services (waiters and waitresses, chambermaids, taxi drivers), the usual rate is about 10% of the price. Hairdressers usualy get R 5.

Weights and Measures
For a number of years, the Republic of South Africa has used the metric system of weights and measures. Similarly, official temperature measurements are now made in degrees Celsius and no longer in degrees Fahrenheit.

Vacations and Holidays
The individual provinces have varying school vacations. The main vacation season is between the beginning of December and the middle of January; there's another, roughly four-week period between

the end of June and the beginning of August; two weeks at Easter, and one to two weeks in September/October.

In future, South Africa is to have 12 official holidays. These are:

January 1 . . . . New Year's Day
March 21 . . . . . . Human Rights Day
April 14 . . . . Good Friday
April 17 . . . . Family Day
April 27 . . . . Independence Day
May 1 . . . . Workers' Day
June 16 . . . . Youth Day
August 9 . . . National Women's Day
September 24 . . . . Heritage Day
December 16 . . . . . Day of the Vow
December 25 . . . . Christmas
December 26 . . . . . . Goodwill Day
. . . . (Boxing Day)

If a holiday falls on a Sunday, it's celebrated (i.e., shops and businesses are closed) on the following Monday.

Youth Hostels

You can get general information about the country's youth hostels from the South African Youth Hostel Association National Office, 101 Boston House, Strandstreet, Cape Town 8001, tel. 021-4191853, fax: 021-216937. There are youth hostels in Barrydale (Western Cape), Beaufort West (Western Cape), Cape Town-Muizenberg, Cape Town-Camps Bay, Cape Town (3), Durban, East London, Hermanus (Western Cape), Johannesburg, Kimberley (Northern Cape), Hazyview (Eastern Transvaal), Sabie (Eastern Transvaal), Marquard (Free State), Pietermaritzburg (Kwa-Zulu/Natal).

To stay in a hostel, you need an international membership card; this can also get you various price reductions for train tickets, car rental, and other things. You can get more information at the youth hostels themselves; at the large information center in Cape Town, the organization has its own counter. Many bookstores in the United Kingdom, Ireland, the United States, Canada, Australia, and

New Zealand also sell a listing of international youth hostels.

Low-cost accommodations (preferably for longer stays) are also avaiable at the YMCA and YWCA (Young Men's/Women's Christian Associations). For information, contact the South African National Council of YMCAs, Head Office, P.O.Box 31 045, Braamfontein 2017, tel. 011/339-1385, fax: 339-7184 and: YWCAs National Headquarters, PO Box 5436, Johannesburg 2000, tel. 403-2423.

ADDRESSES

Diplomatic Representation in South Africa

Australia. Embassy, Fourth Floor, Mutual & Federal Centre, 220 Vermeulen St., Private Bag X150, Pretoria 0001, tel. (012) 325 4315, fax: 323 0557.

Canada. 5th floor, Nebank Plaza, Church and Beatrix Streets, Pretoria, PO Box 26006, Arcadia 0007, te;. (012) 324 3970, fax: 323 1564.

Great Britain. *Embassy*: Greystoke, 225 Hill St., Arcadia, Pretoria 0001, tel. (012) 433121, fax: 433207. *Consulate:* 10th floor, Federated Insurance House, 320 SMith St., PO Box 1401, Durban 4000, tel. (031) 3053041, fax: 3074661.

Ireland. 8/9/10 London House, 21 Loveday St., Johannesburg 2001, tel. (011) 836 5869.

U.S.A. *Embassy:* 7th floor, Thibault House, 225 Pretorius St., Pretoria 0001, tel. (012) 284266. *Consulate:* 4th floor, Broadway Industries Centre Foreshore, Cape Town 8001, tel. (021) 214283. *Consulate:* 29th floor, Durban Bay House, 33 Smith St., Durban 4001, tel. (031) 3043734.

GLOSSARY (Afrikaans)

eeu = iu . . . . Sneeuberg
eu = öi . . . . Keurboom
oe = u . . . . Bloemfontein

oo	= ou	. . . . Koopman
ou	= au	. . . . Hout Bay
sch	= at the end of a word: ss	
		. . . . Kirstenbosch
ui	= eu-i	. . . . Muizenberg
uu	= eu	. . . . Suurberg
v	= f	. . . . Ventersdorp
y	= ey	. . . . Lydenburg

1 *een*	11 *elf*	21 *een en twintig*
2 *twee*	12 *twaalf*	30 *dertig*
3 *drie*	13 *dertien*	40 *veertig*
4 *vier*	14 *veertien*	50 *vyftig*
5 *vyf*	15 *vyftien*	60 *sestig*
6 *ses*	16 *sestien*	70 *sewentig*
7 *sewe*	17 *sewentien*	80 *tagtig*
8 *ag*	18 *agtien*	90 *negentig*
9 *nege*	19 *negentien*	100 *honderd*
10 *tien*	20 *twintig*	1000 *duisend*

departure	. . . . *vertrek*
arrival	. . . . *aankoms*
goodbye	. . . . *tot siens*
train station	. . . . *stasie*
gasoline	. . . . *brandstof*
cheap	. . . . *goedkoop*
thank you	. . . . *dankie*
excuse me	. . . . *ekskuus*
good	. . . . *lekker*
shop	. . . . *winkel*
good day	. . . . *goeie middag*
information	. . . . *inligting*
yes	. . . . *ya*
no	. . . . *nee*
left	. . . . *links*
right	. . . . *regs*
street	. . . . *pad*
expensive	. . . . *duur*
detour	. . . . *Ompad*
when	. . . . *wanneer*
what	. . . . *wat*
how	. . . . *hoe*
how much	. . . . *hoeveel*
where	. . . . *waar*
room	. . . . *kamers*

AUTHOR

Marianne Fries studied German, history, and geography; worked for many years as an editor for a publisher of encyclopedias; and has published articles for years on the subject of South Africa. She is grateful to **Werner Gordes**, press officer of the tourist office SATOUR, for his help and advice during the writing of this book.

PHOTOGRAPHERS

Archiv for Kunst and Geschichte,
Berlin   18, 24, 26, 200, 210L, 219
Albers, Pieter   34, 138, 167L
Bondzio, Bodo   37, 41, 44, 47, 70, 78, 85, 132/133, 139, 150, 154, 173, 183, 193, 212, 213
Bondzio, Zdenka   184, 206/207
Deutsche Presse-Agentur   27, 224, 232
Friedrichsmeier, Hartmuth   21, 23, 157, 162, 163, 164, 167R, 208/209, 216, 222
Fries, Marianne   19, 59, 62/63, 98, 100L, 100R, 126, 127, 128, 166, 185, 189, 190, 194, 210R, 217L
Henninges, Heiner   cover
Hinze, Peter (Freelance Press)   73, 89, 97, 233
Hoffmann, Per-Andre   90, 102, 112, 134, 149, 151
Janicke, Volkmar E.   116, 123, 129, 142, 155, 188
Kristallmuseum Riedenburg   220R
Pansegrau, Erhard   8/9, 12, 15, 30/31, 35, 38, 45, 46L, 46R, 52, 55, 60, 67, 68, 69, 74L, 74R, 77, 80/81, 87, 93, 95, 96, 99, 105, 106, 117, 120, 121, 141, 145, 158, 170, 171, 172, 178/179, 180, 191, 198, 211, 220L, 221, 230, 231L
Scheibner, Johann   10/11, 14, 28/29, 39, 42, 50/51, 72, 76, 94, 107, 186, 187, 192
Roth, Hans-Georg   20, 82, 86, 140, 143, 146, 147, 152, 153, 159, 160, 165, 229
Schmidt, Friedrich   40, 57, 64, 228
Tourist Office of South Africa   17, 22, 56, 92, 101, 104, 110/111, 118, 119, 124, 125, 144, 169, 196/197, 202, 203, 204, 214, 217R, 227, 231R

Explore the World

NELLES GUIDE

Explore the world
NELLES GUIDE
THAILAND

Explore the world
NELLES GUIDE
AUSTRALIA

Explore the world
NELLES GUIDE
VIETNAM

AVAILABLE TITLES

Australia
Bali / Lombok
Berlin and Potsdam
Brittany
California
  Las Vegas, Reno,
  Baja California
Cambodia / Laos
Canada
  Ontario, Québec,
  Atlantic Provinces
Caribbean
  The Greater Antilles,
  Bermuda, Bahamas
Caribbean
  The Lesser Antilles
China
Crete
Cyprus
Egypt
Florida
Greece - *The Mainland*
Hawaii
Hungary
India
  Northern, Northeastern
  and Central India

India
  Southern India
Indonesia
  Sumatra, Java, Bali,
  Lombok, Sulawesi
Ireland
Kenya
Malaysia
Mexico
Morocco
Moscow / St Petersburg
Munich
  Excursions to Castels,
  Lakes & Mountains
Nepal
New York - *City and State*
New Zealand
Paris
Philippines
Prague / Czech Republic
Provence
Rome
South Africa
Spain - *North*
Spain
  Mediterranean Coast,
  Southern Spain,
  Balearic Islands
Thailand

Turkey
Tuscany
U.S.A.
  The East, Midwest and
  South
U.S.A.
  The West, Rockies and
  Texas
Vietnam

FORTHCOMING

Corsica
Israel - with Excursions
  to Jordan
London, England and Wales
Portugal
Sri Lanka

Nelles Guides – authorative, informed and informative.
Always up-to-date, extensivley illustrated, and with first-rate relief maps.
256 pages, appr. 150 color photos, appr. 25 maps
UK £ 8.95   USA US$ 14.95   AUS $A 21.95